HOW CUSTOMERS THINK

Gerald Zaltman

HOW CUSTOMERS THINK

Essential Insights into the
Mind of the Market

Harvard Business School Press
Boston, Massachusetts

Library of Congress Cataloging-in-Publication Data

Zaltman, Gerald.
    How customers think : essential insights into the mind of the market /
Gerald Zaltman.
        p. cm.
    Includes bibliographical references and index.
    ISBN 1-57851-826-1 (alk. paper)
        1. Consumer behavior—Psychological aspects.   2. Consumers—Psychology.
    3. Marketing—Psychological aspects.   4. Creative thinking.   I. Title.
    HF5415.32 .Z35 2003
    658.8'342—dc21

                                                                2002011666

The paper used in this publication meets the requirements of the American National
Standard for Permanence of Paper for Publications and Documents in Libraries and
Archives Z39.48-1992.

To all my doctoral students

Contents

Part III Thinking Differently and Deeply

Preface

Neither art nor science stands still in representing

our visible and invisible worlds. Marketing, as both art

and science, can't stand still either.

PETER DRUCKER, arguably the leading observer of management today, suggests that businesspeople stand on the threshold of the "knowledge society." In this society, a company's competitive advantage will come from an historically underdeveloped asset: the ability to capture and apply insights from diverse fields, not just from business. Drucker notes that many CEOs of large U.S. firms who were "appointed in the past ten years were fired as failures within a year or two," partly for not cultivating this asset.[1] Their failures ultimately resulted from woefully flawed paradigms for navigating an increasingly precarious environment—a situation not unlike that of the crew on the *Titanic*. Indeed, most marketing managers operate from a paradigm—a set of assumptions about how the world works—that prevents them from understanding and serving customers effectively.

Elliot Ettenberg, chief executive officer of Customer Strategies Worldwide LLC in New York City, summarized the current state of affairs in a recent article published in *The Economist*. In Ettenberg's words, "Everything else has been reinvented—distribution, new product development, the supply chain. But marketing is stuck in the past."[2] The article argues that a far deeper and better understanding of consumers is "a much harder task than describing the virtues of a product. While consumers have changed beyond recognition, marketing has not."[3] These changes in consumer behavior include increased skepticism about business (especially marketing), more assertiveness, greater sophistication, less loyalty to companies and individual brands, and major concerns about privacy and security.

The world has changed, but our methods for understanding consumers have not. We keep relying on familiar but ineffective research techniques and consequently misread consumers' actions and thoughts. The products and communications that we create based on those techniques simply aren't connecting with consumers.

In this "knowledge-explosion epoch," then, the limitations of our current marketing paradigm loom ever larger. Despite the fact that many of the assumptions underlying this paradigm characterize Western thinking in particular, they undermine the quality of thinking that informs marketing everywhere in the world. How so? Because businesses based in non-Western cultures have adopted Western ways, and Western firms have exported their biases to their non-Western operations.

The Challenge of Change

So why don't we just change our paradigm? Because it takes courage and patience to alter deeply entrenched existing paradigms. As history has shown, people who can't envision a different worldview often fight to maintain the current one. The Catholic Church, for example, couldn't accommodate a heliocentric view of the universe, prompting Galileo to renounce the earth's revolving around the sun. When someone challenges our current thinking, we human beings tend to resist.[4] Our resistance increases when the challenge forces us to reconsider not just *what* we think (that is, the content of an idea) but also *how* we think (the process). For example, learning that customers do not think in words forces us not only to embrace an unfamiliar idea about the thought process but also to think differently about communicating with customers. Vincent P. Barabba of General Motors notes, "Managers will throw a lot of money at a problem before they'll ever consider having to change the way they think about it." Overturning a paradigm requires changing many formal and informal assumptions, expectations, and decision-making rules that govern our thoughts and actions.⁵ Unfortunately, the phrase *paradigm shift* has become so clichéd that when people utter it, they generally mean a new fad rather than a fundamental shift in thinking patterns.

Another problem is premature dismissal. Too often, managers discard sound ideas without giving them a fair hearing. This intolerance often has roots in an unhealthy if hidden disdain for learning. In an address to an international group of agribusiness leaders at the Harvard Business School, Peter Brabeck-Letmathe, vice chairman and CEO of Nestlé—a company that actively seeks to understand brain functioning and emphasizes organizational learning—observed that marketers "treat personal common sense as superior to science-based knowledge and to what the humanities have to tell us." Another CEO of a leading global consumer products firm goes even further: "If [marketers] read popular business magazines, they feel on top of things. They disdain anything else. People with these attitudes would not last in any other profession." This appraisal may seem harsh, but all of us can name disdainful colleagues.

That said, resisting new ideas is actually healthy as long as we don't do so simply because they fall outside our cognitive or emotional comfort zone. *We must suspend our judgment about an unfamiliar idea when we first encounter it* and ask ourselves, "Would we value this idea if it were true?" If we answer yes, then we should critically examine the merits of the idea. The endnotes throughout this book should help readers do just that. They provide both supportive and contrary sources about particular ideas and findings, identify the diverse domains that are relevant, and forever change how we ask questions about customers, interpret the answers, and use that information. The endnotes are pathways into frontiers where different fields intersect.

The most troubling consequence of the existing paradigm has been the artificial disconnection of mind, body, brain, and society. Though systems theory is not new to managers, it hasn't dented their conceptualization of consumer or manager behavior and how they affect one another. Only by reconnecting the splintered pieces of their thinking about consumers can companies truly grasp and meet consumers' needs more effectively—and thus survive in today's competitive and rapidly shifting business environment.

Connections among Communities

As disciplines grow, they specialize and fragment, presenting two challenges to marketers. The first challenge is to acknowledge that the distinctions made between disciplines do not reflect how people actually live their lives. Thankfully, we human beings don't experience life the way companies or universities delineate it. The second challenge is that we must explore many disciplines, since the most promising knowledge frontiers typically exist at the boundaries *between* fields rather than at the fields' respective centers.

In many ways, this book is about connections, including those among or between:

- disciplines ranging from neuroscience and linguistics to anthropology and evolutionary psychology
- new ideas and the new ways of thinking that they may require
- the unconscious and conscious mind
- managers' and customers' minds
- neurons and neural clusters in the brain
- mind, brain, body, and society
- the power of metaphor and its central role in thought
- the malleability of memory
- emotion and reason
- verbal and nonverbal expression
- universally shared human perceptions and values

These connections reveal a consumer very different from the one many managers imagine. To underscore the difference, the book develops several central themes:

- Most of the thoughts and feelings that influence consumers' and managers' behavior occur in the unconscious mind.
- Insightful analysis of consumer thought and behavior requires an understanding of how mental activity occurs.
- Consumers do not live their lives in the silo-like ways by which universities and businesses organize themselves.

- The mind as we think of it doesn't exist in the absence of the brain, body, and society.[6]
- The mind of the manager (including both its unconscious and conscious elements) and the mind of the consumer (and its unconscious and conscious elements) interact, forming the "mind of the market."

Our existing thought systems can accommodate change up to a point. But when enough new insights and changes in our thinking accumulate, the resulting strain demands a paradigm shift. Radically new assumptions, expectations, and decision rules emerge, like a butterfly morphing from a caterpillar. As in the gradual twisting of a kaleidoscope, a multitude of small modifications eventually yields a substantially different picture.

A Quick Tour through the Book

How Customers Think is organized into three parts. Part I, Preparing for an Expedition, begins with a frank look at the state of marketing today. Chapter 1, A Voyage from the Familiar, examines the difficulties many companies face in becoming customer-centric. We explore the fallacies about customer thinking that underlie these difficulties and that marketers must leave behind. Then we ready ourselves to imagine a whole new way of "thinking about thinking"—a new marketing paradigm.

In chapter 2, A Voyage to New Frontiers, we look more closely at the new marketing paradigm. We consider the advantages of the interdisciplinary approach and explore the new paradigm's implications. We encounter some startling realizations: For example, as much as 95 percent of consumers' thinking occurs in their unconscious minds; much thinking surfaces through metaphors; consumers' memories are much more malleable than we thought; and marketers' *unconscious* minds influence consumers' thinking as much as their *conscious* minds do.

The chapters in part II, Understanding the Mind of the Market, detail the features of the new paradigm through examples of how companies today apply the paradigm's principles, with remarkable results.

Chapter 3, Illuminating the Mind: Consumers' Cognitive Unconscious, explains the unconscious mind and why marketers should study it. The unconscious mind (which the conscious mind allows us to consider) is one of the most important forces behind our decisions. It accounts for 95 percent or more of all cognition.

Chapter 4, Interviewing the Mind/Brain: Metaphor Elicitation, discusses how to match research questions with the appropriate research methods. The chapter spotlights metaphor. We discover how often metaphors crop up in human communication and how vital they are for understanding consumers' deepest thoughts and feelings. Market researchers can use innovative interviewing techniques to help consumers express their thinking through metaphors. The insights gained through these processes often remain far beyond the reach of traditional research methods. An appendix to this chapter provides more detailed guidance about eliciting deeply held consumer thoughts and feelings.

Because we must answer many important questions by exploring the unconscious mind, chapter 5, Interviewing the Mind/Brain: Response Latency and Neuroimaging, describes two new techniques for tapping into the unconscious mind and interpreting our findings. Still in their infancy, response latency and neuroimaging techniques complement metaphor elicitation techniques. The chapter also discusses several limitations of focus groups, which many managers still consider effective for interviewing the mind.

Chapter 6, Come to Think of It, explores the nature of thought and how conscious and unconscious cognitive processes work together. It addresses the importance of identifying thoughts about a topic that otherwise different consumers share. We examine how thoughts bundle together—and why those associations matter to marketers. We also discuss how consensus maps can capture the connections among consumers' thoughts and help us identify opportunities for enhancing the effectiveness of our marketing efforts.

In chapter 7, Reading the Mind of the Market: Using Consensus Maps, we look at the malleability of the mental models that a market segment shares and how various marketing efforts can reshape them. Marketers can remap these models by introducing new concepts or by reinforcing or even underplaying existing ones, while also introducing new associations among constructs or changing the strength of associations among them. We also look at how different consensus maps or shared mental models interact with one another.

Chapter 8, Memory's Fragile Power, discusses how memory works and emphasizes the reconstructive nature of memory. That is, consumers' memories are always changing—often without their awareness. Each time they revisit a memory, they change it, sometimes a little bit and sometimes a lot. Marketers can affect this reconstructive process by influencing the kinds of consumption-experience memories that consumers create.

Chapter 9, Memory, Metaphor, and Stories, weaves together themes from preceding chapters. The chapter shows how memory, metaphor, and story connect. Memories are story-based; consumers reconstruct them each time and use them to re-present past experiences. But memories are also metaphors; they "stand in" for other thoughts and experiences. The overlap of memory, metaphor, and storytelling strongly influences consumers' consumption experiences and behaviors. By providing particular metaphors, marketers can guide customers in weaving their stories of past, current, and future experiences in the marketplace. Consumers, in turn, use their own metaphors to express thoughts and feelings about those experiences.

Chapter 10, Stories and Brands, shows how memory, metaphor, and storytelling contribute to brand building. It demonstrates how brands are represented by bundled constructs, or consensus maps that filter how consumers perceive, process, and respond to marketing stimuli. A brand is itself a metaphor for this meaning. The chapter argues that consumers and marketers cocreate these meanings, these outcroppings of the mind of the market.

In part III, Thinking Differently and Deeply, we expand the picture beyond customers' and consumers' thinking. Chapter 11, Crowbars for Creative Thinking, shows managers ten ways to "break out of the box" when thinking about consumers and marketing—and how they can help their colleagues to do the same. This chapter doesn't recommend wholesale changes in thinking, but rather using temporary alternatives when customary habits of mind fall short. Drawn from various disciplines, the principles here can help marketers to manage consumer relationships more effectively.

Chapter 12, Quality Questions Beget Quality Answers, develops a theme common to several of the "crowbars" in chapter 11. The theme suggests that new ways of thinking start with better ways of asking questions. The chapter provides eight guidelines for developing the core research question to address, independently of the method used to investigate it. Every answer to an effective question contains the seed of another important question. The questions that marketers pose to consumers and the way they present them greatly affect the quality of information gathered.

Chapter 13, Launching a New Mind-set, is a caution against slipping into "business as usual" attitudes and practices. The sinking of the *Titanic* resulted from a failure to question two and a half decades of practice. These practices, in turn, encouraged the crew to disregard available information indicating that they should change course. The iceberg and certain design flaws in the *Titanic* simply enabled flawed thinking to wreak its toll. Similar patterns of thinking prevail today among managers, and a similar fate awaits them if they fail to rethink what they know about marketing. The ideas in *How Customers Think* are a starting point for better representing the mind of the market. Marketing managers, like any artists or scientists, should not hesitate to challenge those who insist on being frozen in an old paradigm.

Sources of Insight

The ideas in this book derive from current research by leaders from multiple disciplines. Despite its seemingly unrelated origins, this knowledge is vital for understanding and managing consumer relationships. While the book draws heavily on insights from many fields beyond marketing, I selected these insights based on their relevance to marketing practice. Four sources have especially influenced the selection of knowledge for inclusion in this book.

One source is the Mind of the Market Laboratory at the Harvard Business School, including members of its corporate Advisory Council.

The Mind of the Market Lab, which I codirect with Stephen M. Kosslyn, a world leader in cognitive neuroscience, provided a testing ground for many of these ideas. The Mind of the Market Lab is itself an unofficial offspring of Harvard University's Mind/Brain/Behavior Initiative (MBB). MBB is an interdisciplinary group of internationally known scholars that meets regularly to explore problems such as addiction, the meaning of (ir)rationality, placebo effects, memory distortion, learning and brain plasticity, and the impact of society on brain development. In the course of several years of involvement in MBB and the Mind of the Market Lab, I have benefited from interactions with some of the world's most gifted scholars and executives.

In the same spirit, I have benefited greatly from my interaction with graduate students in the Customer Behavior Laboratory, a course I teach at the Harvard Business School, most recently with Professor Luc Wathieu. In addition to sharing their early work experience and responses to new ideas, many of these students remain in touch, relating their experiences as they apply ideas in this book in their work. They have provided many examples of successful implementation of these insights. They have also shared examples of the problems that can arise when managers ignore these ideas.

A third source involves the many practitioner and academic reviewers of various drafts of this manuscript (acknowledged individually elsewhere). Their collective expertise spans all of the ideas presented here. These individuals offered invaluable insight into which ideas to include and which examples would best illustrate them.

A fourth source of ideas and examples comes from Olson Zaltman Associates, led by Dr. Jerry C. Olson, a world leader in consumer psychology. He and my immediate OZA colleagues and their clients have provided me with the opportunity to apply and further develop important ideas in a wide variety of marketing settings. The partnerships OZA has created with forward-thinking practitioners inform many of the insights shared in this book.

Finally, in these chapters you'll encounter certain terms borrowed from a wide range of disciplines, and so some of their meanings may differ from common usage. The following glossary groups these terms in a way that tells a story about consumer thinking and previews the ideas in this book.[7]

Glossary of Key Terms

Thinking: The use of mental processes; activities of the brain involved in storing, recalling, or using information, or in generating specific feelings and emotions. Also called cognition and mental processes. For example, when a woman who was participating in a General Mills study about nutrition noticed a new breakfast food on her friend's countertop, she recalled and compared her children's reactions to other breakfast foods against her assessment of the new food and its manufacturer ("They usually lead the pack").

Thought: The outcome of thinking, conventionally called beliefs, attitudes, and evaluations. For example, the above *thinking* produced the *thought* in the woman's mind, "I'll try that product," which she expressed by saying aloud, "I'll give that a shot." Sometimes we confuse "thinking out loud" with the actual process of thinking and with the thoughts that we express "out loud." Although we may be aware of a memory or a new idea having popped into mind, we are likely oblivious to the internal processes that yielded it. Thus, any "thinking out loud" occurs after the fact and is almost certainly incomplete.

Conscious thought: Thoughts that we can articulate because we are fully aware of our own existence, sensations, and cognition. Also called the cognitive conscious mind. For example, the woman's decision to try the product was a *conscious thought* that she shared with her friend. It emerged from many thoughts, some of them conscious but most of them unconscious, such as her favorable view of the company, her need to find more appealing food for her children, and her willingness to take a risk.

Unconscious thought: Thinking outcomes of which we are unaware or vaguely aware and struggle to articulate; mental activity outside conscious awareness. Also called the cognitive unconscious mind. Obviously, using our conscious mind for actions like tying our shoelaces or chewing food would simply take too long; thus our unconscious mind has helped us survive and evolve as a species.

Concept: An unambiguous, sometimes abstract, internal representation that defines a meaningful grouping or categorization of living and nonliving objects, events such as experiences, and thoughts. We have concepts for "new product," "family," "children's food preferences," "manufacturer of nutritious food," "nutrition," "tree," "dog," and so on. Concepts help us interpret new information and experiences and decide how to act on them.

Construct: The label or name tag a manager or researcher gives to a conscious or unconscious consumer thought that the manager or researcher has identified. Marketers can use constructs to understand consumers' thinking and to communicate among themselves and with consumers about products. For example, the General Mills research and management team found that many consumers express different versions of the thought, "They are junk-food magnets," when describing their children's nutritional behaviors. This thought bundles together three *concepts:* children, junk food, and attraction. The General Mills managers and researchers gave this thought bundle a name—"negative nutrition"—a construct that they defined in a specific way and illustrated with several quotations and sensory metaphors from consumers. The team later discovered that this construct called many other constructs to mind for consumers.

Neurons: Brain cells active during thinking. (Neurons do other things as well.) Neurons receive signals from other neurons or from sensory organs, process these signals, and often pass them along to other neurons, muscles, or bodily organs. Thoughts and emotions arise from the activation and interconnection of these brain cells.

Neural cluster: A group of neurons that are activated and stimulate each other when we think. They hold hands, so to speak. Also called a neuronal cluster. These neural clusters produce thoughts, labeled by constructs.

Neural pathway: The route followed when one neuron or group of neurons affects others; the connections among clusters. Every thought has an associated neural cluster, just as every residence has an address or every community has specific geographical coordinates. For example, the woman's thought about her kids, "They are junk-food magnets," stems from the activation of a particular cluster of neurons. Since different neural clusters stimulate one another using neural pathways, the woman's different thoughts may involve many different clusters.

Brain: The organ that houses neurons used in thinking. (Brains also house many other functions.)

Cerebral cortex: The brain's convoluted or wrinkled surface, where many of our mental processes occur.

Mind: The product of conscious and unconscious thinking in the brain, produced by interactions among groups of neurons and involving thoughts and feelings.

Mental model: A set of associated thoughts formed when neural clusters influence each other; used to process information from and respond to an abstract event. A mental model is like a road map that identifies different communities and their connecting routes. Consumers use this map whenever they encounter something new or contemplate a decision. For example, a study of mothers in Italy on the topic of children's nutrition detected connections in their thinking among the following thoughts: being a teacher, how other mothers view them, rewarding children, pride, their own childhood memories about eating, and self-esteem. These associations sometimes took on positive qualities and other times, negative ones.

Consensus map: A mental model that different people use in similar ways or that a group of people share. A consensus map represents the convergence of consumer thinking on a common mental model. For example, in the above study of Italian mothers, individual study participants expressed more than twenty of the same thoughts, resulting in more than twenty constructs. Moreover, for most of the participants, each construct connected to at least one of the other constructs in exactly the same way. Since individual consumers have such remarkably

similar mental models, businesses can segment markets
according to consensus maps.

Human universals: The categories of thought and action found in
every culture, regardless of how diverse, such as justice and
punishment, protecting the young, and caring for the ill. Universals include several core metaphors such as journey, balance, and transformation as well as fundamental archetypes.
Consensus maps reflect these universals for a given group or
segment, no matter how broad or narrow the group's definition. In fact, the more deeply we understand consumers who
share a common problem, the more we notice similarities
among those consumers. Furthermore, these shared common
denominators remain stable over time, making them a much
sounder basis for marketing strategy than surface-level differences.

Metaphor: The representation of one thought in terms of another.
This book uses the term broadly to include analogy, simile, and
many other nonliteral devices to convey information. For
example, the woman's children aren't literally "junk-food magnets." The woman was simply using the *idea* of a magnet to
convey certain qualities about her children's attraction to junk
food. Metaphors are vehicles for transporting unconscious
thoughts to conscious awareness when marketers probe for the
thinking behind them. When the interviewer in this study
asked the woman to say more about the expression "a cat with
nine lives" (stimulated by a picture of the family cat that the
woman brought to the interview), she responded with comments that suggested qualities of resilience, focus, determination, patience, parental obligation, the teacher role, and nurturing. All of these constructs linked to the construct "family
nutrition." Other consumers used different metaphors to
express these same ideas.

Figurative language: The use of metaphor to convey thoughts and
help interpret customers' deepest shared thoughts and feelings.

Literal language: The use of the exact meaning of words or other
images to convey thoughts. Such language can take various
forms; for example, an oral statement that the consumer first

experienced the new product at a friend's home, or a written statement in a survey about the probability of the consumer's children liking the product. Managers not only identify but also *interpret* consumers' deepest, shared thoughts and feelings by eliciting such spoken or written comments from consumers and then taking those comments at face value.

HOW CUSTOMERS THINK

Part I

Preparing for an Expedition

Chapter One

A Voyage from the Familiar

Management is our universe,

the consumer its center,

and imagination its boundary.

A FTER YEARS OF RESEARCH and development, a consumer-goods company launches a new soft drink—only to see it dry up in the marketplace. Focus group participants salivate over a new personal digital assistant (PDA) and express their intention to buy—but don't when the PDA goes on sale two months later. We ask customers what they want, we give it to them, and then we watch them snap up our competitor's goodies instead. *Why?* Why do approximately 80 percent of all new products or services fail within six months or fall significantly short of forecasted profits?[1] As the half-lives of existing goods and services shrink, firms need new products to grow revenues.[2] The cost of mistakes is high—lost revenues, low customer satisfaction, low employee morale.

Believe it or not, the reasons for failure boil down to a common, deceptively simple truth: Too many marketers don't understand how their own and their consumers' minds interact. Consider figure 1-1. What do you see?

FIGURE 1 - 1

What Do You See?

From *Mind Sights* by Roger N. Shepard, © 1990 by W. H. Freeman.
Reprinted by permission of Henry Holt and Company, LLC.

At first, you'll likely see one of two creatures, a rabbit or a duck. Now show this picture to a few friends or colleagues. Which did they see first? This exercise demonstrates a very important point: Two people can look at the very same data and have two totally different interpretations.[3] It happens all too often in market research, frustrating managers and consumers alike. Managers say, "We showed you a rabbit, you swore that you'd buy it if we made its feet bigger, and so we did—but now you're not buying it, and so we're not listening to you anymore." Consumers retort, "No, you showed us a duck and we told you that we wanted bigger feet on it. Now you're offering us a rabbit with four huge paws. You don't listen, and so we're not talking to you anymore." Both parties cite the same data to prove their respective points. This often causes managers to ignore customers because they believe that customers don't know what they want, let alone what is technically possible. However, from a cognitive standpoint, no one can even respond to a radically new or unheard of product or service idea without some frame of reference, as ill-suited or ill-developed as it might be. Understanding existing frames of reference is essential if they are to be brought into alignment with the possibilities created by new technologies.

The Need for an Interdisciplinary Approach

George S. Day, the Geoffrey T. Boisi Professor of Marketing and director of the Mack Center for the Management of Technological Innovation at the Wharton School of the University of Pennsylvania, notes that over the next few years, every industry will change dramatically because of technology. To exploit new opportunities, managers must know significantly more than they currently do about how customers think and act.[4] That is, the conscious and, especially, unconscious dynamics of customer thinking must be understood, since these dynamics determine the ultimate commercial success of the technology more than product design or delivery systems.

There's much to learn. Leading neuroscience scholar Antonio Damasio, the M. W. Van Allen Distinguished Professor of Neurology at the University of Iowa College of Medicine, notes, "More may have been learned about the brain and the mind in the 1990s—the so-called decade of the brain—than during the entire previous history of psychology and neuroscience."[5]

Open-minded managers are extending their comfort zones to explore unfamiliar *disciplines,* or communities of thinkers who share the same habits of mind about theory, procedure or methodology, and knowledge usage. For example, neurological research revealed that people don't think in linear, hierarchical ways; figuratively speaking, they don't experience a cake by sampling a sequence of raw ingredients. They experience fully baked cakes. This insight prompted companies like Citibank, Disney, Kraft, McNeil Consumer Health Care, and John Deere to change how they engaged consumers. They're now drawing on previously ignored research from an array of disciplines—musicology, neurology, philosophy, and zoology, along with the more familiar fields of anthropology, psychology, and sociology, among others—to understand what happens within the complex system of mind, brain, body, and society when consumers evaluate products.

Some managers are even importing experts, asking new questions, discovering powerful new knowledge, and then creating products and services that have unprecedented value in the eyes of customers. For example, the managers of one company met for two days with a neuro-biologist, a psychiatrist, an Olympic coach, a specialist in adult intellectual development, and a sociologist specializing in public health matters to examine new ways to use consumer incentives. The meeting generated several innovative and practical ideas, one of which the firm implemented within two weeks. In the next seven months, the effectiveness of its consumer-incentive program soared by almost 40 percent.

Marketers are also gaining a new perspective on how their *own* minds work—how their subconscious mental processes influence the way they reach out to consumers, shape consumers' responses (sometimes in unexpected and undesirable ways), and distort their own interpretations of consumers' behaviors and verbally expressed responses. Moreover, marketers have begun to see how powerfully the current marketing paradigm shapes the decisions, expectations, and actions of their colleagues—sometimes in ways that hurt strategy formation, budgeting efforts, and other key business activities.

Finally, marketers are beginning to realize that their own minds work in the same way consumers' minds do. That is, a similar mix of conscious and unconscious processes influences them. In fact, many companies are starting to use metaphor elicitation methods to help draw back the curtains on their own thinking as well as that of consumers.

When consumers and marketers interact—both of them operating from this maelstrom of mental activity—something called *the mind of the market* emerges. As we'll see throughout the rest of this book, the ability to grasp or understand the mind of the market and creatively leverage this understanding represents *the* next source of competitive advantage for marketers.

Six Marketing Fallacies

"Marketers must understand how their thinking interacts with that of consumers."[6] We've heard it before, we believe it—but we don't act on it. According to Chris Argyris, the James Bryant Conant Professor Emeritus of Education and Organizational Behavior at Harvard University and a director of Monitor Company, that's the difference between *espoused theory* and *theory-in-use*.[7] "Espoused theory" is what we *say* we believe. "Theory-in-use" is the belief that underlies what we actually do. Sometimes espoused theory and theory-in-use coincide; oftentimes they don't, and the theories-in-use reveal what managers really believe.

For example, many managers would say that, with few exceptions, conducting market research to confirm existing beliefs is a waste of resources. That's their espoused theory. Yet, Rohit Deshpandé, Harvard Business School professor and former executive director of the Marketing Science Institute, notes that over 80 percent of all market research serves mainly to reinforce existing conclusions, not to test or develop new possibilities.[8] Managers *act* as if endorsing current views merits 80 percent of their resources. That's their theory-in-use.

As Argyris and other leading management scientists such as Jeffrey Pfeffer and Robert Sutton point out, knowing better does not automatically lead to doing better.[9] Bad habits die hard, especially in an organizational climate that provides no incentives to take risks, no fiscal resources to collect worthwhile information, and no time to think deeply about such information, let alone keep abreast of well-founded advances in disciplines that study human behavior.[10]

The resulting paradigm in use—the assumptions about how the world works that manifest themselves in marketing's actions—prevents marketers from understanding and serving customers effectively. The following section provides a few examples of limiting theories-in-use to stimulate further thinking and encourage managers to depart from such limiting ideas and practices and to open themselves to more promising and well-founded new ideas.

Consumers Think in a Well-Reasoned or Rational, Linear Way

Many managers still believe that consumers make decisions deliberately—that is, they consciously contemplate the individual and relative values of an object's attributes and the probability that it actualizes the assigned values, and then process this information in some logical way to arrive at a judgment. For example, consumers encounter an automobile, consciously assess its benefits attribute by attribute, and decide whether to buy it. Or consumers pinpoint a particular need—transportation—seek a set of options that could meet that need, evaluate the pros and cons of each option, calculate the cost of overall satisfaction per option, and then make a well-reasoned decision.

Consumer decision making sometimes does involve this so-called rational thinking. However, it doesn't adequately depict how consumers make choices.[11] In fact, some of the very research that originally supported such thinking now pegs this kind of decision making as the exception rather than the rule. As it turns out, the selection process is relatively automatic, stems from habits and other unconscious forces, and is greatly influenced by the consumer's social and physical context.[12]

In reality, people's emotions are closely interwoven with reasoning processes. Although our brains have separate structures for processing emotions and logical reasoning, the two systems communicate with each other and *jointly* affect our behavior. Even more important, the emotional system—the older of the two in terms of evolution—typically exerts the *first* force on our thinking and behavior. More important still, emotions contribute to, and are essential for, sound decision making.[13]

For example, a perfume's fragrance—a product attribute—may evoke a particular memory and an associated emotion in a potential buyer. If the memory triggers a painful emotion, then the individual probably won't buy the perfume, even if the fragrance, price, packaging, brand label, and other qualities meet her criteria. When the consumer departs from these criteria, expressed perhaps in a focus group or in response to traditional interviews, marketers will likely judge her behavior as irrational since they don't understand why she rejected the perfume.[14]

Indeed, decision making hinges on the simultaneous functioning of reason and emotion, as the remarkable case of Phineas Gage reveals. In 1848, while laying a railway bed in Vermont, Gage suffered a severe head injury when a blasting cap exploded nearby. The blow destroyed Gage's capacity for emotion but left his reasoning skills intact. Before the accident, people who knew Gage described him as trustworthy and well balanced. Afterward, they deemed him crass, indecisive, and unsure of himself. He could no longer choose wisely.[15] More recent studies of the effects of brain lesions demonstrate that when neurological structures responsible for either emotion *or* reasoning sustain damage, the affected individuals lose their ability to make the kinds of sound decisions that permit a normal life.[16]

Yet despite claims to the contrary, marketers frequently prefer not to get involved in consumers' emotions.[17] Most managers, once they identify an emotion, interpret its meaning based on how people generally use it in the popular vernacular. When pressed, they'll explore emotions only superficially, failing to acquire a deep understanding of the "anatomy" of a particular emotion. The anatomy of an emotion refers to the many qualities that comprise it and enable an emotion to take on different meanings in different settings. For example, a study of the meaning of "joy" conducted for one of the world's leading brands identified more than fifteen elements of this basic emotion. These insights are leading the firm to a major overhaul of the brand story.

Some companies, such as Coca-Cola, Unilever, Hallmark, Syngenta, Bank of America, Glaxo, American Century, and General Motors, are beginning to conduct "deep dives" on specific emotions in order to understand their subtle nuances and operation. Companies that rely on popular conceptions of emotions usually compound this error by focusing on the more positive end of the emotional spectrum. (Fear is the one exception to this positive-emotion bias.) For example, they focus their attention on how joy influences consumer behavior while remaining unaware of the impact of disgust.[18] Yet disgust—one of the most powerful human emotions—plays a major role in people's selection of cleaning supplies, fabrics, food, and many services where joy is also present.

Consumers Can Readily Explain Their Thinking and Behavior

The limitations of this second belief and the research practices it fosters stem from the assumption that most of our thinking takes place in our conscious minds. In actuality, consumers have far less access to their own mental activities than marketers give them credit for. Ninety-five percent of thinking takes place in our unconscious minds—that wonderful, if messy, stew of memories, emotions, thoughts, and other cognitive processes we're not aware of or that we can't articulate.[19] George Lowenstein of Carnegie-Mellon University, a leader in applying psychology to economics, cautions us against exaggerating the role of consciousness: "Rather than actually guiding or controlling behavior, consciousness seems mainly to make sense of behavior after it is executed."[20] Such information may be relevant, but it is also likely to be woefully incomplete. Self-reporting methodologies like telephone or shopping mall interviews or interviews in a person's home that rely on conscious reflection might not provide any substantial insight into what really motivated a particular consumer action or decision.[21]

For example, marketers assume that consumers can readily inspect and easily describe their own emotions. In fact, emotions are by definition unconscious. To surface them, skilled researchers must use special probing techniques.[22] The consumer whose purchase of a specific perfume is heavily influenced by a memory and associated emotion is unlikely to articulate this reason when a researcher explores the decision with conventional research tools. Why? The operation of our memory and emotions occurs below our thresholds of awareness. Most of what we "remember" and many of the emotions that those memories trigger lie beyond our convenient inspection, despite their powerful influence on us.

For example, when asked why they purchase an expensive brand of chocolate, people may be emphatic that they do so as a gift for others. But the truth may differ: Many of these same people actually make those purchases for their own immediate consumption. Moreover, the reasons for doing so involving guilt and joy lie beyond normal conscious inspection and require a skilled interviewer to help the consumer bring them to a level where they can be examined consciously.

In fact, forces that consumers aren't aware of or can't articulate shape their behavior far more than marketers might think. A manufacturer of ingredients used to make paints wanted to understand why firms were willing to pay some suppliers a price premium for an essentially commodity product. The manufacturer identified some traditional reasons, such as an unwillingness to rely on any one source. But by probing deeply, it uncovered an even more important feeling (related to self-esteem) among purchasing agents. The company was then able to strengthen its relationships with purchasing agents by acknowledging the feeling most closely related to self-esteem during sales calls.

Still, marketers continue to misuse surveys and focus groups in an effort to get consumers to explain or even predict their responses to products. Standard questioning can sometimes reveal consumers' thinking about familiar goods and services *if* those thoughts and feelings are readily accessible and easily articulated. Yet these occasions occur infrequently. Fixed-response questions, in particular, won't get at consumers' most important thoughts and feelings if the manager or researcher has not first identified them by penetrating consumers' unconscious thought. Most fixed-response questions and focus group moderator questions address at a surface level *what consumers think about what managers think consumers are thinking about.*

Consumers' Minds, Brains, Bodies, and Surrounding Culture and Society Can Be Adequately Studied Independently of One Another

Marketers believe that they can neatly divide and understand consumers' experiences into "buckets," such as what goes on in their minds, what their bodies are doing, and what's unfolding in their surroundings. Moreover, they assume that what goes on in each "bucket" has little to do with what's going on in the others.

In reality, *consumers do not live their lives in the silo-like ways by which universities and businesses organize themselves.* Rather, the mind, brain, body, and external world all shape one another in fluid, dynamic ways. To truly understand consumers, we must focus not on what's happening with one of these four "parts" but on the interactions *between* the parts. So, for example, when we learn about consumers' psychological processes, our insights become richer and more actionable when we understand those processes' cultural and neurological origins. In fact, the mind as we think of it doesn't exist in the absence of the brain, body, and society.[23] In any system—especially living ones—each part constantly influences and is influenced by the others. The most well-known examples involve blind taste tests in which the simple lack of brand information alters participants' taste experience. Further, what is considered a food delicacy in one cultural setting would cause violent physical reactions in a different setting.

Of all the fallacies, this one will likely prove the most stubborn to correct. Nevertheless, research on the integration of mind, body, brain, and society will increasingly challenge the notion that all four of these components are disconnected.[24] For example, studies have revealed that people from different cultures experience physical pain differently, depending on their view and treatment of pain. Other studies demonstrate that social class influences the incidence of heart disease, even when factors such as education level, knowledge about health care, use of medical services, diet, lifestyle, and other factors are taken into account.

Consumers' Memories Accurately Represent Their Experiences

Marketers also tend to think of consumers' brains as cameras—mechanical devices that take "pictures" in the form of memories. Furthermore, they assume that those memories, like photographs, accurately capture what the person saw. They also believe that what a consumer says she remembers remains constant over time, and that a shopping experience a consumer recalls today is the exact same experience she recalled a week ago or will recall some months from now.

But our memories are far more creative—and malleable—than we might expect. Indeed, they're constantly changing without our being aware of it and, as we shall see in chapter 7, memories are metaphors. For example, a major European retailer discovered that an experience recalled by survey respondents differed depending on the way the survey questions were sequenced (and even on the color of the paper the survey was printed on). That is, the cues involved in retrieving a memory, such as the sequencing of questions about it, alter what is recalled.

In another study, a major manufacturer of appliances found that differences in the way a focus group discussion began produced very different recollections among consumers about what it was like to purchase a specific appliance using the Internet. As a comparison point, the researchers used the memory that each participant reported to the person who recruited him for the focus group. A "confederate" planted in each group and unknown to the moderator posed as an active participant. The confederate elicited different accounts—that is, different memories—from the real participants by beginning the discussion in a positive or negative way and by providing nonverbal cues such as frowning, smiling, and so on while real participants presented their views. Nearly every reported memory was changed, and in about half the cases some of the changes were significant. (In a follow-up telephone call approximately two weeks later, most participants described yet a third version of the episode.) The results of this study revealed the well-known "mind guard" phenomenon. Through this process, one person, by silent agreement within the group, becomes the protector of an emerging consensus and often harshly prevents new ideas from entering the discussion.

Consumers Think in Words

Marketers also believe that consumers' thoughts occur only as words. Thus they assume they can understand consumers' thinking by interpreting the words used in standard conversations or written on a questionnaire. Of course, words do play an important role in conveying our thoughts, but they don't provide the whole picture.[25] People generally do not think in words. For example, brain scans and other physiological-function measures demonstrate that activations among brain cells, or neurons, *precede* our conscious awareness of a thought and precede activity in areas of the brain involving verbal language. In fact, these latter neuronal areas become active only later, after a person *unconsciously* chooses to represent these thoughts to herself or to others using verbal language.

Consumers Can Be "Injected" with Company Messages and Will Interpret These Messages as Marketers Intend

The belief that consumers think only in words makes marketers assume that they can inject whatever messages they desire into consumers' minds about a company brand or product positioning. Because of this belief, marketers in effect view consumers' minds as blank pages on which they can write anything they want—if only they can find a clever enough way of doing so. Thus marketers judge the effectiveness of, for example, an advertisement by asking consumers how much of the ad they recall and whether they liked the presentation. The beliefs behind these marketing approaches run contrary to a rich tradition of research on how people create meaning.

When consumers are exposed to product concepts, company stories, or brand information, they don't passively absorb those messages. Instead, they create their own meaning by mixing information from the company with their own memories, other stimuli present at the moment, and the metaphors that come to mind as they think about the firm's message.

For example, consumers can accurately repeat messages from health care authorities about the recommended frequency for oral care checkups and the reasons why they should visit a dental hygienist every six months. Dentists and other health care professionals tell this story repeatedly. Yet although many consumers can replay this story when asked, they actually experience another, quite different story. This other story includes significant skepticism about the true need to visit a dentist every six months. A dental-referral service obtained this insight and the consumer thinking behind it only after carefully analyzing the metaphors that consumers used to describe their dental-office visits. For example, one consumer used a picture from a child's fairy-tale book, specifically Little Red Riding Hood, to describe his feelings that health care professionals fabricated this advice. As this visual metaphor was explored further and the interviewer probed beyond the initial charge that the advice is made up, the person described dental professionals as the deceptive wolf. This revealed his judgment that they are motivated only by self-interest.

The lesson in these examples? The messages consumers take away from a communication may be very different from the ones that a company intended to convey. Moreover, simply asking people what story they heard or believe is behind a marketing message does not reveal what story they have actually created for themselves.

Improving Practice

Taken together, problematic theories-in-use such as those mentioned in this chapter, among many others that managers must move away from, suggest several underlying themes that marketers must understand if they hope to advance their work. For one thing, consumers' decision making and buying behavior are driven more by unconscious thoughts and feelings than by conscious ones, although the latter are also important. These unconscious forces include ever-changing memories, metaphors, images, sensations, and stories that all interact with one another in complex ways to shape decisions and behavior. In addition, consumers aren't like machines; marketers cannot take them apart in order to understand and change them, as we might disassemble a clock to see how it works or to fix it. Rather, consumers are complex living systems and not subject to the kind of manipulation so confidently claimed in the popular press. As such, they operate from conscious and unconscious forces that mutually influence one another—and that are difficult for outsiders to see and measure, let alone alter.

In falling prey to the six misconceptions just outlined, marketers make some predictable errors that can destroy even the most carefully thought out product launch. These errors fall into three categories: mistaking descriptive information for insight, confusing customer data with understanding, and focusing on the wrong elements of the consumer experience.

"Knowing That" versus "Knowing Why"

Many marketers view consumers' thinking and behavior as commodities that lack subtlety or depth. This assumption is especially obvious in the case of business-to-business marketing. Thus marketers fail to dig more deeply into the forces below surface-level thinking and behavior while conducting market research. For example, knowing *that* customers prefer a container that has a round shape rather than a square shape is important. Knowing *why* they prefer this shape is even more important, because it may suggest a desirable configuration that is neither round nor square.

So when a Canadian container manufacturer discovered too late that the preferred package design revealed by a careful conjoint study among its client's customers was simply the lesser of three evils, they had to undertake a costly redevelopment process. Had they understood the "why" behind expressed customer preferences, they would have discovered their error in time to produce a still better design right from the start.

The error hurt both the manufacturer and its client. The manufacturer could have collected essential information for a small additional cost in the original investigation. Instead, it found itself collecting data at a much greater cost, repeating the conjoint study. However, even this expense was small compared to the lost time and the damage to the firm's relationship with its client.

The manufacturer's error did not lie in its use of conjoint analysis but in the firm's failure to dig more deeply into the "why" behind the "what" of customer thinking before conducting the analysis. Though all the details are not important here, these managers and research-team members made a major—and incorrect—assumption. They believed that customers would interpret a midpoint on a scale used in the study as indicating indifference (no strong feelings one way or the other). In fact, they interpreted the midpoint as signifying ambivalence (conflicting strong feelings). If the company had known this ahead of time, it could have used this knowledge to guide the design of its research and better interpreted the results.

Data Quantity Does Not Assure Data Quality

Along these same lines, marketers believe that by gathering a huge quantity of consumer data, they've automatically acquired a deep understanding of consumers. But data volume and understanding are not the same. Indeed, most data that managers tend to collect—such as demographic data, purchase intent, and attribute preferences—yield only surface-level information about consumers. These data are not very helpful by themselves, because they serve largely as proxies for other, more important forces or decision influences.

For example, managers seldom stop to ask what chronological age is really measuring. One firm discovered that differences between two age groups actually involved differences in the importance of social connection and independence. Rather than relying on age, the firm found a better way of grouping people based on these variables and greatly improved the value of their segmentation strategy. In this case, the managers stopped to ask what really lay behind the differences in the two age groups—aside from the fact that their subjects were born in different time periods—and sought more direct and reliable measures of social connection and independence.

Worse still, marketers collect the wrong types of data primarily because these types are *easy* to obtain. This is akin to the old joke about the drunk who is searching for his glasses under a street lamp. When a passerby asks the drunk where he lost his glasses, the drunk points to a distant spot in the darkness. Incredulous, the passerby asks the drunk why he's not looking in that distant spot. The drunk replies, "Because this is where the light is." Poor-quality thinking cannibalizes high-quality thinking. In fact, poor-quality thinking confuses fast answers with wise answers, ignoring that quality thinking takes time.

Why is a deep understanding so much more valuable than surface-level data? It enables marketers to apply the knowledge they gain from data to new situations. For instance, a company that understands what the phrase "nurturing my clothes" means to consumers in terms of fabric softeners might not only produce a more successful softener; it might also develop other valued clothing-care products that eliminate wrinkles, preserve colors, and extend fabric life.

A deep understanding of consumers also enables marketers to find common drivers of behavior shared by otherwise diverse target markets. That is, the deeper one digs into consumers' thoughts and feelings, the more one finds commonalities across segments. These commonalities will likely be more important determinants of choice and tend not to change very quickly. For example, one firm offering oral care products conducted an in-depth study of how consumers in Asia, Europe, and North and South America experienced the concept of oral care. Four key factors influencing the choice of oral care products were identified as present in each of these regions. Three of these had been missed by prior research. The firm greatly streamlined its advertising development process and budget by focusing on these four factors, while also being attentive to the different ways in which these factors surfaced in different countries.

Without a deep understanding of consumers—that is, without knowing consumers' hidden thoughts and feelings and the forces behind them—marketers can't accurately anticipate consumers' responses to product designs, features, and ideas that cannot be tested directly with consumers because of time, budget, or competitive reasons. This ability to anticipate consumers' responses based on deep knowledge about them lies at the heart of skillful marketing. As many writers on technological innovation stress, a deep understanding of customers is the only sound basis for developing marketing strategy for discontinuous innovations.

However, true understanding takes work. For example, to grasp what "nurturing clothes" really means, a company must go beyond gathering information about just the functional and psychological benefits of clothing care (for example, longer clothing life or the wearer's attractive appearance). Specifically, the company must understand what "nurturing" means to consumers on a deeper level. (For many, it means serving as a caregiver.) The firm must also know why and when consumers feel their clothing merits nurturing. Many consumers view their clothing as a personal "container" or an extension of the self. Thus, when they feel the need to nurture themselves, they may also need to nurture their clothing—as a major producer of women's hosiery recently discovered.

Marketers only compound the problem of surface-level data when they extract surface *meaning* from the data. Specifically, they rely on their first impressions of the data rather than allowing time for deeper or more counterintuitive insights to emerge. Often their first impressions prove incorrect or incomplete. For example, a European-based automaker experienced this problem when it concluded too quickly that word-of-mouth communication among consumers was the culprit behind a serious problem plaguing the company. The company then developed a strategy to combat negative word of mouth. Since the company hadn't taken the time to discover the deeper causes behind the problem, the new strategy failed to solve the problem. Indeed, the situation only worsened in the meantime.

The Complete Consumer Experience

In addition to confusing lots of data with lots of understanding, marketers also attend to the wrong level of consumer experience. Specifically, they focus 90 percent of their market research on the attributes and functional features of a product or service and their immediate psychological benefits, at the expense of their emotional benefits. For consumers, emotional benefits stem in part from the important values and themes that define and give meaning to their lives. Though a product's attributes and functional benefits are important, they represent just a small part of what really drives consumers.

For instance, a Nestlé Crunch Bar has immediate sensory benefits such as taste, texture, and sound. But these benefits also evoke powerful emotional benefits, such as fond memories of childhood and feelings of security. When Nestlé focused its marketing efforts on just the sensory benefits of the candy bar, it not only lost sales—it also opened the door for competitors to eat their way into the chocolate-bar business.

Marketers also underestimate the scope of the consumer experience.[26] They believe that this experience consists of responses to specific events that unfold in specific periods of time—such as what happens during the time someone spends at a category display in a supermarket or between a TV advertisement and a visit to a store. They focus on these aspects of the consumer experience primarily because they can most easily address them.

But viewing the consumer experience in this way can be hazardous to a company's financial health. A German snack-food company discovered this first-hand when it realized that mothers' decisions to buy the company's product in stores depended only partly on product placement, point-of-purchase cues, and pricing. The more powerful forces behind the women's purchasing decisions consisted of their beliefs about teaching proper nutrition practices to their children, among other things. As it turned out, these beliefs included principles governing how and when to reward children with exceptions to nutritious eating (that is, with snack foods). Until the company learned to present its product in a way that was consistent with ideas about good nutrition and special treats, it missed out on major sales opportunities.

Finally, marketers rarely grasp the full extent of the consumer experience because they don't ask enough questions. Rather, they form answers based on first impressions, and then ask only those questions that verify their hypotheses. For example, because of anecdotal evidence reinforced by focus-group research, a manager at a major U.S. credit-card company decided that young adults prized ownership of credit cards for one reason in particular. She thus had a hypothesis in mind that implied a basic research question focusing on this specific reason.

An expensive survey was designed that (not surprisingly) "proved" her hypothesis—because she had framed the more specific survey questions specifically to confirm her conclusion. Moreover, she had done so without being consciously aware of the bias in her survey design.

If this manager had not focused on one particular answer, she might have learned that the initial question wasn't the most valuable one to ask. In fact, she could have explored a more fundamental question about the meaning of credit-card ownership that could have yielded much richer information. Indeed, just as she was conducting her survey, a competitor began looking beyond the idea that young people value credit cards for the one reason the manager had identified. The competitor uncovered multiple underlying reasons—and discovered that they can change for individual customers depending on the context each time they use their cards. The competing company designed a far more effective marketing campaign based on its new knowledge—and won a significant share of this target market.

We must envision and embrace new ideas and find new ways to gather information if we hope to create a new paradigm. Managers who want to conduct truly insightful consumer analysis must progress through the lower two levels depicted in figure 1-2, acknowledging that mental activity emerges from the interaction of social and biological processes. Otherwise, they'll face the same precarious future as the ousted CEOs that Drucker describes.

FIGURE 1 - 2

Insightful Consumer Analysis

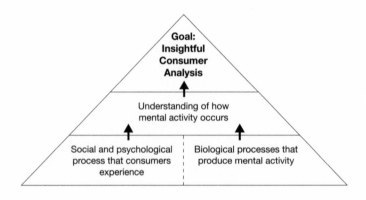

Customer-centricity

Nothing affects an income statement's bottom line as much as its top line—gross billings, the initial parameter within which all other "lines" operate. Marketing owns the top line, ultimately a measure of a firm's *customer-centricity,* the degree to which it focuses on latent as well as obvious needs of current and potential customers. High customer-centricity involves two acts of hearing or listening:

1. The customer "hears"—truly understands—that a firm's offerings merit a purchase.
2. The firm hears—truly understands—through skillful listening what current and potential customers are saying in their native language about their deep thoughts and feelings.

These qualities suggest two simple propositions:

1. The more skilled marketers are in listening to customers, the more effective their marketing strategies will be in establishing the value of the firm's offerings.
2. The more clearly current and potential customers understand the value of the firm's offerings, the larger the top line will be.

A customer-centric firm, then, avoids technological arrogance—the notion that customers are passive and must be aggressively sold rather than skillfully heard. Skillful listening tells the management team how large a challenge they face, especially in terms of meeting latent needs. This intelligence leads to better teamwork and a winning business model and marketing plan.

A customer-centric firm understands how people can interpret the same data differently, why they see one creature more readily than the other, and how to respond so that those who must see a duck can do so without preventing others from seeing a rabbit. It also enables those customers who think that they want to see a rabbit also to see the duck when that's in their best interest. This extraordinary core competence requires insights from several disciplines about how the mind works. Indeed, much of *How Customers Think* involves helping both managers and their customers to see beyond their first impressions.

Embracing New Knowledge through Imagination

To change the current marketing paradigm, we must envision completely new ways of thinking and open ourselves to ideas that initially may seem trivial or irrelevant to business. A lively imagination, and even a sense of play, can help.

To that end, let's start our paradigm-shifting voyage by exercising our imaginations. Picture yourself hosting a dinner party. This party is no ordinary gathering. Your guests range from zoologists and art historians to physiologists, financiers, and neurosurgeons. They're milling around, sampling the hors d'oeuvres, and introducing themselves to one another. Even more unusual, you've provided them with a list of questions to discuss, including:

- Why does art matter in everyday life?
- What role do memories play in daily life?
- What is eating yogurt like?
- How do people feel about genetically engineered foods?
- What constitutes caring?
- What does cleanliness mean?
- What do global account managers experience?
- How does having a major new insight feel?
- Why pay a premium for a commodity ingredient?
- What role does breakfast play in the relationship between a mother and her children?
- What does "feel good" mean?

Granted, such a diverse group of guests would probably not mingle easily at a real party. But if you *did* orchestrate such a gathering, the resulting conversations would yield priceless information for marketers who want to understand how consumers decide whether to buy their products or services.

Thus, this book serves as a surrogate party. The quotation that appears at the beginning of this chapter expresses its central tenet. Our ability to tap into consumers' minds is limited only by our imagination; that is, *our ability to reproduce images and concepts, reshape or recombine them into new images and concepts, and anticipate what the experience of these new thoughts might be like.*[27]

We desperately need imagination to transform how we do business. Not only do we need more imaginative strategies for understanding consumers, we also need new ways of thinking about and using the information we glean from these efforts. We need both *imaginative knowing* and *imaginative doing*.

The Tyranny of "Or"

Envisioning this strange party can help us stretch our thinking processes, but the party has another purpose as well: to break down the artificial distinction between theory and practice or, as the line is sometimes drawn, between basic and applied research.

Vincent Barabba calls the building of artificial and unnecessary distinctions "the triumph of the tyranny of 'or' over the greater good of 'and.'" Barabba is right: Many topics do not fall exclusively into either the theoretical or the practical realm (any more than they belong to only one discipline). Theory and practice are nested within one another. When we split them apart and leave them that way, we lose valuable insights. Scientists often split things apart, but with the goal of better understanding how they work together.

Marketing managers—who already feel overwhelmed by proliferating data, tougher decisions, conflicting advice, and a ticking clock—will find many of the ideas in this book brand new and disquieting, because they come from places where most marketers rarely tread. But readers can rest assured: The ideas discussed here all meet two important criteria for breaking down the walls between theory and practice and between disciplines. First, *they are firmly grounded in the scientific research of multiple disciplines*—that is, the formal research that supports every idea in *How Customers Think* meets each discipline's standards of internal and external validity.

Beyond traditional standards of validity, the ideas in this book also *address real consumer phenomena*—that is, they have "implementable validity." According to Chris Argyris, *implementable validity* means that an idea lends itself to effective action. However, putting an idea into action requires that we use the knowledge explicitly, such as thinking aloud about it in the form of a causal proposition. For example, pharmaceutical research validates the following causal proposition: Medications have greater efficacy when physicians use metaphors to explain how or why a new medicine works. A parallel business-oriented causal proposition might be: A company can enhance consumers' experience with its product by using metaphors that communicate how or why the product works. Drake Stimson, a marketing director at P&G, credits this principle for making Febreze the most successful new product launch in Procter & Gamble's history. By using metaphors effectively in its introductory advertising for Febreze, a product based on a patented new molecule, P&G basically doubled first-year sales over what conventional thinking would have predicted.[28]

The term "customer" in the book's title reflects a tradition in marketing that embraces both business customers and ultimate consumers, although the book covers more of the latter than the former. Marketing managers in both industrial and consumer settings have applied nearly all the ideas in this book in both business-to-business (B2B) and business-to-consumer (B2C) contexts. However, readers shouldn't confuse the *successful* use of valid ideas with their *widespread* use. Otherwise, we wouldn't need this book.

Viewed with an open mind, these ideas can unlock the riches offered by a diversity of perspectives and help managers win satisfied customers. Multiple perspectives can also help marketers avoid the all-too-typical trap, captured in figure 1-3, in which managers and researchers mistake their own reflections for those of consumers.

In your journey through this book, keep in mind that, above all else, the book is about quality thinking—which takes time, energy, the occasional suspension of disbelief and doubt, and an attitude of serious play. Quality thinking also requires the courage to look bad or feel silly or uneasy for a short time in order to succeed in the longer term. As with multiple viewings of an engaging photograph or painting, each subsequent encounter with an intriguing idea can reveal something different.

FIGURE 1 - 3

"For crying out loud, gentlemen! That's us! Someone's installed the one-way mirror in backward!"

As you'll see, this book draws on the latest research from a wealth of disciplines. These insights often offer alternative—and far more effective—ways of seeing and understanding consumers. The book also includes examples of how real marketers, in real companies, have applied this understanding successfully. By understanding more deeply and more fully the true nature of the consumer's mind, marketers can ask the right questions, get the right data, and interpret that data in fresher, more effective ways. The first step to this deeper understanding is to begin imagining what a new worldview might reveal.

Chapter Two

A Voyage to New Frontiers

We are not candy-coated biological pellets rattling around

in a social world independent of our biological world.

—Anne Harrington, "Getting Under the Skin"

O F THE MANY different social and biological disciplines from which marketing can benefit, brain science is one of the most important. To understand the emerging paradigm for consumer research, marketers must appreciate the power and complexity of the human brain.

This remarkable organ contains 100 billion neurons, or cells, and perhaps as many as 1 trillion. The cerebral cortex, the outer covering of the brain where cognition occurs, is about the area and thickness of a cloth napkin at an upscale restaurant. Relatively new in evolutionary terms, the cortex houses about 30 billion neurons that form a vast network of about 1 million billion connections, creating neural circuits that stimulate conscious and unconscious thought and behavior. How vast is this network? The number of particles in the known universe is 10 followed by approximately 79 zeros. The number of neural-circuitry connections possible is 10 followed by more than a million zeros.[1] It's vast.

In reuniting artificially splintered fields of study, the new paradigm reestablishes the connections among brain, body, mind, and the social world that the old paradigm artificially detached. These four components are connected in one seamless, dynamic system. They each influence—and are influenced by—one another. For example, our brains interact with the social and physical world around us; the body mediates this partnership. The body senses information about the world, generates chemical and physical responses that create emotions and thoughts, and moves in response to the brain.

The alliance of brain, body, mind, and society is mutually informing and fully codependent.[2] One can't exist without the others. The brain's nearly countless neurons and interneural associations receive part of their ordering from the external world. For instance, social forces strongly influence which neurons gain or lose prominence or importance and which connections among them will form, be reinforced, or become extinct.[3] Michael Tomasello, a cognitive scientist and codirector of the Max Planck Institute for Evolutionary Anthropology in Germany, points out how social forces have shaped the human brain:

> *The 6 million years that separate human beings from other great apes is a very short time evolutionarily, with modern humans and chimpanzees sharing something on the order of 99 percent of their genetic material. . . . There simply has not been enough time for normal processes of biological evolution involving genetic variation and natural selection to have created, one by one, each of the cognitive skills necessary for modern humans to invent and maintain complex tool-use industries and technologies, complex forms of symbolic communication and representation, and complex social organizations and institutions.[4]*

So how have humans acquired these cognitive skills so quickly? According to Tomasello, the key mechanism has been social or cultural transmission, which works exponentially faster than organic evolution. Our social environment has developed concurrently with our biological characteristics and intellectual capacities.

Figure 2-1 depicts the interconnectedness of brain, body, mind, and society as a three-dimensional pyramid with four corners. For every individual (whether marketer or consumer), each of the four components occupies a corner of the pyramid and influences every other component. Whenever one component changes, the others do as well, below our awareness in the cognitive unconscious. Occasionally, the results of these interactions enter our conscious thoughts. Have you ever savored a "delicacy" in the presence of a guest from a different cul-

FIGURE 2 - 1

The New Paradigm of an Integrated Mind-Brain-Body-Society

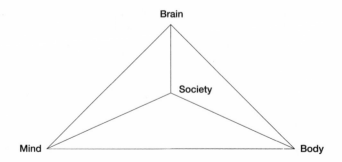

ture and noticed that guest grimacing in disgust? Or has another culture's "delicacy" disgusted you so that you got queasy just looking at it?

Marketing lies at the hub of these interactions. That's why the other fields of discovery are critical to effective marketing practice. Companies like General Motors, Experience Engineering, IBM, Hewlett-Packard, Procter & Gamble, and the Coca-Cola Company are learning more about consumer needs, satisfaction, and loyalty by studying the totality of the brain-mind-body-society system's four components than by examining the parts individually. A leading European electronics firm recently launched a research program to understand how the tactile experience of personal communication devices varies among consumers around the world and how those differences manifest in their usage behavior. However, too many managers study customers as if only one of the four components mattered and end up eliciting the wrong information from consumers, interpreting it incorrectly, and developing products and services that underwhelm the marketplace.

Why? Because turning one's worldview inside out is scary, difficult work.[5] After all, we form our assumptions about how the world works very early in life—long before we learn how to examine our beliefs objectively. Our worldview is deeply embedded and hard to see, let alone change. Also, scientists whose work could help us open up the pyramid often communicate unintelligibly and seemingly inconsistently to nonscientists.[6]

Anne Harrington, science historian and director of Harvard University's Mind/Brain/Behavior Initiative, offers an evocative image that may help managers more easily understand the systemic nature of the pyramid:

> [H]uman beings are . . . like sponges. Sponges, of course, are animals who are saturated by the ambiance in which they live, and whose physiology presupposes the presence of that ambiance. It would not make sense to speak of the physiology of sponges on the one hand, and the watery "context" in which they live on the other hand; the water is part of the internal works by which these animals function.[7]

We are not, as Harrington notes further, hard, candy-coated biological pellets rattling around in a social world that is independent of our biological world.

The partnership between the brain and society takes on even more weight when we start thinking about the mind of the market—that all-important interaction between marketers' and consumers' conscious and unconscious minds. As with consumers, marketers' experiences with the outside world strongly influence their thoughts, abilities, and emotional responses. For example, if you grew up with parents and teachers who encouraged you to notice anomalies or unusual occurrences, then you may be especially adept at spotting emerging consumer trends. If you enjoy embarking on risky new adventures outside of work, you may take more risk with a new market research method in your job. Such interactions between mind and environment also feature feedback loops that either reinforce or discourage a manager's behavior. For instance, if an adventurous type works in an organization that discourages risk taking, he or she may eventually take fewer risks at work.

Among consumers, the experience of a problem, the search for goods and services to solve it, and the evaluation of these offerings all derive from the mind-brain-body-society partnership. For instance, the social context assigned to an object can produce markedly different physiological reactions. In one experiment, people were presented with an odor that the researchers told them came from an aged cheese. Most people reacted in a mildly aversive way to it but indicated a willingness to taste the cheese. The researchers told another group of participants who received the same odor that the smell came from old gym socks. As you might expect, these people recoiled from the odor.

The Mind of the Market

As we saw above, the mutual-influence structure represented by the brain-body-mind-society pyramid shapes the thinking and behavior of each marketer and each consumer. What happens when a "marketer pyramid" and a "consumer pyramid" come together, when marketers and consumers interact? The result appears in figure 2-2. As the figure shows, marketers and consumers influence one another on both a conscious and unconscious level. Marketers have failed to tap into the unconscious level where pyramid dynamics are most active.

As an illustration, consider the possible influences at work in the purchase of a car. A man who drives a sports car may have deep-seated emotional reasons, not just practical ones, for buying it. He may want others to perceive him as youthful, daring, sexy, and aggressive. Cultural influences, such as advertising and the car-buying habits of other people, may have fostered those internal desires. They may have roots in

FIGURE 2 - 2

The Mind of the Market

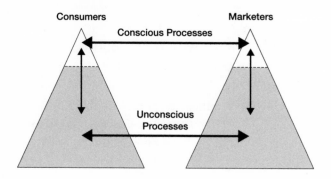

childhood events, like seeing a suave young uncle in a red-hot sports car with an attractive passenger.

At the same time, these internal desires and early influences are what make advertising or other forms of social influence so effective. These desires enable the aspiring sports-car driver to create meaningful experiences based on the information he sees in an ad and his experiences in test-driving, purchasing, and using the vehicle. Thus, "outer" marketing activities play an essential role in evoking the "inner world" of consumers. A consumer's decision to buy a particular product doesn't arise solely from either world—it arises from the interplay of those two worlds. The failure to understand that a consumer's inner world can powerfully transform a marketer's outer-world message leads to most product-development failures.

In the last few years, tremendous advances in sociology, anthropology, cognitive neuroscience, and psychology (to name but a few fields) have helped managers to understand the dynamics shown in figures 2-1 and 2-2.[8] We've learned more about how marketers' unconscious assumptions and expectations influence which questions they choose to ask consumers, how they frame those questions in a survey, whom they select as participants in a study, and which analytical tools they use.[9] These unconscious processes shape what information consumers provide—and what they don't.

Unconscious processes among consumers also influence their *responses* to marketers' questions. For example, the order in which researchers pose questions can make a big difference in the answers they receive, as the following example illustrates. A consumer-satisfaction question in a survey conducted in Japan by a European automaker consistently indicated a high satisfaction rating. A question about repair frequency followed later in the survey. When the automaker asked the question about repair frequency first, the satisfaction rating decreased and the reported repair frequency increased. Both changes were significant. By sequencing the questions differently, the survey designers unknowingly primed consumers' responses in different ways—all without *anyone's* awareness. The carmaker's managers accidentally became aware of the priming, and the company had to revisit its conclusions about consumer satisfaction in its global markets.

A Closer Look at the New Paradigm

If the brain-body-mind-society pyramid represents the heart of the new paradigm, then how might the rest of it appear? To envision this, keep these two principles in mind from figures 2-1 and 2-2:

- Culture and biology go hand-in-hand.
- The mind of the market emerges from the interaction of consumers' and managers' conscious and unconscious minds.

The contours of the new paradigm reveal startling truths about the nature of human communication, thought, emotion, and memory. We glimpsed these realities in chapter 1; in the rest of this chapter, we'll examine them more closely. Remember to suspend your judgment to avoid prematurely dismissing an idea; instead, ask yourself, "If this idea were true, would it change how I think or what I do?" If the answer is yes, then explore further.

Thought Is Based on Images, Not Words

Human thought arises from what neuroscientists call images. These topographically organized neural representations occur in the early sensory cortices—an admittedly rather technical description. When neurons are sufficiently activated—that is, when a sound, sight, or other stimulus turns them on and causes the connections between them (the synapses) to fire—we may experience those electrochemical discharges as conscious thought.[10] An important difference exists between *how a thought occurs* (neural activity) and *how we consciously experience a thought,* if at all, once it occurs. So we must carefully distinguish among how thought happens, what stimulated it in the first place, and how the thought is expressed afterwards. Words can trigger our thoughts and enable us to express them. That's why people believe that thought occurs largely as words.

The neural activities, or images, involved in thought are not necessarily images as we usually think of them. However, since about two-thirds of all stimuli reach the brain through the visual system, we often experience images (as neuroscientists think of them) visually as well as verbally and in other ways. Stimuli leading to a thought may take many forms.[11] For example, the neural activity stimulated by the fragrance of coffee on a walk to work may produce a picture in our mind's eye of reading the morning paper at the coffee shop. We may even hear a response in our mind's ear—"Yeah, I've got time" or "No, I'd better not"—or even voice these conclusions aloud when walking with someone else.

Neural activity may be *stimulated* by sound, touch, motion, background feelings such as moods, and emotions.[12] The neural activity may also be *expressed* in these and other ways. For example, a Coke advertisement can stimulate neural activations. The consequences of these activations—for instance, the recall of an experience of sharing a Coke with a friend, reaching for a Coke, and tasting it—involve other neural activations. Thus different kinds of images or thoughts are linked to one another and occur together.

As we've seen, verbal language factors into the representation, storage, and communication of thought.[13] But despite its great importance in facilitating thought, *verbal language is not the same as thought*.[14] Yet managers persist in seeing thought as word-based. Indeed, "the view that thought is internalized conversation is widespread," Jonathan H. Turner explains in his book, *On the Origins of Human Emotions: A Sociological Inquiry into the Evolution of Human Affect*. Turner continues:

> But a moment of reflection would reveal this to be impossible. If thinking were merely covert talk, we would seem very dim-witted, since talk is a sequential modality and hence very slow. . . . [While] we can often slow the process of thinking down by "talking to ourselves," this kind of thinking is the exception rather than the rule. . . . [The] subordination of other sensory inputs under vision shapes the way humans actually think: in blurs of images, many of which don't penetrate our consciousness.[15]

Examples of people who have thought without language—ranging from deaf-mutes in preliterate societies to adults with brain dysfunction—have received substantial attention.[16] Nobel Prize winner Gerald Edelman has observed that "conceptual capabilities develop in evolution well before speech."[17] Stephen Pinker, Peter de Florez Professor in the Department of Brain and Cognitive Sciences at the Massachusetts Institute of Technology, asks and answers the following question:

> Is *thought dependent on words? . . . Or are our thoughts couched in some silent medium of the brain—a language of thought or "mentalese"—and merely couched in words whenever we need to communicate them to a listener? . . . The idea that thought is the same thing as language is an example of what can be called a conventional absurdity. . . . There is no scientific evidence that languages dramatically shape their speakers' way of thinking.*[18] (emphasis in original)

Cognition, then, shapes language, not the other way around. We develop particular verbal terms to express thoughts—neural activities—that matter to us. Of course, these important concepts are reinforced as new generations of speakers learn existing terms. The connotation of "Please be quiet" differs from that of "Shut up!" because we have developed a need to express the shades of meaning in each phrase. The *existence* of these phrases doesn't create the different thoughts and feelings that they express. If a phrase or word has no relevance or meaning to us, then we won't retain it. When we encounter new ideas through verbal communication, they root themselves within a preexisting system that gives them relevance. Different cultures emphasize different thoughts; that's why each verbal language has expressions not found or readily translated by other languages.[19]

We must view "language" in a multimodal way that includes many channels of communication, not just literal speech. This principle factors into the use of psychodrama wherein body language helps surface insights about individual and organizational issues that verbal language alone can't reveal. Similarly, a key part of metaphor-elicitation techniques involves the creation of visual stories or collages that uncover consumers' and managers' hidden thoughts and feelings.[20] By engaging the language of visual imagery, we enable a richer verbal description of inner feelings. For example, in a study of the hosiery-wearing experience, women who created collages were able to articulate far more clearly than those who did not create collages the nature of their conflicting feelings about wearing hosiery.

Most Communication Is Nonverbal

Experts generally agree that most human communication (as much as 80 percent) occurs through *nonverbal* means. These means include touch; vocal intonations; gestures; body posture; distance; sense of time; eye contact, gaze, and pupil dilation; and visual cues such as apparel and adornments. Through these nonverbal channels, people exchange messages and meaning.[21]

Tone and manner of speech (also known as *paralanguage*) also influence this exchange. For example, a person who says "Yeah, right!" may communicate the exact opposite message by using a sarcastic tone of voice. The way in which we present our spoken statements—especially if we combine tone of voice with other cues such as gestures—conveys a great deal of meaning. The resulting message may communicate our true feelings or thoughts far more than our spoken words do. Marketers who rely too much on analyses of printed consumer transcripts miss out on these messages. For example, an R&D lab at a major communications company performed a voice-pitch analysis of customer responses to a service satisfaction question. Voice-pitch analysis is a method for isolating various psychological states present while a person is speaking. The lab concluded that a high level of uncertainty was present in many of the most positive responses given. That is, although the literal statement customers provided indicated high levels of satisfaction, the uncertainty expressed in their voices indicated considerably less satisfaction. Had the company relied only on literal verbal language, they would have had false confidence in their service delivery systems.

Knowing how to interpret paralanguage is important in many marketing settings, such as telemarketing, face-to-face selling, and voice-over advertising. Researchers have conducted some especially intriguing studies involving "voice masking," in which a speaker's actual words are masked but his or her tone of voice remains distinguishable to study participants. According to these studies, our judgment about the value and merit of a speaker's statements hinges on our evaluation of his or her tone of voice. For example, if we think that a speaker sounds honest or sincere, we will likely give his or her literal message—the actual words he or she is speaking—more weight. Indeed, in the event of an apparent contradiction between tone of voice and spoken statements, listeners will believe the former over the latter. Thus, the paralanguage of sales personnel or spokespeople in a televised commercial may influence consumers' behavior far more than the literal content of their message.

Edward T. Hall's classic work *The Silent Language* provides further evidence of the power of paralanguage. Hall identifies ten "primary message systems" involved in human communication.[22] Only *part* of one of the systems he identified—interpersonal communication—involves verbal language. The other nine systems rely on nonlinguistic forms of communication.

This surprising power of paralanguage becomes less surprising when we examine the development of spoken language. As it turns out, spoken language emerged relatively recently in human evolution. Moreover, written, phonetic-based language developed even later, about 5,000 years ago, as a byproduct of our ability to detect the edges of shapes.[23] With so much evolutionary practice, our brains are far better at sensing and interpreting paralanguage than they are at understanding spoken or written language. Yet most market research tools rely on literal language to capture information, synthesize and report survey responses, draw conclusions from focus groups, and trace literal data such as those from scanners. Thus, *a great mismatch exists between the way consumers experience and think about their world and the methods marketers use to collect this information.*

Metaphor Is Central to Thought

Metaphors, the representation of one thing in terms of another, often help us express the way we feel about or view a particular aspect of our lives. For example, if a man says, "My hair is my signature," he doesn't mean that he uses his hair to sign his name. Rather, he means that something about his hair signals what kind of person he is to others. This metaphor is therefore rich with meaning about identity, individuality, and the significance of other people.

Metaphors stimulate the workings of the human mind.[24] By one estimate, we use almost six metaphors per minute of spoken language.[25] Through brain-imaging technologies, researchers better understand the neural bases of metaphor. For example, although both halves of the human brain enable literal and figurative language (which includes metaphor), the right half is more strongly associated with metaphoric language.[26]

Why do we think so often in metaphors? They help us interpret what we perceive in the world around us; indeed, they help us perceive the world, period. They help us see new connections, interpret our experiences, and draw new meaning from those experiences.[27] Metaphors also affect imagination.[28] Philosopher Mark Johnson explains, "Without imagination, nothing in the world could be meaningful. Without imagination, we could never interpret our experience. Without imagination, we could never reason toward knowledge of reality."[29] Speaking metaphorically, *metaphor is the engine of imagination.* In fact, the use of metaphor together with visual imagery lies at the heart of all major advances in science, according to Arthur I. Miller, professor of history and philosophy of science at University College London.[30]

Metaphors are so basic to our thinking that marketers and their audiences alike are often unaware of them. As we'll see, market researchers can glean valuable knowledge by encouraging consumers to use metaphors. Why? Because metaphors can help bring consumers' important—but unconscious—thoughts and feelings to the surface.[31] Indeed, metaphor constitutes a powerful tool for unearthing the hidden thoughts and feelings that have such a profound influence on consumers' decision making. Indeed, consumer researchers around the world have found using metaphors effective in helping people to bring their unconscious experiences into their awareness and then to communicate those experiences.[32]

Many metaphors also reveal what's called "embodied cognition"—the referencing of our sensory and motor systems to express our thinking.[33] Examples of such metaphors abound: "I hope you *see* what I mean" or "get the *point*"; "I don't wish to get too *far ahead* of myself" or "*in over my head*"; "I hope these ideas don't *put you off*" by "*being beneath* you" or "*sounding unbalanced*"; and "I want these ideas to *reach* people" with different "*viewpoints.*"

Emotion's Partnership with Reason

As we saw in chapter 1, most market research methods are biased toward reason and away from emotion.[34] Marketers collect and interpret survey and other consumer information as if consumers' decisions stemmed primarily from conscious, logical processes. Why? It's less messy to interpret the resulting responses from consumers. Consumers share only the logical aspects of their decision-making process because marketers ask for those aspects—and conscious, logical thoughts are much easier to articulate than emotions.

Few managers would dispute the importance of emotions in their own and consumers' decision making (their espoused theory), yet in their behavior they persist in their pro-reason bias (their theory-in-use). Managers and researchers collect and present information as if decisions derive from conscious processes (in particular, from logical inference), in which emotion has only a bit part in the drama of making decisions. This approach reflects a bias, itself a reflection of powerful emotional drivers, that decision making *ought* to involve as little emotion and as much reason as possible. This bias, in turn, may produce unreliable data.

The pro-reason bias in research is half-right. It is also half-wrong. Multiple, complex reasoning systems do work together during decision making. And as we saw in chapter 1, so do multiple systems of emotion.[35] More important, both sets of systems collaborate. *Reason and emotion are not opposites; they are partners who occasionally disagree but depend on one another for success.* Joseph Turner elaborates:

> To select among alternatives requires some way to assess the relative
> value of these alternatives, and this ability to assess alternatives is tied to
> emotions. Emotions give each alternative a value and, thereby, provide a
> yardstick to judge and to select among alternatives. This process need not
> be conscious; and indeed, for all animals including humans, it rarely is.
> Thus to be rational means also to be emotional; and any line that
> we draw separating cognition and emotion fails to understand the
> neurology of cognitions. *One can't sustain cognitions beyond working
> memory without tagging them with emotion.*[36]

That is, if an idea doesn't have emotional significance for us, we're not likely to store it and therefore won't have it available for later recall.

Studies of patients with particular patterns of brain damage (including the classic example referred to earlier involving Phineas Gage) reveal that when reasoning systems are intact but emotional capacities damaged, poor decisions result. The same outcome occurs when emotional systems are intact and reasoning capacities damaged. The separation of reason and emotion, however convenient, is misleading, according to Antonio Damasio:

> *The lower levels in the neural edifice of reason are the same ones that regulate the processing of emotions and feelings. . . . Emotion, feeling, and biological regulation all play a role in human reason. The lowly orders of our organism are in the loop of high reason.*[37]

The emotion–reason partnership argues for using research methods that enable both reason and emotion to surface and reflect their coexistence and mutual influence.[38]

Most Thought, Emotion, and Learning Occur without Awareness

According to most estimates, about 95 percent of thought, emotion, and learning occur in the unconscious mind—that is, without our awareness.[39] As important as it is, consciousness is the end result of a system of neurons processing information in largely unconscious ways.[40] Feelings, the conscious experience of emotions, are only the tip of the iceberg. Now picture, if you will, a few seals lounging on the top of the iceberg. The few seals represent our limited ability to hold more than a few chunks of information at this tip of our consciousness at any one time. If new seals arrive, others must go.

In marketing, much knowledge about consumer decision making is based on information gathered through verbal protocols (telephone interviews, group meetings, questionnaires) that rely on self-reflection and self-awareness. In other words, these methods are largely confined to seeing only what is on the tip of the iceberg. However, as leading neuroscientist Joseph LeDoux cautions: "We have to be very careful when we use verbal reports based on introspective analyses of one's own mind as scientific data."[41]

So much of our knowledge is unconscious or tacit that we can never be fully aware of all that we know. We often devise surprising new answers by synthesizing information at hand, which is a basic function of our inductive and deductive thinking skills. These unconscious thinking processes use existing "data" to produce conscious thoughts that consist of new answers.[42] For example, long-intimate couples can usually answer questions about how their partners would react to unexpected events because of their deep understanding of each other. This understanding enables them to infer their partner's future reactions based on past behavior. Similarly, managers who deeply understand their consumers may accurately anticipate their responses to a new product before the firm presents it. By synthesizing existing knowledge, a manager may know implicitly whether a proposed consumer incentive will achieve a particular unit sales goal. Sales personnel know automatically when to begin closing a sale, although they may struggle to explain this knowledge.

Because most knowledge is hidden, surfacing it presents a major challenge. Managers can use metaphors involving both conscious and unconscious processes to address this challenge. By evoking and analyzing metaphors from consumers, marketers can draw back the curtains on consumers' tacit knowledge, encourage consumers to look in, and then share what they see so that managers can create enduring value for customers in response to the insights revealed.

The Importance of Socially Shared Mental Models

As we've seen, thought occurs when neurons become active. Different groups of neurons—thoughts—communicate back and forth with one another. One thought literally leads to another, which may lead back again to the earlier thought. Sets of connected neuronal groups constitute mental models, or what researchers sometimes call *scripts* or *schema*. Mental models help us interpret the flood of stimuli and information that our brains absorb from the world around us. Because we simply can't process all of the incoming information entering our brains, we need a system to filter it, to group it, and to otherwise render it more understandable.

For the sake of efficiency, our mental models help us decide which information to attend to and what to do with it. For example, people's mental models determine their approach to ill-structured problems, their attraction to a particular auto design, their disposition toward snack foods, and their conduct in an upscale boutique shop. Can you imagine a situation where mental models are absent?[43] Probably not.

Moreover, groups of people—as diverse as purchasing agents for chemicals used in industrial paints, European consumers of Coca-Cola, or parents bringing their children to Disney World—share important features of their individual mental models.[44] Called *consensus maps*, these shared features can yield valuable insights for marketing strategy development.[45] *In fact, consensus maps are possibly the single most important set of insights that a manager can have about consumers.* Consensus maps, when surfaced through metaphors, reflect consumers' unconscious and conscious thoughts and feelings as well as the commingling of emotion and reason.

As you might imagine, human beings possess an extraordinary number of mental models, although most of them lie dormant at any one time. When they *are* activated by our experiences, we're generally not aware of their activation. We often become aware of our mental models only when an experience dramatically contradicts those models and the expectations that lie at their core.

The notion of mental models is well established in the social and management sciences.[46] Quantitative methods in these fields have greatly improved our ability to depict mental models, especially those elements that otherwise different individuals have in common. The task of *managing* mental models—or, more important, the consensus maps that reflect a market segment's common thinking—is less well developed as a formal activity. However, as managers use new insights from various disciplines to understand consumers' deeper thoughts and feelings, they will likely become more proactive in reshaping their customers' consensus maps.

The Fragile Power of Memory

People tend to think of a memory as a snapshot of a past experience that can fade or be lost over time. However, if we view the human experience as the intersection of mind, brain, body, and society, then memory becomes a creative product of our encounters, beliefs, and plans. This creative product develops at a preconscious level; that is, we're not aware of its development. Rather than a printed photograph, managers will see a memory reconstructed each time it's recalled. Sometimes, the differences from one activation to another are small and unimportant, such as recalling our name. Other times, they are larger with great consequence, as we have learned from eyewitness testimony research.[47]

Furthermore, marketing is a major source of influence on what consumers recall. That is, marketing efforts such as product and service development and delivery not only make memories possible in the first place, communications about them also alter consumers' subsequent recollections of product or service experiences. This is one of the important ways in which managers' conscious and unconscious minds influence consumers' minds. As we shall see, memory is story-based and, together with universally shared archetypes and core metaphors, memory affects the stories or coherent meanings that consumers create about brands and companies. The consensus maps shared by consumers represent a kind of diagram or outline of these important stories.

The rapid accumulation of insights about human behavior reveals the outlines of a new way of understanding consumers' thoughts and behavior. While the conscious and unconscious minds are active partners, consumers' unconscious minds contain the vast majority of relevant information for managers. As we'll see in part II, marketers can uncover this information through a variety of innovative research tools and techniques.

Understanding the Mind of the Market

Chapter Three

Illuminating the Mind

Consumers' Cognitive Unconscious

Most of what we know we don't know we know.

It usually seems that we consciously will our

voluntary actions, but this is an illusion.

—*Daniel Wegner,* The Illusion of Conscious Will

IMAGINE A FILTER that enables you to see, in color, the variations in the heat intensity of objects. Through such a filter, a fresh loaf of bread cooling for fifteen minutes resembles a rainbow as different parts of the loaf lose heat at varied rates. The bread retains its usual shape and texture, but looks far more interesting through this filter. Now imagine a similar filter applied to consumers' unconscious thoughts. More colors appear than any fireworks show could ever hope to display. These new colors represent the hidden treasures in the shadows of the mind—the cognitive unconscious. Learning to see and use these colors is the major frontier managers must explore as they seek new insights into consumers' thinking and behavior. Indeed, most influences on consumer behavior reside at this frontier; consumers encounter these influences and process them unknowingly.[1] Firms that most effectively leverage their explorations of this frontier will gain crucial competitive advantages.

Equally important, consumers will benefit as well. The limitations managers face using surface-oriented research methods are also limitations on consumers. Consumers are empowered, instead, when research methods are used that allow them the freedom to explore and express their innermost thoughts and feelings along with those on the surface.

The term *cognitive unconscious,* sometimes called the unconscious mind, refers to the mental processes operating outside consumers' awareness that, together with conscious processes, create their experience of the world. As used in this book, the term does not refer to psychoanalytic concepts, although those too have an important presence in the unconscious mind and merit treatment all on their own.[2] Before we explore the unconscious mind, let's discuss its relationship with the conscious mind.

Being Human

We share a great deal with other creatures.[3] For instance, 98 percent of our genes are common to those of chimpanzees. They and other species maintain elaborate social hierarchies, as do we. Ants, for example, have castes; systems to organize labor and food cultivation; characteristics such as altruism, sacrifice, care for the injured, and sharing in times of scarcity; and the ability to mount preemptive military strikes, follow norms of reciprocity, and so on.[4]

Their intricate communication structure, which is based on taste and smell rather than sight and sound, enables them to coordinate complex activities and to convey such things as the exact location of food and whether to pursue it. Other creatures display degrees of thinking, emotions, feelings, and certain kinds of intentionality—the sense that doing one thing leads to another. The latter might take the form of giving a false impression for individual gain, such as fooling a predator or a competitor for food, or attracting a mate.[5] Much of what we know about human emotion comes from the study of other animals due to such similarities.[6] Thus, neither social activities nor the existence of emotions and feelings are uniquely human. *Rather, our ability to reflect on these states and activities and to make considered judgments about them makes us special.* The human aptitude for self-awareness and self-reflection, then, is what differentiates us from every other living creature. We refer to this ability as "high-order consciousness," or just "consciousness," in this book.

Consciousness is a developmental process in humans. An infant's capacity for awareness grows as it learns what the mind is and what the mind does.[7] At around eighteen months, children begin to consider hypothetical situations involving basic human concerns such as abandonment, fear, change, and love—matters that begin to involve awareness of awareness.[8] Our state of consciousness varies over our lifetime and even over the course of a day. Elements of it appear and disappear while we work, walk, sleep, and dream.

High-level consciousness serves an important purpose. In response to the question, "What is consciousness for?" the late Harvard University philosopher Robert Nozick answered, "to help us make considered choices."[9] These choices, and the higher levels of consciousness they require, are created through social and technological changes.[10] High-order consciousness evolved to cope with an increasingly complex social world that demanded the ability to learn in new situations.[11] For consumers, these complexities can be challenging and even a source of complaint. For six consecutive years, consumers in developed economies have rated the proliferation of product choices one of the top five issues of concern.[12] Consumers like the idea of many choices, but not the mentally taxing efforts to cope with them.

Where Does It Come from Now?

Hungarian goulash has a particular flavor; when you take a bite there is one overall taste. Any chef will explain, however, that the combination of spices and ingredients mix and mingle through the cooking and eating process to create a unique essence that is goulash. Diners may not consider the preparation involved; they taste only the result. High-order consciousness is a little like Hungarian goulash. We focus on the overall outcome, not on the complex process that produces it. Whatever its evolutionary origins or developmental history, *high-order consciousness emerges from, and is defined by, its base ingredients: lower levels of awareness and unawareness.*[13]

Whether or not the base of the goulash or the source of high-order consciousness is initially recognized, it comes about only through the exercise of other activities and component parts. John R. Searle, a leading contemporary philosopher at the University of California at Berkeley, notes that for something to be unconscious, we must in principle be able to bring it to a conscious level.[14] Gazing at our goulash, a food connoisseur most likely couldn't describe in detail how a particular flavor came about, but after enjoying the total taste experience, he could probably deconstruct it. Vague awareness and unconscious information emerge in our conscious mind and we can guess what's in the goulash after all.

The 95–5 Split

Consciousness is crucial in daily life for many obvious reasons. However, an important fact and one of the key principles of this book is the 95–5 split: At least 95 percent of all cognition occurs below awareness in the shadows of the mind while, at most, only 5 percent occurs in high-order consciousness.[15] Many disciplines have confirmed this insight. John Haugeland explains this idea eloquently:

> *Thus, compared to "unconscious processing" . . . conscious thinking is conspicuously laborious and slow—not a lot faster than talking, in fact. What's more, it is about as difficult to entertain consciously two distinct trains of thought at the same time as it is to engage in two distinct conversations at once; consciousness is in some sense a linear or serial process in contrast to the many simultaneous cognitions that are manifest in [unconscious action].*[16]

Nobel laureate and neuroscientist Gerald M. Edelman and his colleague Giulio Tononi note that the "occurrence of a single conscious state rules out billions and billions of other conscious states, each of which may lead to different potential consequences."[17] To come to conscious awareness a thought must emerge from its primary and highly crowded habitat in the unconscious mind. The processes that determine which of a near-infinite array of possible states from this habitat enters consciousness are themselves unconscious. "Most of the data available to us from the external world and from our bodies never enter consciousness," wrote J. Allan Hobson, psychiatrist, director of the Laboratory of Neurophysiology, and a leading sleep researcher.

> We process many inputs automatically, and we have no conscious idea of the vast amounts of data that are saved or discarded. But consciousness is supra automatic in that it is the mental attribute that allows us, occasionally at least, to transcend automaticity.[18]

Consciousness allows us the freedom to understand unconscious events. To quote Edelman and Tononi once again: "Unconscious aspects of mental activity, such as motor and cognitive routines, and so-called unconscious memories, intentions, and expectations play a fundamental role in shaping and directing our conscious experience."[19]

Consciousness evolved to help us critically review past actions, plan, and organize choices to make in new situations. Not surprisingly, marketing managers and researchers focus mostly on conscious consumer thinking. They ask consumers to think consciously about specific topics and respond within formats convenient for both consumers and managers. They also observe consumer behavior directly or indirectly using large databases and providing their own highly conscious interpretations. These activities make sense; they seem easy and logical.

But this focus mistakenly ignores arguably the most significant feature of higher order consciousness: the ability to recognize and explore the unconscious mind.[20] *The 5 percent of our thinking that is highly conscious enables us to confront the other 95 percent of mental life below this stratum.* This ability is also a quality of being human. We can contemplate what we're aware of, but many other elements are at work. Therefore, the managerial tendency to focus on conscious consumer thought, while understandable and natural, also blocks managers' access to the world of unconscious consumer thought and feeling that drives most consumer behavior.

Owning a bicycle and knowing how to ride it are important for taking a bike trip. However, *a meaningful journey requires a willingness to get* on the bike. Similarly, the conscious mind permits meaningful travel in the unconscious mind only if we commit to such a journey. When managers forgo such a trip to understand consumers, they are like the well-intentioned stranger who claims to know us from photographs, videos, or one arbitrary encounter, but lacks any real knowledge of who we are. Like the cartoon of the scientists in figure 1-3, these strangers look at themselves backwards and typically see only the conscious elements staring back.

If everyone knows that so much thinking is unconscious, then why do managers (and researchers) miss the mark? Partly because we become enamored with (and distracted by) ourselves and our own reflections, like a puppy that enjoys chasing its own tail. As psychologist Daniel Wegner of Harvard University states, "The illusion of will is so compelling that it can prompt the belief that acts were intended when they could not have been. It is as though people aspire to be ideal agents who know all their actions in advance."[21] Our experience of consciously willing an action does not mean that we consciously produced it. Far from it.

Typically, we ask consumers to consider and comment on their own ideas and others' in focus groups or to provide careful, conscious answers to careful, consciously developed survey questions. We analyze aggregate consumer data through the crafted lens of particular quantitative models and experimental designs. Through these activities, consumers and marketers alike get caught up in the explicit issues brought to their attention by researchers and managers. *This approach feels right because it employs the very mechanisms that are the assumptions of the approach.* The logic is of this sort: "The data collected, based on my assumptions, support those assumptions." Indeed, consumers do learn from their satisfying and unsatisfying choices by identifying those biases or decision rules that led to their wise choices and to their mistakes. Relying on their innate storytelling capacities, consumers can reasonably account for their behavior when asked, especially when managers facilitate the storytelling with questions or other cues.

These reasoned accounts are unlikely totally wrong. The critical issue is how complete they are. If a puzzle has only three pieces and you have two of them, then you can probably figure out what third might be. If the puzzle has 500 pieces and you have only a few important ones, the larger picture will forever remain a mystery. Sometimes, the puzzles that marketers open have only a few pieces and other times, a great many. The latter case, typically the most important one, requires tapping into high-order consciousness and digging deeper into the unconscious mind for a more complete picture. The very existence of our high-order conscious mind gives us the capacity to understand the unconscious foundations on which it rests. Unfortunately, often we become entranced by our awareness of our awareness and ignore the unconscious mind that makes it all possible.

The Unconscious Mind in Action

We needn't search long or far for examples of the unconscious mind in action.

- The social context of eating has enormous impact on consumers' experience. This experience includes how foods taste, what sounds seem pleasant or harsh, and what strikes the person as repulsive or appealing. The exact same dinner will taste different depending on whether one is dining with a close friend or an unpleasant stranger.
- Many more units of a product are sold at a price of $9.99 than at $10.00. Certainly the one penny savings on identical products does not account for this.
- The correlation between stated intent and actual behavior is usually low and often negative. For example, more than 60 percent of consumers participating in an at-home test of a new kitchen appliance indicated after trying the product that they were "likely" or "very likely" to purchase the appliance in the next three months. Eight months after the product's introduction, only 12 percent of these consumers actually made a purchase. A survey among those who did not follow through on their stated intent found that most consumers couldn't explain their behavior.
- Blind taste tests may suggest that consumers prefer formulation A over formulation B by a significant majority. Yet when

consumers know the formulations' brand names and can see their packaging, they strongly prefer B.

- Consumers using both a store brand and a national brand of an over-the-counter medication insist that they know the two brands are identical except for price. However, when their symptoms are severe, the great majority of these same consumers use the higher-priced name brand. Moreover, if the medicine is for a child or spouse, the purchaser will almost always select the national brand. Unconsciously, the buyer believes that the national brand works better and is therefore better for her loved ones.

- A stimulus that appears only for milliseconds and doesn't register consciously can affect responders' future behavior. For example, a European manufacturer was testing a sensing system that measured the speed of a vehicle and the distance of an object in the vehicle's direct path. When the system detected a certain combination of speed and object distance, it displayed the message "Brake!" on the vehicle's windshield. In simulated driving tests, the system increased reaction times of test participants. The R&D staff experimented with different message intervals, such as one or a few seconds during which the alert would appear. Interestingly, the fastest reaction time occurred when the message flashed subliminally, so quickly that people were unaware of reacting to it.[22]

- When judging sincerity in advertising, consumers unconsciously select many of the cues. Moreover, both creative staffs and consumers remain unaware of consumers' selection of these signals. For example, in a Mind of the Market study, Maya Bourdeau found that, in judging sincerity, both consumers and creative staffs unconsciously use criteria related to *neoteny*, or people's fascination with infants and baby animals. Neotenous characteristics include large, round eyes and high foreheads that remind us of infancy, innocence, and naïveté. People perceive messages transmitted by a baby-faced person as more sincere because they see babies as innocent and honest. However, neither the consumers nor the creative personnel in this study were consciously aware of the power of neoteny.

These examples are, to use a cliché, just the tip of the iceberg of the unconscious mind. Nevertheless, they raise important challenging questions. Currently, managers' notions that consumers engage in calculated rationality strongly guide their approach to consumers.[23] But price, demonstrated product effectiveness, and even consumers' confidently stated claims simply don't reliably predict what consumers will actually do. When using traditional research methods, managers must augment the idea of calculated rationality with equally sensible but typically invisible insights.

From Unconscious Decision to Conscious Action

The areas of the human brain that involve choice are activated well before we become consciously aware that we've made a choice. That is, decisions "happen" before they are seemingly "made." In fact, unconscious judgments not only happen before conscious judgments, but they guide them as well. A cleverly designed study by Antoine Bechara, a neuroscientist at the University of Iowa, and his associates tested this idea. The study participants included normal individuals and patients who had suffered damage to the prefrontal lobes of their brains—the structures responsible for decision making.[24] Bechara's team asked both groups to perform a task using four decks of cards, two of which were advantageous decks and two disadvantageous. Playing mostly with the advantageous decks produced an overall gain of money, while the disadvantageous decks produced an overall loss. The researchers tracked the number of cards that each group drew from each deck and monitored changes in participants' skin temperature, awareness of their progress in the game, and attitude.

The study generated interesting findings. For instance, before they realized that two decks were "bad," but after they experienced all four decks, the normal participants generated high anticipatory skin-conductance responses when they pondered making a choice from a "bad" deck. They did not consciously know that they were about to pull a card from a disadvantageous deck. However, their high anticipatory skin-conductance responses *before* they took a card from the bad deck revealed their unconscious reaction to the game's parameters. The patients with prefrontal brain damage displayed no such distinction even after they had identified the good and bad decks. In fact, they disregarded this knowledge as they continued playing the game. At some level, the normal patients recognized that choosing from a bad deck was a bad strategy. They arrived at this decision without the added assurance provided by conscious knowledge. Whether they perceived it, the normal patients used their unconscious learning from prior experience to inform their future decisions.

Often our actions seem to derive from conscious decisions when we actually made them much earlier. For example, imagine that you are walking where people have seen poisonous snakes. Suddenly, you notice a coiled object under a bush. This sight triggers an immediate, unconscious activity involving the amygdala, a subcortical area of the brain involved in certain emotions. The activity in the amygdala triggers an immediate defensive act: You freeze or perhaps step back. This rapid, complex action involves a number of brain and other physical systems working simultaneously to produce an action that we can consider only *after* it occurs.[25]

Human beings store images in a part of the brain called the hippocampal system. Images related to snakes comprise your explicit memories of actual interactions with snakes, garden hoses, or perhaps tree roots that resemble snakes. If you see an object that more closely resembles a snake than a garden hose, then your innate plan for dealing with dangerous snakes kicks in. If you realize that the object is a garden hose, then your awareness unfolds unconsciously as you retrieve various images, compare them, and then evaluate them before consciously deciding how to react. If the object more closely resembles a tree root, then you resume walking. Your heart may race a little faster, your muscles may tense, and you may even blush. None of these critical responses ever required conscious thought. If they did, our species would have gone the way of the dodo bird. After all, when faced with a possibly dangerous snake, who has the time to think about a response? Our unconscious processes often protect us better than our conscious processes do. A conclusion that we consciously experience ("That snake is dangerous") already happened in our unconscious mind. Our *awareness* of it takes the form of an inner voice saying that it's okay (or not) to continue what we were doing (strolling through the woods). *That inner voice creates the illusion that we have made a conscious decision.*

The Neurological Foundation of the Unconscious Mind/Brain

As we saw in chapter 2, the brain is an extraordinary and still mysterious organ. Consider again the small but important cerebral cortex, which factors into thinking, speech, and complex movement patterns. The cerebral cortex has approximately 30 billion neurons, which serve as the building blocks for thought. And as it turns out, different neurons like to "talk" with one another. Thus, they form clusters akin to conversation groups or chat rooms. These clusters form what are called *constructs* or specific thoughts and ideas. Moreover, these clusters like to communicate or gossip with one another. These "conversations" involve reasoning processes linking constructs. That is partly why the same idea may trigger different thoughts among different people or even in the same person at different times.

Most of the brain spends its time communicating with itself; only infrequently do we consciously witness these conversations.[26] Put differently, conversations among neurons and groups of neurons are generally quiet; they involve a silent language we do not "see" or "hear." What do neuronal groups talk about? They converse about actions, feelings, and thoughts. Occasionally, the results of these conversations bubble up into our consciousness, and we become aware of them. Other times, we may have a "feeling" that the conversations are occurring, but we may not be able to grasp their nature. Most of the time, though, we have no idea that they're taking place. Whether we perceive it or not, the activity of the brain gives rise to the mind, which consists of tools for thinking.[27] Cognitive neuroscientists say that the "mind is what the brain does" and use the term "mind/brain" to denote this concept.

The Processes behind the Unconscious Mind

Consciousness is the awareness of awareness and is a prerequisite for healthy functioning in a complex society.[28] It influences our ability to make choices—as well as marketers' ability to understand consumer behavior. Market researchers can certainly acquire valuable information at consumers' conscious level relatively easily through standard research methods. For example, through surveys they can obtain useful information about preferred package designs when they present consumers with clear alternatives.

However, approaches that depend on conscious thinking often do not go far enough. This isn't surprising when we remember that conscious activity represents only about 5 percent of human cognition. As George Lowenstein suggests, the *conscious* mind explains actions produced by *unconscious* processes. And, as scientists in several disciplines point out, these explanations are often woefully incomplete. For instance, a product-development team at a graphics software firm used a focus group consisting of ten dissatisfied users of their new software to better understand customer complaints. The team predicted that the users would express dissatisfaction with the clarity of the instructions and the confusing nature of certain icons. Thus, they asked the moderator to explore these areas. Indeed, discussions in the focus group identified the instructions and icons as main sources of trouble. The company improved these features—but complaints decreased only marginally. Later, while using in-depth, one-on-one storytelling to develop advertising for this and related products, the firm identified another, more serious source of consumer dissatisfaction. A group setting relying on the conscious exchange of ideas had failed to surface this more serious issue.

Unconscious processes generally serve us well. In fact, as the earlier example about encountering a possible snake suggests, what people sometimes mean by intuition or gut reaction is really the manifestation of distilled wisdom accumulated in our unconscious mind. In the marketplace, unconscious processes enable us to make purchase decisions more efficiently and effectively than we could if we had to consciously process every relevant factor. Moreover, many unconscious processes—for example, our ability to acquire and use verbal and nonverbal language—are innate.[29]

We acquire many other components of our unconscious mind simply through having different experiences.[30] In fact, the unconscious mind learns quickly. We quickly transform good and bad experiences into tacit rules of thumb that guide us when we encounter new situations. We then adapt to those new situations and acquire new social norms without conscious thought. The unconscious mind also serves as a repository for skills and other forms of knowledge that we learn consciously but that become automatic through repeated use. These skills range from walking, tying our shoes, and dreaming in a second language to knowing when a consumer is ready to commit to a sales offer.

Working in partnership with each other, the innate and learned components of the unconscious mind powerfully enable us to take action. For instance, they can produce a response to potential danger so quickly that we become aware of the response only *after* it has occurred. Or they may cause us to continue working on a mental task even after we seem to have put it out of our minds; for example, when we suddenly recall a name that was "on the tip of our tongue" hours ago. This information retrieval often catches us by surprise because, at the moment it occurs, we've made no conscious effort to prompt it.

The Interaction of Consumers' and Managers' Unconscious Minds

Recall figure 2-1, which depicted how consumers' and managers' thinking interacts. It was noted that when managers think about consumers, they do so using both conscious and unconscious levels of thought, since important thinking tools reside at each level. The same is true of consumers when they consider a firm's offerings. The managers' conscious and unconscious levels of thinking commingle with one another and, ultimately, commingle with the same processes among consumers. In this way, the mind of the manager is present in the mind of the consumer, and vice versa.

Two examples will help illustrate the subtle interactions that can occur between marketers and consumers. In a study of unconscious communication, dental patients received a placebo painkiller during a typically painful dental procedure. The patients experienced a lack of discomfort *only if* the dentists also believed that the treatment they administered was an authentic painkiller. Unconscious behaviors emanating from these dentists reinforced their patients' belief in the placebo. However, when the dentists knew that the treatment was not authentic and merely pretended it was, patients experienced considerable discomfort. (All patients involved in the study were undergoing the same procedure with the same likelihood of pain.) Something in the disbelieving dentists' unconscious behavior signaled to the patients that the supposed painkiller was a sham. Patients processed and acted on this nonverbal cue *unconsciously* while *consciously* believing that they had received an authentic painkiller—and the dentists unconsciously colluded in maintaining this belief.

A second example comes from a proprietary experiment sponsored by a professional association. Not surprisingly, this study found that a salesperson's confidence in a product (his belief in its efficacy) is an excellent predictor of sales success. But even more interesting, the representative's confidence conveys in subtle, nonverbal ways a sense of authenticity that "adds great persuasive power even when [the equipment] is not the best available. Confidence contrived does not work." Like the dentists who believed they were using a real painkiller, salespeople who truly believe in their product will influence customers in their favor. The unconscious expression of belief by sales personnel is a powerful cue that customers process both consciously and unconsciously. Thus, the first "sale" must be to the sales representative.

A Closer Look at the Placebo Effect

Much of marketing is about placebo effects. The term *placebo* is Latin for "I shall please." In common usage, it carries with it negative connotations of fakery, trickery, falseness, and sham. This is unfortunate, because the so-called placebo effect is very real, and stems from actual neurological mechanisms. Although the technical quality of goods and services is crucial in providing satisfying consumption experiences, an important part of consumers' total experience with a firm's offerings results from what consumers believe and expect these offerings to deliver. When product quality declines, so do the added benefits created by the mind of the consumer.

How does the placebo effect work? Our beliefs, expectations, and possibly prior experiences cause biological changes roughly equivalent in magnitude and effect to those produced by chemical substances known to have the same effects. For example, naturally occurring painkillers in the brain, called endorphins, are similar in chemical structure to opium-derived narcotics and act much like morphine. When a *placebo* analgesic is administered to postoperative patients, many of them experience an easing of pain. Their belief that they have taken an authentic painkiller is enough to stimulate *naturally occurring* pain-killers.

This and other research shows that, for many people, the belief or expectation of a positive outcome can trigger the same physiological processes and hence produce the same benefits as an artificial substance. In fact, in most studies of the effectiveness of a medication, between 35 percent and 50 percent of participants receiving the placebo treatment show the same improvements as those being treated with the actual medicine. This is not based on self-reports of patients, but on monitoring of physiological conditions. For example, one recent study involving antidepressants used brain-scanning techniques to show that patients who improved following placebo treatments and those who improved after receiving an actual antidepressant medication (38 percent and 52 percent, respectively) showed changes in activity in the same area of the brain.[31] People who did not respond to either the placebo or the antidepressant showed no change in this same area of the brain. The placebo effect is so real and so grounded in neurochemistry that it occurs even in other animal species, such as rats, that presumably are not subject to "tricks of the mind" or high-order conscious expectation. Research of this sort indicates that the placebo effect can operate through conditioning, not just through conscious expectation and belief.

Most scientists generally accept that the placebo effect produces a significant amount of the benefit derived from an authentic medication. This benefit is additive; it supplements the benefits already provided by the active ingredients or intervention. For instance, one popular over-the-counter treatment for stomach distress doesn't kick in until at least thirty minutes after ingestion. However, many frequent users report significant relief within the first twelve minutes. This relief is very real and is accompanied by changes in body chemistry. The actual treatment takes effect later, sustaining the positive experience. In doing so, it reinforces the expectation of more immediate relief—and therefore its delivery. This phenomenon demonstrates the combined action of expectation, conditioning, and authentic treatment. The power of this combination has far-reaching implications in the world of medicine and beyond. The benefits of placebo-only treatments, however, often decline rather soon. But when coupled with an authentic treatment, placebo benefits continue.

As we've seen, belief factors into the placebo effect. For example, participants in one experiment were told that a substance they would be asked to drink might induce vomiting. After drinking the liquid, nearly 80 percent of the participants actually vomited. When they received a placebo "antidote" to stop their vomiting, their condition improved almost immediately. As you may already have guessed, the antidote was the same inert substance but in a different color.

An experiment reported by V. S. Ramachandran demonstrates the power of the mind to reshape the body's neurological systems.[32] Although not strictly in the domain of placebo effects, the experiment tapped into the mysterious world of what's known as phantom pain. Common among amputees, phantom pain is pain perceived in a missing limb. This pain, often excruciating, may occur in various ways. In one sufferer, it took the form of a vivid sensation that the person's missing hand was uncontrollably curling up in a clenched fist, causing agony as the fingers dug mercilessly into the palm. Using a special system of mirrors, the researchers asked the man to insert his *intact* hand into a transparent box that superimposed the reflection of the intact hand's actions onto the reflection of the missing hand. Thus, the missing hand appeared to mimic the actions of the intact hand:

> Robert looked into the box, positioned his good hand to superimpose its reflection over his phantom hand, and after making a fist with the normal hand, tried to unclench both hands simultaneously. The first time he did this, Robert exclaimed that he could feel the phantom fist open along with his good fist, simply as a result of the visual feedback. Better yet, the pain disappeared. The phantom then remained unclenched for several hours until a new spasm occurred spontaneously. Without the mirror, his phantom would throb in pain for forty minutes or more. Robert took the box home and tried the same trick each time that the clenching spasm recurred. If he did not use the box, he could not unclench his fist despite trying with all his might. If he used the mirror, the hand opened instantly. . . . We have tried this treatment in over a dozen patients and it works for half of them.[33]

Referring to another patient undergoing the same treatment, Ramachandran notes, "This is a mind-boggling observation if you think about it. Here is a man with no hand and no fingernails. How does one get nonexistent nails digging into a nonexistent palm, resulting in severe pain? Why would a mirror eliminate the phantom spasm?"[34] Much of Ramachandran's book, *Phantoms in the Brain,* provides a neurological and social answer to this question. He explains:

> *Everything I have learned from the intensive study of both normal people and patients who have sustained damage to various parts of their brains points to an unsettling notion: that you create your own "reality" from mere fragments of information, that what you "see" is a reliable—but not always accurate—representation of what exists in the world, that you are completely unaware of the vast majority of events going on in your brain.*[35]

This discussion of placebo effects demonstrates the power of the unconscious mind to produce very powerful and beneficial experiences over and above those expected from the technical merits of the product. Consider the extra experience that people have when they know that they're consuming their favorite brand compared to the lesser experience of their brand in a blind taste test. We'll probably discover that this special functioning of the mind accounts for loyalty to a brand or service provider, especially in commodity products. While the mind of the manager may ultimately yield the technical features of a product or service, the mind of the consumer adds significant value about the consumption experience. Rather than treating these consumer sources of added value as frivolous, we must understand and encourage them. They factor into the consumer's storytelling process when creating brand meaning, covered in chapter 7.

Mechanisms Underlying the Unconscious Mind/Brain

A number of mechanisms support the operation of the unconscious consumer mind. We look more closely at these mechanisms in the following sections.

Priming

Imagine that you're conversing with someone, and the person happens to casually mention the word *doctor* during the conversation. Then he shows you a jumble of letters in which the letters "n," "u," "r," "s," and "e" are embedded, among many other letters. The person asks you to find a word in the seemingly random bunch of letters. As research reveals, under these conditions you would probably quickly find the word *nurse* in the jumbled letters. The prior mention of the word *doctor* has *primed* your thinking. It has caused you to focus your attention unconsciously in a way that another phonetically similar word (such as *curse*) would not. Though the priming process has a powerful effect on our thinking, we are generally unaware of it. For example, in the above scenario, you'd be unaware that the word *doctor* enabled you to identify the word *nurse* more quickly than you would have without priming.

Similarly, the music played in retail settings can significantly increase or decrease the amount of time consumers spend in the store, which can affect sales volume. In one experiment commissioned by a major European retailer, researchers found no significant differences in shoppers' *self-reported* time spent in three store situations: no music played; music designed to decrease shopping time; and music designed to increase shopping time. However, shoppers' *actual* time spent in the store differed as predicted across the three situations. Although most participants perceived the presence of background music in the store, few could accurately describe the style being played. Thus, their decision to stay in the store longer, or to leave more quickly, happened unconsciously. Moreover, the researchers found no differences in the impact of the music on time spent in the store between those who recalled music playing and those who did not. Even if the presence of the music didn't register consciously, at least as measured by the ability to recall music later, it still influenced shoppers' behavior without their knowing it.

Sometimes information can prime unwanted actions or thoughts. For instance, stop-smoking campaigns often backfire, prompting smokers to light up more often. This backfiring stems from so-called trigger cues. Even if a billboard communicates the obvious health hazards of smoking, the giant cigarette in the graphic display may activate a smoker's unconscious cravings. One advertising campaign designed to discourage illicit drug usage featured a visual of drug paraphernalia in unpleasant surroundings to highlight the disease and victimization. All the ad's viewers consciously—and accurately—understood the message in the ad, regardless of whether they'd used drugs or were recovering drug addicts. However, the images only heightened recovering addicts' desire to relapse. The ad made these individuals' recovery so difficult that it was withdrawn. We will revisit the topic of priming later in this chapter.

Adding Information That "Isn't There"

Our senses, acting on environmental cues, help us *create* our understanding of the world around us. For example, in the words of Harvard University biologist John Dowling, visual perception is "reconstructive and creative. . . . The image that falls on the retina is two-dimensional, yet we live in a three-dimensional world. . . . Not only does the visual system use the information impinging on the retinas, but it draws on visual memories and experience to construct a coherent view of the world."[36] The third dimension comes from unconscious inferences drawn by applying our tacit knowledge and rules.[37] Thus, we unconsciously use judgments based on one set of cues to create judgments about other matters. Figure 3-1 is an example of this phenomenon.

After viewing this figure for three or four seconds, people ranging from fifth graders to senior executives offer remarkably similar accounts of the scene. As they see it, the figure shows a large creature with an angry expression on its face chasing a smaller creature who looks frightened. Note that this "story" comprises several elements: social relationships (one creature chasing another), emotions (anger and fear), intention (render harm and seek safety), and physical orientation (large and small, and locomotion).

As you may have guessed, both creatures are identical in every way. Without being aware of it, we use several visual cues to infer the story in the picture. In this case, the converging lines suggest a hallway or tunnel and create the optical illusion that one of the creatures is farther in the distance than the other. A lifetime of experience with depth perception tells us that, if two objects look identical in size but one appears farther

FIGURE 3 - 1

Two Creatures in a Hallway

From *Mind Sights* by Roger N. Shepard, © 1990 by W. H. Freeman.
Reprinted by permission of Henry Holt and Company, LLC.

away, then it must be larger than it actually looks. Since we "see" one creature as farther down the hallway, we "know" that it's bigger than the creature that appears closer. If the converging lines disappeared, then we'd deem the two creatures identical in size. When the two appear the same size, viewers will likely not infer that one of them is chasing and menacing the other; this particular social element evaporates.

Yet figure 3-1 has another intriguing lesson: Even after we learn that the creatures are identical in every way, *one still looks bigger* to us. Our unconscious processes keep producing an experience that contradicts and prevails over our conscious knowledge. Moreover, after learning the truth about the creatures in the drawing, people who initially judged one creature larger than the other still take longer to scan the "larger" creature in their mind's eye.

The perception of an angry look on the "larger" creature and a frightened look on the "smaller" creature, together with the judgment that one is chasing the other, reflects the ability of the unconscious mind to add emotional meaning to and define relationships between characters in a scene. This phenomenon speaks volumes about our natural, automatic capacities to generate stories based on just a few cues as we discuss in chapter 9, Memory, Metaphor, and Stories.

What does all this imply for marketers? Physical, social, and psychological settings and a consumer's emotional state—all of which comprise what researchers call *context*—profoundly shape consumers' interpretation of images, as well as sounds, smells, and other incoming sensory information.[38] Visual cues, such as the lines suggesting a hallway, prompt us to generate information ("One creature's chasing the other" or "The big one's angry") that simply does not exist in the actual image. How our brain receives and processes sound causes us to judge the direction from which the sound is coming, the distance of its source, and the event causing the sound. These judgments create other judgments telling us, for example, whether we should feel threatened or comforted, angry or amused. However, we are aware only of the judgments, not the sophisticated processing that produces them. As with placebo effects in medicine, our minds are very active creating or providing qualities not otherwise presented by a stimulus, be it a supposed painkiller or wine from a famous vineyard.

Let's explore this process further. When viewing figure 3-2, most people will "see" a triangle (as well as pizza and the video character Pac-man). Many people will even see the white inside the triangle to be brighter than the white outside of it. New brain-imaging techniques show us that the brain records the lines as if they were actually present.

In the same way, consumers record as present an experience with a product or service that they expect to be present even if it's not. Absent information is counted as present. Thus, if consumers know they are sipping their favorite beverage, they add special qualities to the consumption experience such as smooth taste, smoky flavor, a relaxing feeling, and so on. In a blind taste test, these added qualities do not materialize, because in such tests brand name does not play a part in participants' expectations. Blind taste tests can help marketers develop

FIGURE 3 - 2

What Do You See Besides Pacmen?

new product formulations before introducing them as brands. However, in these early developmental stages, marketers should also analyze the impact of environmental cues, such as package design, brand name, and logo, on the consumption experience.

Brand meaning is even more elusive than marketing researchers previously thought, because consumers' predispositions generate thoughts and feelings toward the brand that unconsciously influence their reaction to that brand. They fill in missing information, which becomes as real to them as if it were physically present in a product or in promotional materials. Consumers add qualities to a familiar brand just as they see the missing lines in figure 3-2. These qualities are experienced as real and duly recorded in the brain as such. They *are* real, because consumers' minds (more than the brand) have supplied them with that information. Remove any knowledge of the brand, and the special qualities tend to disappear.

Subtracting Information That *Is* There

Our minds also subtract information. Information one would expect to be visible isn't. We often believe we take in more information than we actually do. For example, in one study, researchers showed participants a short video in which a pendulum in the center of the picture swings dramatically back and forth. With the first version of the video, mud splashes appear randomly on the screen. In this version, viewers didn't see the pendulum moving. With a second version of the video, in which the mud splashes are removed, viewers did notice the movement of the pendulum—and were surprised that they missed it in the earlier version.

In another experiment, participants counted the number of times a basketball is passed among a small group of people, as shown on a video.[39] In the video, a gorilla walks past the group—but viewers don't mention seeing the animal. When the researchers showed the video *without* first asking the subjects to count, the gorilla becomes the most conspicuous element of the scene. In the first version of the experiment, the focus on counting causes people to unconsciously subtract the gorilla, a presence otherwise remarkable.

We subtract details from our experiences because we have a limited capacity to hold information at a level of conscious inspection. We can't afford to attend to cues that are not obviously relevant to the task at hand if we want to perform that task well. Yet participants' subtraction of the gorilla in the previously described experiment doesn't necessarily mean that they completely discounted the gorilla from the experience. In all likelihood, had these same participants seen a photo showing a large number of different animals (including a gorilla) soon after viewing the film, their eyes would have moved first to the gorilla.

This tendency to subtract information explains the frequent phenomenon in which people recall an advertisement but not the product being advertised. What engages our attention is not the brand but some other element of the message. In another example, a manufacturer of marine engines brought a group of boat builders to a marine-engine production plant to impress on them the quality and care with which the engines were manufactured. The plant manager had developed a specific list of "learning points" he wanted to convey to the builders. After the visit, the builders recalled very few of these points while evaluating the experience. Upon investigation, the company discovered that several graphic and clever safety and motivational posters intended for employees had distracted the visitors. These posters were removed, and during the next visit the boat builders successfully retained the learning points.

Figure 3-3, also shown in chapter 1, graphically demonstrates a variation of the information–subtraction phenomenon. When viewing this figure, most people first see either a duck lying on its back or a rabbit nibbling grass. Very few people will see both animals at once.

After staring at it, people eventually see whichever animal they missed at first. The two views will then continue to alternate; viewers see one animal and then the other. Even when they know that both animals are present, most people can still see only one at a time. Seeing one animal requires them to deny unconsciously the presence of the other; they know it's there but can't see it.

This phenomenon, in which awareness of one idea requires the suppression of another, helps explain why people may view a brand differently at different times. The context in which a brand is viewed will favor the surfacing of one interpretation over another. Thus, a duality or paradox emerges in consumers' perceptions of a product or service. For

FIGURE 3 - 3

What Do You See?

From *Mind Sights* by Roger N. Shepard, © 1990 by W. H. Freeman.
Reprinted by permission of Henry Holt and Company, LLC.

example, a person may describe Coca-Cola as invigorating or relaxing in one setting and as an American symbol or a universal icon in another context. Package recipients judge the delivery of a package by Federal Express as slow or fast depending on their own social and psychological conditions—even if the actual delivery timing is constant. For instance, if a recipient is eager to receive the package, he will perceive the delivery time as slow.

These alternating perceptions involving the interaction of unconscious and conscious processes suggest that firms must be particularly sensitive to that element of a duality that occurs most often in consumers' conscious minds and what may cause a shift to the unconscious. Companies can then build in cues in the design of a service setting or a product and its packaging and advertising that will encourage activation of the more "silent" element in the duality.

The unconscious mind represents a significant frontier where marketers may establish secure beachheads of competitive advantage. Certainly no firm can claim to understand consumers without colonizing this land of opportunity. Indeed, companies must grasp how conscious and unconscious thinking interact with and shape one another if they want to mine the treasures hidden in this frontier. Equally important, marketers must also understand how their own unconscious minds influence marketing mix and other key decisions. Finally, the mind of the market consists of the interactions of both managers' and consumers' conscious and unconscious thinking, adding yet another challenging complexity. The mind is what the brain does, and managers must pay considerable attention to the mechanics and paradoxes that characterize it.

Interviewing the Mind/Brain

Metaphor Elicitation

Imagination is the soul of the mind

and metaphor its primary nourishment.

The elaboration of metaphors is an

imaginative form of rational thinking.

—*Richard E. Cytowic*

MARKETING PROFESSIONALS have numerous research methods at their disposal, including one-on-one interviewing, surveys, ethnographic studies, projective techniques, and focus groups. All have their strengths and weaknesses. This chapter begins with a short commentary on research methods, then focuses on metaphors that transport unconscious, tacit thought to a conscious level where it may be examined. The next chapter reviews two additional methods for interviewing the mind.

About Research Methods

All research methods involve compromises with reality.[1] Researchers prefer more than one method whenever possible, because human thought and behavior are too complex for any one method to capture fully. Also, when different methods converge on the *same* insight, the researcher can feel greater confidence in its soundness. Excepting focus groups, which have little grounding in any science, the most commonly used market research methods all have situations in which they are and are not appropriate to use.

Marketers must develop and use research methods that dig deeply into the mind of the market by taking new approaches as well as improving upon old ones. Traditional quantitative and qualitative methods work well in several circumstances: when managers have substantial brand and category knowledge, when little has changed among consumers or in the competitive environment, where consumers can readily articulate what they think, and where issues of recall are not present or relevant. For example, the brand manager who wants to know what opinion leaders think about an established brand might use a survey, especially if she knows the relevant drivers of purchase. If she wants to study the opinion leaders' vocabulary, she could conduct a focus group exclusively of such leaders.

Tactical issues usually suggest traditional techniques. For example, statistical analyses of questionnaire data or opinions expressed in focus groups can help identify the most attractive package design. Marketers can use scanner data to determine which products to promote together or whether to discontinue a particular promotion; in-store observations and scanner data together to assess the value of particular product placements within stores; statistical analyses of scanner data, simulated settings, and store exit interviews to assess the effects of lighting, music, and other in-store environmental cues on purchase volume; and user observations to determine the utility of an established product or a prototype of a new product.

Standard research methods address basic marketing issues such as: How do purchase frequency and store preference differ among market segments and are they changing? How has market share changed among competing brands? Do consumers prefer product attribute bundle A over bundle B? Is the taste of formulation A preferred over formulation B?

Standard methods falter in addressing such important issues as: What frame of reference do people use when thinking about a brand?

Why do consumers prefer one attribute bundle over another? What role does a product play in consumers' lives? How do consumers feel about the basic problem a product is designed to solve? What do people mean by "good health," "luxury," "managing money," or "a company I can trust"? Why are consumers loyal to a particular brand? What are the dimensions of the customers' total experience with a product? What latent needs are causing consumers to use a product differently in different situations?

In these cases, marketers need methods that go beyond what customers can readily articulate—that get at what people don't know they know. This is more critical than ever before, as rapid technological change requires managers to understand consumers' latent needs. Put differently, people's responses to very new products and services are governed by their deeply held and hard-to-express thoughts and feelings rather than by surface-level attitudes and opinions. The more radical the product, the more important is the unconscious mind in accounting for the acceptance or rejection of the innovation.

The most limiting aspect of research, however, does not stem from inherent compromise but from human nature. That is, the *person using a method*—rather than the *method itself*—most determines both the benefits and problems that the method will generate. These *limitations come largely from the inappropriate matching of a method to a problem.* Sometimes, too, researchers forget or ignore the compromises that a method entails and present findings as more robust and reliable than warranted.

Trained in mathematical sociology, I favor survey research and techniques that require thoughtful statistical analysis. Advances in mathematical analyses permit more sophisticated inferences and promise to dig deeper into customers' and consumers' unconscious minds.[2] These inferences, however, must still be informed by important advances about how customers think. They must also build on deep initial explorations into relevant thoughts and feelings, the building blocks of sound quantitative inferences. The new insights from several disciplines introduced here, plus recent advances in qualitative investigations to be discussed here, should benefit the more quantitatively oriented researchers.

I highly regard various observational techniques when skilled observers use them, whether in laboratory settings, a consumer's home, a retail store, a customer's office, or a manufacturing plant. At the same time, these techniques simply cannot uncover all the important aspects of consumers' unconscious and conscious thoughts and feelings. Given the prominence of the unconscious mind, or the cognitive unconscious, we must augment existing research methods with methods designed specifically to probe unconscious cognition.[3]

"Penetrating the Mind by Metaphor"[4]

As we saw in chapter 3, the unconscious gives the orders and the conscious mind carries them out. Or, as Gerald M. Edelman and Giulio Tononi, authors of *A Universe of Consciousness: How Matter Becomes Imagination,* put it, "Unconscious aspects of mental activity, such as motor and cognitive routines, and unconscious memories, intentions, and expectations play a fundamental role in shaping and directing our conscious experience."[5]

If the unconscious mind is so powerful—and so elusive—must managers and consumer researchers despair of ever surfacing the treasures within it? Happily, no. Researchers from various disciplines have developed numerous devices for mining the unconscious and using those revelations to create real value for consumers.[6]

One particularly intriguing device involves metaphors.[7] By inviting consumers to use metaphors as they talk about a product or service, researchers bring consumers' unconscious thoughts and feelings to a level of awareness where both parties can explore them more openly together. The appendix to this chapter provides guidance for doing this.

Because metaphors can reveal cognitive processes beyond those shown in more literal language, they can also surface important thoughts that literal language may underrepresent or miss completely.[8] For this reason, specialists in clinical psychology and psychiatry are increasingly using metaphor elicitation to help patients make unconscious experiences progressively more conscious and communicable.

Metaphors direct consumers' attention, influence their perceptions, enable them to make sense of what they encounter, and influence their decisions and actions.[9] Therefore, understanding and influencing consumers' thoughts and decisions—and designing more valuable offerings for them—requires an exploration of the metaphors they use.

Like much research on metaphors, this book treats them broadly to include similes, analogies, allegories, proverbs, and the like. All of these forms express one thought in terms of another. Historically, novelists and poets have used vivid imagery in metaphors to express love, desire, pain, and life in general. However, metaphor making is a fundamental aspect of the mind.[10] Indeed, metaphors have a neurological foundation, which accounts for their prominence and operation.[11] Different social contexts, ranging from a people's overall cultural environment to small social cliques, affect the way these wirings operate.

More firms are using metaphors as a formal way of understanding their customers.[12] Some use consumers' metaphors to develop entire new lines of business. For example, Hallmark launched a new division based on the insights gained from consumer metaphors relating to memory. A major European-based cosmetics company has used three core metaphors it discovered in consumers' thinking to develop new beauty-care product lines. Still other firms, such as Bank of America, Samsung Electronics, Procter & Gamble, Schieffelin and Somerset, DuPont, and Diageo, have used consumer metaphors to generate new product and service ideas. Other companies, including Glaxo Wellcome, Immunex, Hewlett-Packard, McNeil Consumer Healthcare, Mercedes, and the Story Development Studio, have made explicit use of metaphors for understanding auto design preferences; the experience of medical conditions such as high cholesterol, rheumatoid arthritis, and erectile dysfunction; home health care issues; and audience reactions to film and television programming content. In all cases, these firms spent considerable time understanding the basic nature of metaphoric thought, not just examining the consumer metaphors they found interesting. Then they adapted their communications and offerings to meet the needs represented in consumers' metaphors, based on knowledge of *how* metaphors work. Metaphors have a strong presence in advertising. For example, the muscle-bound man climbing out of a bottle to clean floors, the giant in the washing machine, and the Rock of Gibraltar all represent security and strength. The challenge, however, is to make tacit thinking about metaphor explicit so that the powerful role of metaphor in consumer (and manager thinking) can be leveraged more effectively.

Metaphors can hide as well as reveal thoughts and feelings.[13] An example comes from a study conducted for the Lifetime Television network on how women see their day. One interview participant brought with her a picture of a solitary tree growing in a barren landscape. Initially, the interviewee used this picture to describe her sense of loneliness, a lack of help in raising a preschool-age son, and the absence of recognition of her struggles. In short, the tree represented the woman's solitary effort. Later, when the interviewer revisited the image in a different way with the interviewee, an additional—and dramatically different—interpretation of the picture emerged from the interviewee. (Remember the rabbit-and-duck picture in chapters 1 and 3?) In this alternative interpretation, the tree represented the woman's sense of achievement and her courage in the face of difficult odds. Other women who used different metaphors echoed the dual meaning of the lonely but strong tree. As a result, the network incorporated these ideas into a film script about strong but lonely women.

When properly elicited and interpreted, consumers' metaphors can uncover deep as well as surface-level thoughts.[14] Wini Schaeffer, a Motorola manager, describes how the use of metaphors has "enormous implications for positioning products. . . . You get answers to questions that you never thought to ask. I can't imagine you'd get that from a survey."[15] DuPont researcher Glenda Green describes how metaphor-based research provided the first positive things they could act on in their marketing of hosiery. The metaphor research provided "intensity, texture, and depth that we'd never gotten from other studies . . . bringing out subtleties related to sexual issues that you don't get in a straight interview. Also, rather than a love-hate attitude toward hosiery, we discovered something more complex, a like-hate relationship." As a result, hosiery manufacturers and their distributors changed their ads to include images of sexiness and allure along with images of super-competent career women. One company began including cards with a yin-yang symbol in its packaging to acknowledge the like-hate feelings woman held, and on the other side of the card, a personalized quote to convey a message of understanding and female affirmation.[16]

If managers understand the full range of metaphors consumers use to think about a product, they can design more effective communications about the brand and increase the likelihood of a purchase. For example, managers at a major Midwestern bank found that their small-business customers used metaphors relating to vitality when evaluating banking services. In response, the bank designed more meaningful materials to communicate with these customers in a way that spoke to the need for vitality. A leading architectural firm has used metaphor-elicitation techniques with their residential and commercial clients to help align architect and client thinking.

A Closer Look at Embodied Cognition

Many metaphors consist of references to physical motion, bodily sensations, or sensory experiences. This "embodied cognition" isn't surprising: We begin creating metaphors early in life in order to make sense of our world. The systems we experience most intimately at this and later stages throughout our lives are related to our bodies. Consequently, many metaphors rooted in our sensory and motor systems link the outside world with the brain. Here are just a few everyday examples:

"I *hear* what you are saying" reflects comprehension.
"You'll *see*" forewarns or predicts a future state.
"Those rules *stink*" indicates repugnance and dissatisfaction.
"What a *touching* scene" conveys a special feeling about a situation.
"She's a *pain*" indicates irritation.
"Don't *get ahead* of yourself" suggests slowing down.
"She's a *go-getter*" describes motivation.
"He's *falling behind* in his payments" describes tardiness.
"I'm feeling really *up*" describes a mood.
"He lords it *over* us" portrays an attitude.
"Lend a *hand*" refers to a request for or offer of assistance.
"I got a *kick* out of that" describes a type of reaction.
"She's *in* it *up* to her *neck*" suggests trouble.

Numerous disciplines provide evidence that abstract thought is often rooted in sensory and motor systems. That is, we use our senses and our bodies as metaphors to represent ideas that have nothing to do with the specific sense or body part. Since these systems have one purpose—to inform us about the world and help us navigate within it—not surprisingly, we rely on them to help us represent our abstract thoughts and actions.[17] Neuroscientist Antonio Damasio has this to say about embodied cognition:

> The lower levels in the neural edifice of reason are the same ones that regulate the processing of emotions and feelings, along with the body functions necessary for an organism's survival. In turn, these lower levels maintain direct and mutual relationships with virtually every bodily organ, thus placing the body directly within the chain of operations that generate the highest reaches of reasoning, decision making, and, by extension, social behavior and creativity. Emotion, feeling, and biological regulation all play a role in human reason. The lowly orders of our organism are in the loop of high reason.[18]

And as linguist George Lakoff and philosopher Mark Johnson explain:

> [From a biological perspective,] it is eminently plausible that reason has grown out of the sensory and motor systems and that [reason] still uses those systems or structures developed from them. . . . [This] explains why our system for structuring and reasoning about events of all kinds should have the structure of a motor-control system.[19]

Embodied cognition in metaphors is universal among human beings. Every culture and every society uses such expressions, although they may emphasize different senses and motor systems in expressing particular thoughts. Box 4-1 provides additional examples of embodied-cognition metaphors, all of which are present in one form or another in all cultures. Because embodied cognition is so basic and automatic, we often fail to appreciate such metaphors' special power to reveal more complex, hidden meaning.[20]

Box 4-1

Sample Metaphor Categories

Linguist Andrew Goatly has identified several metaphor categories that apply across cultures.[21] Notice the prominence of embodied cognition, as well as references to the impact of the natural world on our physical world, in this classification scheme. Metaphors from diverse market research projects conducted by Olson Zaltman Associates illustrate each category.

Human qualities: *Dead, lively, living, overwork, bring to mind, dissect, mutilate, flesh out, body, backbone, head, shoulder, heart, scar, hand.* The project conducted for Lifetime Television concerning how women picture their day brought forth the following quotation in reference to an image of a heavily damaged ceiling: "That is how my heart feels all day. It wears a big scar."

Plants/vegetables: *Take root, uproot, transplant, plant, blossom, bud, barren, green, seasoned, peel, grow.* While exploring the learning environment at General Motors, one executive described his responsibilities this way: "The first thing I had to do was to nurture new ideas and have patience while they grow. Give them a chance to bloom."

Games: *Volley, ball's in your court, kick off, start the ball rolling, opponent, goal, strike out, foul, win.* The CEO of a services firm who described difficulties in recruiting talented personnel explained her initial philosophy for finding promising talent: "We didn't want people who hit singles all the time. We wanted the grand slammer, the person who scores touchdowns, not goals."

War/fighting: *Battle of wits, in-fighting, truce, attack, strike, defend, resist, bombard, fire away, shoot mouth off, shoot down ideas, point blank, ammunition, flak, double-edged sword, combative.* The same services-firm CEO also noted: "We were shooting ourselves in the foot. In any event, we have stopped sabotaging ourselves and are pretty aggressive with anyone promising."

(continued)

Liquids: *Spout, leak, pour, spit, brim over, dry up, in midstream, torrent, stream, against the tide, mainstream, new wave, hold water, drained, test the waters, hot water.* A study on what it means to have breakthrough thinking in globally networked organizations illustrates the liquidity of ideas. As one CEO participating in the study commented, "One breakthrough idea can be a tidal wave sending people scurrying to higher ground for protection. . . . But people are just afraid to swim in moving waters, they prefer wading in a stagnant pool."

Walking/running: *Run over/through, as the saying goes, he goes over and over, stop, ramble, wander, sidestep, roundabout, falter, halting, stumble, retreat, find your way, passage, maze.* A project involving trial users of Febreze, a spray-on product for removing odors from fabrics, produced a number of motion metaphors: "People will be tripping over themselves to get this stuff." "Before using this on my clothes you could see people step back from me when I got near; I guess it was all my smoking."

Food/drink: *Food for thought, half-baked, raw, sweet, rehash, spill, drink in, chew on, ruminate, digest, regurgitate.* A project for the Story Development Studio analyzing a script for a feature film invoked several food and drink metaphors: "I thought it would be just warmed-up leftovers from *Police Academy*." "This had my stomach going." "It'll be just another puke film."

Money: *Cheap, rich, payback.* A study for Citibank concerning retail banking operations provides these examples: "The place oozes money . . . not because it's a bank, but the marble floors and even the smell inside says 'class' like a house from the 'Rich and Famous.'" In a study of attitudes toward financial planners, the money-as-wisdom metaphor was evident: "If they [financial planners] are so smart, why aren't they rich?"

Cloth/clothing: *Texture, material, weave, tag on, tailor, fabricate, decorate, embellish, padding.* The Lifetime Television project involved many clothing metaphors. For example: "You just don't outgrow some memories the way you do your jeans." "I wish the creeps could be in my shoes even for an hour, even fifteen minutes. . . . They'd button their mouths up fast."

Movement/transfer: *Drop, release, throw, pass, take back, exchange, put, pose, place, catch, gather, extract, find, store, hold, hang on, vacillate, tough going, advance.* A Procter & Gamble study of consumers' weekly grocery experiences provides this example: "I wish I could just chuck the whole experience out the window." Someone who engaged in boutique shopping said: "[V]isiting a boutique even if I don't buy anything is a kind of rush. It sort of raises my mood."

Vehicles/vessels: *Launch, go under, captain, crash, run, embark, torpedo, lifeline, pilot, wreck, harbor.* Another project addressing parent-child relationships produced several vehicle-related expressions: "After an hour with the kids shopping for school, I'm a complete wreck. They drive me crazy." "Dealing with him is like being on a roller coaster, except that on a roller coaster you know it's going to end soon."

Weather: *Atmosphere, climate, sunny, dark, gloomy, hot, cold, cloud, frosty, storm.* A project about motivation among R&D teams in an electronics company provides these examples: "[The team leader] blows hot and cold; you just can't forecast his reaction." "The team can be all excited until he calls the meeting to order, and then it's like a cloud moving across the sun." "Compared to my last company this is a breath of fresh air."

Vision: *See, overlook, watch, search, transparent, faint, murky, indistinct, enlighten, screen, picture, sketch, sparkle, bright, blind, focus, short-sighted.* Vision is a fundamental metaphor for expressing comprehension ("I see what you mean"), an unusually perceptive person ("She's a true visionary"), an attitude ("See?" as in "I told you so"), and so on. Probably no other sense is used so often in metaphor in so many different ways. For example, a project on sincerity in advertising generated such expressions as "I could see right through them," "It's all smoke and mirrors," and "They try to pull the wool over your eyes"—all of which referred to the firms that had created the ads.

(continued)

Places: *Lot, sphere, spot, near to, away from, enter, exit/leave, occupy, fill/empty, void, abandon, possess, sucked into, tied to, exclude, boundary/line.* A project on spirituality encountered references to "finding an inner void," "filling a void," "abandoning my roots," "falling into a rut," "becoming one with the universe," and "leaving old ways behind." An investigation of people's attitudes toward germs generated expressions such as, "They are everywhere," "Germs know no boundaries," "It's like a doctor's office, not a lived-in home."

Social Constructions

As box 4-1 suggests, people in all cultures face the same basic problems and key events in life; not surprisingly, they display similar responses to those problems and events at a fundamental level. For example, every society has developed belief systems involving justice and punishment, commerce, and the production of goods and services. Many social beliefs and practices pertaining to community, religion, family, games, and work have coevolved with and even influenced our physiology.[22] Expressions of these fundamental domains appear in every society's day-to-day speech, although different societies use different expressions. For instance, consider the domains of family and community, religion, and sports.

FAMILY AND COMMUNITY:
- "She's in a *family* way" refers to a pregnancy.
- "She's like a *sister* to me" conveys a sense of bonding.
- "Somehow we never *connected*" describes the absence of a solid relationship.
- "She got left *out*" refers to social exclusion.

RELIGION:
- "He's the high *priest* of comedy" suggests professional status.
- "What an *angel*" expresses appreciation.

- "She's full of the *devil*" describes a character trait.
- "Whatever *possessed* me" indicates loss of control.
- "Stop *preaching* at me" rejects someone's behavior.
- "He received the family's *blessing*" describes acceptance.

SPORTS OR PLAY:

- "She hit a *home run* with that speech" represents success.
- "He *scored* points with employees" reflects making a good impression.
- "He *struck* out" expresses failure.

These core institutions—sports, religion, politics, family, law, and many others—inspire a number of expressions that we use to convey thoughts completely unrelated to those institutions. Moreover, many of these expressions combine social, sensory, and motor metaphors. For example, "heads of state" command "foot soldiers," and in most societies "higher up" is better than "lower down."

Metaphors in Action

So far, we've had just a glimpse into how some companies have used metaphor elicitation to better understand consumers. But managers have also used metaphor to help understand their own thinking. The following examples shed light on both uses of metaphor.

"They Try to Skin You"

In this study, researchers asked consumers to collect pictures from any magazines, newspapers, and other sources of their choice that represented the thoughts and feelings that came to mind when they thought or heard about a particular credit-card company. Participants were to bring these pictures to an interview and talk about them there.

One consumer offered a picture of a meat cleaver to express the treatment she experienced from this firm. "They try to skin you," she commented. Later in the interview, her interpretation of the image shifted. Originally, she had spoken of the company as being the aggressor, but later she described the meat cleaver as a weapon she used against the company. Specifically, in a composite image that she created near the end of the interview, she depicted the meat cleaver as severing a credit card. In the picture, several other former consumer "victims" wielded the handle of the knife. By engaging in this activity, these consumers transformed themselves into "victors" in a battle with the company. Without the added stimulus of the pictures, such deep thoughts and feelings as these might have remained hidden during the interviews.

"Godzilla Should Go Away"

Metaphors can also help managers understand their own thoughts and actions. For example, one global industrial-goods manufacturer used metaphor elicitation to explore executives' experiences with innovation within the company. (More and more firms are using this technique to address internal organizational issues, especially issues about change, learning, and diversity.)

Below is an excerpt from one three-hour interview. The italicized words are those of the interviewee. The picture of Godzilla that is referenced is just one of several pictures that the manager was asked to find before coming to the interview that would help describe the experience of being innovative in the company.

> *[T]here is a picture of Godzilla. Godzilla depicts people who are the protectors of the old way of doing things. Maybe that is management.*

How do you feel toward the Godzillas when it comes to innovation?

> *I feel that Godzilla should go away and let the people learn how to defend themselves or go on the offense to stop whoever is coming. I would call this ingenuity and innovation. Down the leg of Godzilla is the word "Princeton" because of the style Princeton uses when it plays basketball, a very slowed down style, very methodical, but they do win most of the time. So I'm not saying that's a bad process, but I think it hinders the innovation process, because it slows it down.*

So, how would you relate that to the way you approach innovation?

I would be on a different team—one that's full of a lot of people who can play on a team, but have individual characteristics.

Any reason why Godzilla is as big as it is?

Yeah, Godzilla is tough to handle, very strong, built on "This is the only way of doing things," which has worked [in the past]. It's hard to beat Godzilla.

As a metaphor, Godzilla represented this manager's view of senior managers who protected old ways that impeded learning, moved methodically and slowly, and, ultimately, obstructed innovation. This particular manager preferred to be on a team that valued and encouraged individual expression. At a deeper level, she expressed feelings about the power of the status quo, a lack of speed at the company, the need to fight a discouraging internal attitude, and isolation.

As it turned out, many others in the firm shared these feelings. The revelations generated by the metaphors compelled senior management to take action. They decentralized and simplified the process of initiating new plans and procedures to offer additional autonomy to people. Months later, an audit found that more new ideas emerged successfully in the eight months after these changes than had emerged in the prior two and a half years.

"Negotiating with a Gorilla with a Huge Chip on His Shoulder"

Another study, this time about how industrial customers viewed corporate image, involved a picture of a gorilla. In this project, managers talked about what they believed purchasing agents thought of their company. This information was then contrasted with findings from interviews with purchasing agents about their views of the company. While some ideas overlapped, especially those relating to product quality, their thinking clearly diverged in certain areas. Two of the purchasing agents, reflecting the thoughts of many others, brought in pictures of gorillas. In one case, the gorilla reflected the company's obstinacy in negotiations. In another, it depicted an insensitivity to the purchasing agent's needs. In contrast, managers from the vendor brought positive pictures to describe how purchasing agents saw them, such as people shaking hands, a doctor speaking with a patient, someone tending a garden, and a mother and child baking a cake together. Subsequently, the vendor worked to close the gaps between the managers' and purchasing agents' perceptions of the company and developed a survey based on the issues surfaced by metaphor elicitation. The firm now uses this method periodically to monitor purchasing agent attitudes.

Values-Cues Research

General Motors uses metaphors in its Value-Cues Research program for designing vehicles, advertising, and dealership appearances. In a recent study, GM hired researchers to ask consumers to bring objects expressing "optimism" to a one-on-one interview. One participant brought an image of a champagne flute. The interviewee explained that the flute's simple, open design expressed many things, including the dawning of a new day. GM's designers then used this understanding to convey optimism in their car designs. One design-team member remarked, "It would be impossible to do this relying only on verbal cues. Getting customers to express themselves in the same design vernacular we use goes right to the heart of how we connect with them."

In another metaphor-elicitation project, General Motors' designers asked consumers to show them photos of "friendly" watches. Respondents chose watches that were easy to read and could stand up under abuse. The dominant design features of these watches included a large face, easily legible numbers, and a low-tech, nonindustrial "feel." Study participants also chose watches that appeared "fun." "Fun" was expressed through color; "innocent, silly" shapes; a round face; and designs "that make you smile," look comfortable, and invite comments from others.

To its amazement, the design team also learned that "slight changes in design can drastically change the metaphor conjured up by customers." With watches, as with human faces, the difference between a mean and friendly look can be very subtle indeed. That's why the Value-Cues Research program uses "in-depth one-on-one interviews rather than focus groups to probe deeply and figure out why a subtle change in design produces a major change in the metaphors used to describe one design option versus another," according to Dr. Jeffrey Hartley, a psychologist and manager of Brand Character and Theme Research at General Motors.

By asking consumers to use nonautomobile examples, the researchers gained a more complete understanding of the diverse meanings of "friendly" as potentially relevant to automobiles. In fact, in most of its metaphor-elicitation research, Olson Zaltman Associates asks consumers to bring in pictures that don't show the product in question, but depict their thoughts and feelings about that product, service, or experience. Thus, in a study of the essence of Mickey Mouse, OZA asked consumers *not* to choose pictures relating to or including Mickey or Disney in general. As a result, consumers thought more deeply about the topic and produced more valuable insights than otherwise would have been the case.

Metaphors Involve Mental Models

Metaphors do not exist as words in memory, but as networks of abstract understandings that constitute part of our mental imagery.[23] We call these networks *consensus maps* when a group of people shares them. Figure 4-1 shows a simple consensus map of consumers' understandings of Chevrolet trucks in terms of a rock, in response to Chevy's "Like a rock" advertisement, one of Chevy's most successful. The company designed it based on metaphor-elicitation research with consumers; as a result, it effectively identified the associations present in the thinking of dedicated Chevy truck owners and then, through advertising, established these associations in the thinking of a broader truck-buying public (see figure 4-1).

The phrase "like a rock" inspires four basic associations in consumers' minds: "rock" with "take abuse"; "Chevy" with "reliable"; "Chevy" with "rock"; and "take abuse" with "reliable." When consumers make a connection between the idea of a Chevy truck and the idea of a rock, they attribute certain rocklike qualities, such as the ability to take abuse, to Chevy trucks and translate them into notions of reliability and ruggedness. Figure 4-1 shows how these qualities enter consumers' awareness directly through advertising or other marketing decisions.

FIGURE 4 - 1

Metaphor Structure for Chevy Trucks

These qualities in turn are embodied in the Chevy truck logo. Thus the mutual influence between marketers and consumers flows back and forth, as each responds to the other's metaphorical communication.

Another example of how companies both represent and influence consumers' thinking through metaphor is the Folgers "Coffee Dancer" TV commercial. The ad shows a young woman waking up in the early morning, enjoying a cup of coffee, becoming increasingly alert, and finally participating in an energetic dance rehearsal, presumably later that same morning. The music in the ad starts out slow and then quickens its pace, mirroring the woman's physical movements. The associations here include "Folgers Coffee" and "dance"; "dance" and "energy"; "Folgers Coffee" and "being alert"; and "energy" and "being alert." The ad further symbolizes the idea of alertness through its depiction of the connection between energy and dance. The creative staff of an advertising agency also developed this idea based on its analyses of the metaphors that consumers used to describe the experience of drinking coffee.

Clearly, social and physical experiences interact strongly to produce the metaphors in our minds. Figure 4-2, which shows how one consumer thought about smoking and the neutralization of cigarette smoke in her home, provides a simple framework for thinking about these associations. The figure also reveals the ways in which social and physical experiences work together to influence how consumers communicate about their problems and how marketers can present information about the products intended to solve them.

A company created this figure by eliciting consumers' metaphors describing their experiences with smoking and with using a smoke-neutralizing product for fabrics during in-home trials. One respondent's data illustrates this point. Like others in the same study, this person

FIGURE 4 - 2

The Interaction of the Social and Physical Experience

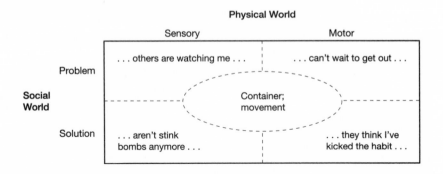

found cigarette-smoke odor to be more than just a sensory experience; it affected her image as a person, a homemaker, and a mother.

According to this consumer, the smell of smoke stuck to her kids' clothing, her furniture, and the inside of her car. She commented, "I feel others are watching me when my kids visit their home." This statement conveys a social problem (disapproval by others) linked to the sense of vision (cell 1 in the figure). Later in the interview, the woman said, "I know when they drop by here to pick up their kids they can't wait to get out." This statement also reflects a social problem ("They can't wait") but is linked to physical motion through expressions such as "pick up" and "get out" (cell 2 in the figure). At another point in the interview, while discussing how the odor-neutralizing product worked, this same participant commented, "Now when my kids go over to a friend's house, they aren't stink bombs anymore." Thus the consumer sees the product as a solution to a social problem because it defuses a "stink bomb" (the smell of cigarette smoke on the kids' clothing; cell 3). The kids' no longer smelling of cigarette smoke suggests cell 4, revealed by the woman's comment, "they think I've kicked the habit." This same consumer described using the product on her car upholstery. She said it enabled her to offer rides to friends without embarrassment. "So long as I get rid of the butts, they think I've kicked the habit"—another example of cell 4.

Notice that the consumer's statements have direct and indirect references to "containers," things that hold other things. This participant mentioned containers such as "a stink bomb," a home (both her own and others' homes), her car, and clothing and upholstery (which absorb cigarette smoke). Thus the researchers placed the word "container" in the center oval to show that it is a more fundamental thought—a core metaphor—that generates the thoughts located in each of the four cells. Another candidate for this center oval is the idea of movement: walking stink bomb; a bomb explodes, spreading its contents; her kids' "going over to" friends' homes; other parents' picking up their kids and being impatient to leave her home; people riding in her car; her "kicking the habit"; and so on.

Using Metaphors to Discover Products That Meet Consumers' Needs

The significance of metaphors for marketing managers comes from their centrality to consumers' imagination. Understanding consumers' metaphors enables managers to imagine the nature of consumers' needs with respect to discontinuous innovations outside of consumer experience and beyond the reach of more conventional, literally oriented research tools. With that information in hand, managers can tailor their communications to consumers, as mentioned earlier. But even more important, they can envision new, more effective ways to respond to those needs through specific products and services. The interplay of consumers' own metaphors with those used in marketing communications also enables consumers to imagine how companies' offerings might satisfy their needs.

In short, metaphors are the primary means by which companies and consumers engage one another's attention and imagination. Consumer needs are metaphors representing potential product ideas to managers who can interpret those needs in terms of new products or enhancements to existing products. Similarly, consumers see a firm's offering as a metaphor—a representation of a potential solution to a problem.

The metaphors a company uses in its advertising messages strongly influence how consumers interpret the messages or see a product's value. Thus firms must take great care in selecting metaphors.[24] Similarly, the right metaphor can cause consumers to "see" information in an ad that is not actually present anywhere in the ad's text or graphics. For example, when consumers view a beverage ad depicting a koala bear, most of them conclude that the beverage is intended to be consumed warm. By contrast, when they view an ad showing a polar bear, they conclude that the drink should be consumed cold. In one study, an ad showing a koala bear paired with a cold beverage produced confusion among consumers.

Establishing the relevance of a product innovation to a consumer need is a challenging task for managers. It requires uncovering the metaphors consumers use when thinking about a problem or need and using those metaphors to develop new products, modify existing offerings, and demonstrate a connection between the products and the consumer's problems. The task becomes even more challenging when consumers don't understand their own needs or how new technologies relate to them. In this case, using metaphor elicitation to help consumers articulate their experiences can prove essential. According to Stephen Cole, an expert on the use of metaphors for developing mail surveys and perhaps the only experienced market researcher holding a doctorate in the field of philosophy:

> Nearly all of the most successful new products I've studied in several industries over the years have involved managers or engineers making clever use of buyers' metaphors in conceiving, designing and introducing new products. The biggest flops [occur] when metaphors are ignored as a way of establishing a real connection with buyers.[25]

Identifying Core Metaphors

Like the thoughts and feelings they represent, some metaphors are surface-level and explicit while others are deeper and more tacit or unconscious. Understanding these deep or core metaphors can help marketers identify some of the most important but hidden drivers of consumer behavior.

Recall from box 4-1 how several basic metaphor categories or themes emerge from everyday phrases and from figure 4-2 how the statements in each cell imply deeper thoughts about containers and movement. Two additional examples will clarify the contrast between surface-level and core metaphors.

Indigestion and the Core Metaphor of "Balance"

A consumer participating in a research project for an over-the-counter treatment for indigestion commented on a picture of dollar bills, "I know that when I eat rich food, I'll pay for it later." Another person remarked on a picture of a chef: "Moderation is the key. You've got to learn what exactly is the right amount [of food] for you and what things accompany other things well." Both people used metaphors of wealth and money—"rich" food and "paying for it." But on a deep level, these metaphors also express the concept of balance. In the first case, the participant alluded to the idea of *moral balance* (the sin of over-indulging is offset by paying later). In the second case, the individual implied the idea of *material balance* (not too much and not too little) and *systems balance* (eating foods that go together).

For both consumers, the concept of balance underpins their way of thinking about indigestion. The first consumer made other observations related to balance, such as: "Some days it's like being on this seesaw. You're up and then you're down. You take something and then you're up again for a little while before plunging back." The second consumer implied a social imbalance when discussing a picture of the scales of justice: "It just isn't fair that some people eat anything they want and get away with it, and I can't. It's not right." Yet neither consumer explicitly mentioned balance or imbalance. Rather, the idea of balance is a kind of magnet around which many thoughts about indigestion cluster. These thoughts then take the form of surface metaphors to convey more specific ideas.

Owing to the prominence of the core metaphor of balance (expressed by nearly everyone in the study), the company decided to make this metaphor the keystone of its indigestion-aid advertising strategy. This concept replaced the idea of relief as the primary benefit of an indigestion aid. Balance and relief are related, but the core balance metaphor expressed consumers' larger need: They sought products that would help restore and maintain their relief *in order to experience balance,* not the other way around. This shift represented a unique positioning in the industry, given that competitors stressed relief as the ultimate purpose of an indigestion aid (without understanding *why* consumers wanted relief).

After the ads aired, the company credited the new strategy with an immediate significant increase in unit sales. Equally important, the company performed this metaphor-research project *before* issuing its creative brief to the advertising agency. By thinking about metaphors early in the creative process, managers could focus on deeper levels of consumer thought and not get bogged down by surface comments.

Telephone Help Lines: Force and Movement

An additional core-metaphor example comes from a study in which a major software provider explored consumers' thinking about the company's telephone help line. In the study, one consumer complained that trying to get "good service from a help line is like banging your head against the wall." Another customer, speaking about the same help line, noted: "[They] respond in a flash. Like greyhounds chasing a rabbit." While each consumer used different imagery and represented dramatically different experiences, both expressions strongly suggested force and movement. Other consumers offered additional statements suggesting force and movement: "the speed of molasses," "getting me going again," "stuck," "slam down the receiver," and so on. While "getting me going again" and "slam down the receiver" suggested increased movement, other phrases—such as "the speed of molasses" and "stuck"— implied a lack of movement. This *absence* of force and movement is especially salient—that is, noticed—among consumers, because people expect help lines to "get them moving again quickly."

In this example, force and movement are core metaphors that guide the expression of more specific (and sometimes contradictory) thoughts and feelings about telephone help lines. By focusing on the core metaphors, the company could tailor its communications and services so as to address *all* its customers' needs, rather than make the all-too-common mistake of trying to address conflicting, surface-level needs.

The company's managers used the metaphor-elicitation research to improve their help line in several ways. For instance, they trained help-line personnel to use movement and force metaphors during conversations with consumers ("Let's conquer the problem," "Let's get you going quickly," and "It's a slam dunk"). The company also added the image of a lightning bolt near the help-line phone number on its packages and in its instructional materials. This image suggesting force and movement reassured potential purchasers that they could get fast, effective help when they needed it.

To identify core metaphors, managers and researchers must make judgment calls about consumers' most profound, unconscious thoughts. This may sound difficult, but we all do this kind of thing all the time. For instance, a colleague may ask us what a person or experience is like, "in a word." Managers use the same process to identify a new market segment based on the dominant shared characteristics within a group of potential or existing customers. Marketers simply must extend this practice to their analysis of surface metaphors so as to discover the core metaphors. The ability to identify core metaphors can be developed with modest training or assistance. It does not require a degree in literature or linguistics or psychoanalysis, but simply a little practice interpreting metaphor-elicitation data.

A Closer Look at Core Metaphors

Like other unconscious processes, core metaphors have a neurological foundation.[26] Indeed, we can think of a core metaphor as akin to the root of a tree: It serves as the foundation of the tree's trunk, branches, and leaves (which are akin to surface metaphors). While each part of the tree is unique, they are all pieces of a whole. However, the roots are essential for the emergence of the trunk and leaves.

Companies find core metaphors helpful in several ways.

- They generate ideas for positioning a product, such as providing *balance*.
- They guide the development of a firm's image; for example, as a *nurturing caregiver*.
- They represent profound needs, such as the need to *transform* a feeling of depletion into one of being refreshed and energized.
- They guide the development of advertising strategy; for instance, showing a breakfast food as being especially relevant to the *transitions* that children make as they grow.

- They signal new product opportunities; for example, when consumers express a lack of immediate *connection* with sources of security while walking in parking lots or unfamiliar places.

Three Core Metaphors about the "Ideal Company"

In a study conducted by the Harvard Business School Mind of the Market Laboratory, researchers asked consumers to share their thoughts and feelings about what a company that truly has their best interests at heart would be like. The participants' responses shed additional light on how managers can identify core metaphors. In this study, consumers again brought pictures to interviews and used them as starting points for their stories. The quotations below are participants' responses to interviewers' probes. The immediate connection between images and words may not always be evident, even though the pictures played a key role in helping participants surface their thoughts. The quotes come from different consumers and reveal three core metaphors: resource, nurturing, and support. Follow-up research has shown these same core metaphors underlie how consumers in several different categories respond to the same issue.

Core Metaphor 1: Resource

Consumers view firms as resources. Specifically, they want companies to either provide them with knowledge or save them time. Indeed, time is a crucial resource for consumers and integral to their judgment of a company's intentions. As the quotes below suggest, consumers want to know that a company is helping them conserve time and maximize the return they get from their investment in "time shopping."

Most people are working, they're raising a family, and when you're looking for something it takes too much effort. If you're shopping sometimes you just want it to be easy . . . not a lot of brain work. Something that you don't really have to put a lot of effort or energy into. . . . If I am shopping, I want it to be easy, pain-free, go in and get it and you're out . . . without the effort and the search.

I'm pretty happy because this purchase is going to do what it says it's going to do. I'm not going to have to return it. I'm not going to have to spend time tracking things down. It's a time-saving device. So I'd say convenience and a time saver.

If [the product] works well or it tastes good, that makes me feel satisfied and I can move on. I don't have to give it any thought. I don't have to put energy into it. I don't have to be angry about it. I don't want to spend time being angry about something or having to then call the company or call and complain and get annoyed and get stressed out.

Consumers also evaluate companies in terms of their willingness to take time dealing with consumers, as the following remarks show.

You feel comfortable dealing with [customer service] when you have to call them on the telephone. They're very nice to you. They don't just try to push you off and make it a quick conversation. They take the time.

Every customer is important and they [the companies] want to make sure that they [the customers] feel welcome when they come to us . . . you truly believe that you're the center of attention and you're the most important customer to them at that time. When something goes wrong, they're there as your backup; you can get in touch with them as they try to fix the problem. They don't just want to sell you something. It makes me feel like I can depend on them.

Core Metaphor 2: Nurturing

Many participants in this study expressed the concept of nurturing in describing the ideal company.

[The company] is a parent. Most parents wouldn't take advantage of their children because they want them to grow. [The company] could also be a gardener. So it could be you and a plant or it could be a mother and son or daughter. A parent always watches over you.

Here is a picture of a mother holding her child on a beach. They're at the edge of the water and she's holding his hand as they're entering the water. She's taking care of him; she's protecting him. She's watching out for him.

Her whole focus is on her child. In regard to a company, they're focusing on the care of their client, the customer. They want to take care of their customer, and there's safety in that. This child is safe, and you can feel safe with a company who cares, and whose focus is on their clients' happiness or safety.

Core Metaphor 3: Support

According to this study's participants, companies that have consumers' best interests at heart provide support when needed—and in the way needed.

I have a picture of a woman teaching a man how to play pool. I liked the way that they're working together to make their shot. She's not showing him how to do it by doing it herself or doing it for him. . . . They're in there together and they're lining it up and she's talking to him about it, but he's doing it. I liked the teamwork and the cooperation. Doing it for sort of the edification of both of them and for a better shot.

Metaphors both invoke and express images of all types—visual, tactile, and olfactory—in a nonverbal form. Metaphors are so basic to the representation of thought and emotion that communicators and their audiences alike are largely unaware of their use and significance in the expression of ideas and feelings.[27]

Metaphors vary in depth. A surface-level statement such as "She's on the fast track to management" or "She moved up the ranks quickly" suggests there is also a deeper level of thinking about advancement in an organization: the idea of movement. The diversity of the metaphors we use and the way they interact with one another create an intricate web of meaning and open windows to our inner thoughts and feelings. Understanding the diversity and importance of deep metaphors in human expression helps marketers tap into consumers' unconscious minds and offer more effective communications and products that meet consumers' needs. The appendix to this chapter introduces a way of interviewing consumers to uncover the deeper meanings behind the metaphors they use.

Appendix

The Metaphor-Elicitation Process

Chapter 4 discussed the importance of metaphors and provided examples of the kinds of thoughts and feelings they can reveal. But how do you conduct a metaphor-elicitation interview?[1]

Box 4-2 provides an example from an Olson Zaltman Associates project with second-generation Hispanics living in several regions of the United States. The project explored participants' thoughts and feelings about being Hispanic in the United States today. One week before the study, researchers asked participants to gather pictures that expressed their feelings about the topic. Through a series of one-on-one interviews, the study ultimately investigated the relationship between the consequences of participants' experiences and the effect of those consequences on their buying behavior. The researchers also examined how participants felt their experiences differed from that of their parents and from those their children might have.

The pictures participants selected were metaphors representing multiple thoughts, feelings, and behaviors. For example, the photograph shown in box 4-2 introduced a number of themes, including masks and hiding, togetherness, support, fear, social acceptance, rejection, identity, the role of spoken language, social embarrassment, and pride. The same image elicited discussion on topics such as participation in public events, half-lives, opportunity, sorrow, learning from one another, acknowledging diversity, roots, strength, and isolation.

Box 4-2

Metaphor-Elicitation Technique

In each of the examples below, the effective probe follows the participant's initial statement. The alternative probe comes next, followed finally by an example of what would have been an ineffective probe.

Image Description Probe: *Can you describe this image for me? What do you see here?*

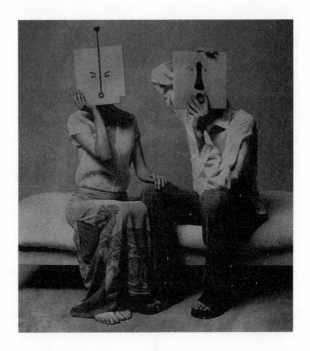

I see a couple, two people, a woman and a man, sitting down and you can tell that they're related, together. 'Cause she has her hand on his knee. It shows body language. And they have a type of mask, sort of a plate in front of them. And it sort of shows their facial expression but really not, kind of hiding who they are. They're sitting down just their knees facing each other, not their faces, and they're holding a mask in front of their face.

Introductory Probe: *And how does this image relate to your thoughts and feelings about being Hispanic in America today?*

Well, I see it as these people are together, but yet they're scared of being accepted. That's why they're putting the mask in front of their face . . . when I see it, I can think of some people that are not from America and when they're in places, they're probably kind of scared of showing who they are, where they are from, because of not being accepted and just being different, and their ways that are, like, not the same as Americans. But yet they're together, they're not alone. So that's why I see them holding on to each other, 'cause that's what they've got. But they're kind of like frightened so they put a mask in front of them to kind of hide.

Effective Probe 1: *Could you tell me more about the mask?*

I can't speak for all Hispanics, but some Hispanics they're, you know, not afraid of showing who they are. But then again I've seen like family members and also friends and in school, I would see some girls that, like, just recently came from Cuba who were like hiding who they are 'cause they feel scared. Maybe everyone's speaking English and they would be scared of speaking in English since they don't speak it properly or like with an accent. So they tend to hide. So I would think that the mask would be like just scared of trying to relate with other people 'cause of communication.

Alternative Probe: *How do you think these people would feel if a gust of wind suddenly blew their masks away?*

Ineffective Probe: *Does this mask hide them from others in America whom they are not like? [This question reflects the interviewer's thinking, not the respondent's thinking.]*

. . .

Effective Probe 2: *How do they create a mask? What do they do when they hide?*

They sit back; try not to socialize with Americans or any other ethnic group. Also, like stay away from different, public crowds. They

(continued)

probably go to just family houses and not go out to different restaurants. They stay only in the Latin type of restaurants. They're scared to go to an American restaurant where you have to speak English. They're scared of going to another restaurant because you must speak English. Imagine if a whole family would go from another country and all of 'em don't know how to speak English, they would be kind of embarrassed to order the food. 'Cause I know my father was, and we would have to order it for them.

Alternative Probe: *Have there been occasions when you have been scared or wanted to hide?*

Ineffective Probe: *Is only speaking Spanish part of creating this mask? [This comment interjects the interviewer's hypothesis that language reveals a weakness and is a reason to put up a mask.]*

. . .

Effective Probe 3: *Does anything happen as a result of being scared?*

It keeps them back from doing things. They live half-lives. That's what my mother says. They came to America probably to either expand or to get away from where they were—as a refugee. They're holding themselves back in a way too—if they don't open up to communicate, they're not going to acknowledge new things. So I think they're holding themselves back with being scared and being intimidated.

Alternative Probe: *Could you say a little more about holding back?*

Ineffective Probe: *Does being scared mean that they avoid embarrassing situations? [The interviewer assumes that "scared" and "embarrassing" are connected and encourages the interviewee to affirm this assumption when they may not really connect.]*

. . .

Effective Probe 4: *Could you say a little more about what happens when they hold themselves back?*

They don't open themselves to all the opportunities that there are in America. And then it's like they got away from their roots for nothing—they don't open up to what there is around here and choices they could have. It makes me feel sad—like I wish that there was something, some type of group or some organization that could help these people that are Hispanic come together and realize that we're all people. And when we all learn from each other, we're not all the same. Even within the Hispanic people, they're not all the same either. So if they all come together to, like, open up and give each other support and to learn new things, it would probably be better.

Alternative Probe: *What is it like to live a half-life?*

Ineffective Probe: *Are they holding themselves back from exploring America? [Here again the interviewer is asking the interviewee to respond to what the interviewer is thinking, not necessarily what the interviewee is thinking.]*

. . .

Effective Probe 5: *"Open up." What does that mean?*

What makes some not afraid is that they'll come very eager to another country. They're saying, "Man, I can't wait!" 'cause they know or they've heard of so many things that are going on in here; how we're expanding. And so they come very eager to probably, like, learn everything that they possibly can, to fill themselves up and achieve as many things as they could. So like they're not really scared. They don't care if they mess up when they talk to an American person. Or they don't care that they don't speak the right English. Or they don't care that they don't know what a certain thing is because it's in English or American. They'll be willing to like stay strong and just learn. And then some are scared.

Alternative Probe: *You mentioned getting away from their roots for nothing. Could you help me understand that better?*

Ineffective Probe: *Would opening up eliminate these feelings of fear? [The interviewer is leading the interviewee to confirm a hypothesis that may not be part of the interviewee's thinking.]*

. . .

(continued)

Effective Probe 6: *What happens to them by staying strong and learning?*

I think being strong is a very good benefit because people see how your character is willing to do so many things, and you'll get opportunities left and right. Things will just come at you and you'll be able to handle it and take it and just fight for it. To me being strong and learning says "give me more" to other people who want to help you.

Alternative Probe: *What have been your experiences about "filling up" that differ from, say, your parents' experiences?*

Ineffective Probe: *Is expanding a benefit of staying strong? [This forces the interviewee to go down a particular path that may not be salient.]*

. . .

Effective Probe 7: *What do you think prevents some Hispanics in the U.S. from opening up?*

Because they feel limited that they're not citizens or 'cause they're not from here they feel limited. Some feel, like, not welcomed or, like, are repressed. They just stay closed in. When they feel like they're not from here, they feel the burdens of not being able to communicate with other people; they're like stopping themselves from doing a lot of things that they probably would have done in their country because they're from there.

Alternative Probe: *What are some of the things that have come at you that you have or haven't handled the way you'd like?*

Ineffective Probe: *Does being a minority prevent Hispanics in the U.S. from opening up? [This doesn't encourage a more in-depth exploration of a complex issue; it encourages a brief surface answer.]*

. . .

Effective Probe 8: *Could you share some of your own experiences, if you've had them, in hiding behind a mask and in opening up?*

When I was a kid I had lots of friends who weren't Hispanic, but the only friends I'd invite home were my Hispanic friends. I was embarrassed that the Anglo friends couldn't speak easily with my parents, and my parents would say funny things to them without knowing it. I always thought they would laugh at me behind my back and tell other kids at school. I know that's stupid. But that's how I felt then. So I kind of hid my home for a long time. I guess I hid my parents even though I was tremendously proud of what they did to get here.

Alternative Probe: *Have you ever felt not welcomed or repressed?*

Ineffective Probe: *It sounds like you've pretty much followed the opening-up path and avoided the mask path, is that right? [This encourages a yes or no response without explanation, and confirms the researcher's thinking rather than presenting an opportunity for new ideas from the interviewee to surface.]*

Box 4-2 also demonstrates effective probing techniques—that is, a way of asking questions to encourage participants to think more deeply. In addition, it shows a different but equally effective probe as well as an ineffective probe (that is, one that would prompt the respondent to respond to the *interviewer's* thinking rather than his or her own thinking).

In addition to using effective probes such as those in box 4-2, the interviewer asked the participant to imagine widening the frame of the photo in any direction and then to describe who or what might enter the picture that would cause the two people to willingly lower their masks.[2] This activity produced additional thoughts and feelings. For example, the participant began talking about the role of teachers, friends, and parents and about how a well-meaning stranger could behave in such a way that a person must grip his mask with two hands instead of just one. When asked to place himself in the picture and describe his feelings and actions, the participant offered still other thoughts.

Clearly, the picture itself was a metaphor. Through effective probing and creative mental activities, the interviewer encouraged the participant to explore and express what lay hidden behind this visual metaphor. For instance, metaphors of force and movement emerged through phrases like "*ripped off* the mask" and "*leaped from* the bench."

The interviewer probed further to elicit even deeper meanings about being Hispanic in the United States today.[3]

Probing versus Prompting

As you might have guessed after reading box 4-2, a good rule of thumb in metaphor elicitation is to *probe, not prompt,* consumers' thoughts and feelings.[4] In probing, the interviewer encourages participants to open up, to look through more windows on their thinking and share what they see. How does an effective probe differ from an ineffective one? The former enables participants to respond in multiple, often unexpected, ways, while the latter prohibits discovery by focusing the participant's attention on the interviewer's assumptions and hypotheses. Over and over again, participants disprove such assumptions. *Ineffective probes actually prompt participants to affirm the expected answer.* When interviewers probe ineffectively, the results reflect the *interviewers'* thoughts, not the participants'. Even if an interviewer has the same thought as a participant, its salience and relevance to the participant will probably differ at that moment.

As a tool for probing further, interviewers can provide "mental hiccups," in the form of offbeat, unusual questions or challenges that can put participants slightly off balance. As they regain their balance, they often express a more deeply held idea. For example, during a ZMET licensing training program at Procter & Gamble, a project conducted for the company's diaper division explored a topic never before studied: mothers' attitudes toward their babies' bowel movements. This may sound like a strange subject to discuss, but it strongly influences women's purchasing decisions for diapers.

To stimulate deeper thinking, the interviewers introduced the following "hiccup":

> *Now I'd like to switch gears a bit and ask you to create in your mind's eye a home movie or video in which there are three characters. One is your baby, of course, one character is you, and . . . yes, you've guessed it . . . the other character is your baby's [participant's preferred phrase for bowel movement]. Assume that the [bowel movement] has thoughts and*

feelings and can express these freely. Take a moment if you like to think about where the three of you are, what you are doing and saying to one another.

Many participants in this project reacted to the hiccup with surprised laughter. But in just a few seconds, most of them began crafting a movie scene that included ideas expressed earlier in their interview, thus underscoring their importance, plus new ideas that this particular step allowed to surface. Although this project was meant as a training exercise, it also produced actionable insights and generated some important ideas. For instance, it provided ideas for advertising involving husbands and suggested product-design changes.

Trust and Training

A metaphor-elicitation interview can be an acutely personal, revealing experience for participants. Thus, mutual trust between interviewer and interviewee is essential. That trust comes with time, patience, and training on the part of interviewers. In particular, interviewers must understand that participants may share an amazing quantity of relevant information during a session. Participants may also become quite emotional as one thought unexpectedly triggers another more intimate or possibly upsetting thought. In these instances, even if the upsetting thought is relevant to the study, the interviewer should avoid pushing the participant to explore it further. The interviewer must navigate the discussion in a way that respects the participant's experience at that moment and his comfort level in sharing intense feelings.

Moreover, skilled interviewers know that socioeconomic status has no bearing on the richness, depth, or number of ideas a participant expresses. For this reason, organizations that conduct metaphor-elicitation interviews insist that participants recruited for a study *not* be screened on the basis of verbal articulateness, apparent analytical thinking skills, or other factors that suggest higher education or professional standing. Too many focus group participant recruiters use screening questions such as "How many uses of a brick can you name?" These kinds of questions are ineffective for several reasons, not the least of which is that people who are screened out may be important represen-tatives of the targeted market. Such screening methods mainly make things easier for the researcher or provide entertaining focus group members for a client to watch. They don't benefit the client because they exclude people who can provide deep insight into the mind of the market.

Chapter Five

Interviewing the Mind/Brain

Response Latency and Neuroimaging

The mind screams volumes in silence.

T HE LAST CHAPTER discussed using metaphor to elicit both unconscious and conscious thoughts and feelings. That approach accesses the content of what consumers think and feel. Other methods also help us learn about what consumers experience unconsciously and are especially helpful where unconscious and conscious perceptions of and reactions to the same event can differ. Unconscious reactions to marketing stimuli are more accurate indicators of actual thought (and subsequent behavior) than the conscious reports consumers often provide.[1]

Methods that tap unconscious perceptions and responses have special value in quantitatively precise testing of certain kinds of thought, such as positive and negative emotions, and thought processes such as the retrieval and encoding of memory. They can also evaluate specific thoughts identified by metaphor-elicitation processes. Two methods are introduced here. Both are valuable in identifying reactions consumers may be unaware of or that they incorrectly report when traditional

Appreciation is expressed to Dr. Fred Mast, Department of Psychology, Harvard University, for his contributions to this chapter.

research methods are used. One traditional research method, focus groups, is also discussed toward the end of this chapter.

Response Latency Techniques

Surveys are most reliable when they ask respondents to consider very familiar issues or to describe a decision they are about to make. Because of the analytical tools that can be applied, surveys can also reveal associations among respondents' thoughts and feelings that might not surface during other kinds of research. However, evidence also suggests that what consumers say in response to an explicit survey question often contradicts what they really feel, intend to do, and actually do.[2] One reason that consumers cannot predict their own behavior is that the contexts in which choices are made, in contrast to those in which answers to questions are given, are very important and equally difficult to anticipate.

One way to avoid such contradictions is to monitor respondents' *response latency;* that is, how long it takes them to respond (by pressing a key on a computer keyboard) to a certain pairing of words or images. The relative quickness of response can suggest the presence or absence of "noise" in their thoughts and feelings that would not be detected in other ways. Traditionally used in psychology, these techniques have consistently produced as good or better indicators of thought and action than questionnaire data. Yet marketers are just beginning to use such methods to study consumer behavior.

Response latency techniques help researchers distinguish between study participants' explicit, consciously held thoughts and feelings and the implicit beliefs that exist outside participants' conscious awareness. Both kinds of cognitive processes have potential importance for managers. However, what a consumer believes explicitly may not affect his actual behavior—similar to espoused theory and theories-in-use among managers. When explicit and implicit thoughts and feelings contradict one another, the implicit ones are the more reliable indicators of future behavior. To discern implicit thoughts and feelings about a product, researchers can use various response latency techniques, detailed in the following sections.

Priming

In one experiment, consumers saw pictures of two brand-name perfume bottles on a computer screen and then viewed randomly presented words that included "alluring," "sexy," "sophisticated," "mysterious," "energizing," "informal," and so on. The participants' task was simply to judge whether strings of letters represented a word or a nonword. After being primed by a picture of one bottle, participants responded (at a computer keyboard) more quickly upon seeing the words "alluring" and "sophisticated" than they did when seeing the words "energizing" or "informal." Moreover, they associated the other brand more strongly with the idea of "informal" than they did with "alluring" or "sophisticated."

This exercise shed light on how consumers compare brands and the extent to which those brands "prime" or elicit certain thoughts. Interestingly, these same perfume associations also came to light in a survey, but not as strongly. If the second brand mentioned had relied solely on the surveys, the company might have erroneously concluded that it could compete with the first brand noted by using a "sophisticated" or "alluring" positioning strategy.

In a somewhat related study in a very different category, the goal was to judge whether particular product designs were uniquely associated with particular concepts. The particular concepts used were first identified using the metaphor-elicitation process discussed in the last chapter. Consumers were presented with visual stimuli along with alternative sets of evocative words. The results showed that the two different product designs the firm was considering were associated with very different concepts. This helped the firm to select the design whose concept best fit its desired positioning strategy. This application was also a validation study undertaken as an experiment by the firm in question. It involved only forty representative consumers, and yet produced the exact same results as a more costly study involving a survey (also based on the metaphor-elicitation insights) of 550 consumers. It produced additional insights as well that enabled the firm to alter its initial positioning strategy.

Recently, this technique was used to test potential names for a new resource center on smoking. It turned out that the participants responded differently to names such as "Life Rather than Tobacco," "Make Smoking History," "Trytostop," and so forth. The response times differed from those in the questionnaire-based data, and, most interestingly, only the priming technique revealed significant differences between the smokers' and nonsmokers' associations. This supports the idea that the results from priming studies are in fact behaviorally relevant and may be especially helpful in naming research.

The Implicit Association Test (IAT)

The implicit association test, or IAT, builds on priming research and measures the relative association of two sets of concepts in consumers' minds. For example, the method can help researchers assess the strength of association between a set of concepts such as "flowers" and "insects" and positive and negative concepts such as "pleasant" and "irritating." As you might expect, the IAT finds greater association between "flowers" and "pleasant" and "insects" and "irritating" than between "flowers" and "unpleasant" and "insects" and "pleasant." Researchers have used the IAT to examine implicit associations in a wide range of contexts, most recently related to specific brands.

In a proprietary application of one IAT study, a clicks-and-mortar distributor identified surprising differences in consumers' online and in-store service experiences. The company refined its strategy accordingly: For certain offerings, it encouraged consumers to visit a physical store, while for others it prompted them to shop via the Internet. The payoffs were greater efficiency in order processing, fewer returns, lower shipping costs, and higher shopper satisfaction.

In another proprietary study of product design for a durable good, response latency measures pointed to the most appropriate set of verbal descriptors for reinforcing the different concepts behind the alternative designs. These results, later supported by consumer choice behavior, countered initial focus group findings and a post–focus group survey.

Implicit Attitudes as Behavior Predictors

Many psychologists argue that implicit attitudes measured through techniques such as priming and the IAT not only reflect consumers' real attitudes, but also more accurately predict their actual behavior. Consumers may sincerely believe their own stated thoughts, but they may not consciously understand the opposing forces that drive their behavior. A just-completed study for a new fast-food offering provides a good example. The company had tested several basic concepts and names, initially using focus groups and later a survey. At the same time, they also conducted a priming study to evaluate proposed names and an IAT study to assess the product concept. The response latency data produced a very different selection of name and concept than that suggested by the focus groups and survey. The company then altered their test marketing plans to allow for testing the two different sets of names and concepts. It became dramatically evident very early during test marketing that sales were superior in the test market site using the name and concept supported by the response latency measures. The firm has decided to use that positioning and name in their national introduction of the food.

Implicit measures offer two benefits that make them better predictors of behavior than explicit measures such as surveys. First, implicit measures uncover attitudes consumers may not be aware of, but that still strongly influence their buying decisions. Second, they reveal the social drivers that affect behavior. For example, if a person wants to be perceived as a health-conscious consumer, he may report on a survey or in a focus group that he does not consume much alcohol and may give negative ratings to various brands in that category. Implicit measures are much less susceptible to demand characteristics in situations in which consumers respond in certain ways because they feel that is what is expected of them. In one study comparing implicit measures with focus groups and surveys, response latency measures returned a different assessment of the size and composition of target markets for alcoholic beverages than did the other methods. People displayed much more positive attitudes toward particular brands and toward alcohol consumption generally.

One of the most interesting examples supporting implicit attitudes as good predictors of behavior comes from studies of stereotypes about elderly people.[3] These participants were first asked to unscramble groups of five words that primed either an elderly stereotype (e.g., "Florida," "wise," "bingo") or a neutral concept (e.g., "thirsty," "clean," "private"). The researchers then timed how long it took people to walk a 9.75-meter hall as they exited the experiment. *They found that subjects who received the "elderly" prime walked significantly more slowly than those who received neutral primes.* Using another word-scramble task, these same researchers found that people who received a "rude" prime (e.g., through words such as "disturb," "intrude," "brazen") were quicker to interrupt an experimenter. Other research finds that covert primes for helpfulness make people more helpful,[4] while intelligence primes (e.g., words that activate a stereotype of a college professor) make people temporarily perform better at the board game Trivial Pursuit.[5]

Implicit Association with Brands

Research suggests that implicit measures may be especially powerful tools for understanding brand meaning and consumers' relationships with brands. Implicit measures may not only give us more confidence in explicit results, they may also give us a richer picture of brand attitude or preference. For example, research comparing associations between juice and soda brands finds that while both implicit and explicit attitudes correspond, an implicit measure (the IAT) may predict *actual* product usage better than self-report measures.[6]

One study employed a widely used explicit self-report measure (CETSCALE) and an IAT to measure the degree of ethnocentrism among U.S. and foreign consumers living in the United States.[7] They found that both U.S. and foreign-born consumers revealed very little ethnocentrism on the *explicit* test. In fact, both groups felt that country of origin for a product was irrelevant in their evaluation of products. However, the IAT revealed a different story. For example, U.S. consumers more quickly associated the U.S. brand Hallmark with the positive attribute "lucky" than they associated the foreign brand Kawasaki with a similar positive term.

Consumers' current mood states are among the important influences on just how they respond to a brand at a given moment. This phenomenon, of long interest to consumer researchers, is illustrated by a response latency study of consumer associations with the brands Ben and Jerry's and Marlboro.[8] As we would expect, the research found positive associations with Ben and Jerry's and negative associations with

Marlboro. But it also discovered that these positive and negative associations are stronger for sad consumers. In addition, mood affected the *correlation* between explicit and implicit measures. When consumers were in a happy mood, explicit measures were good predictors of implicit attitudes. When they were in a sad mood, explicit measures were poor predictors of implicit attitude.

In these ways, implicit measures provide a richer understanding of consumers' evaluation of products and understanding of brands. Moreover, considerable evidence suggests that in many circumstances an implicit measure may be a better predictor of actual consumer behavior. In the future, market research that combines explicit, implicit, and behavioral variables will further reveal the interrelatedness of conscious and unconscious information and its impact on consumer behavior.

Neuroimaging Techniques

Advances in the brain sciences have spawned new questions and provocative new answers regarding the mind's workings. Innovative technological methods for studying the brain have accelerated this progress. These technologies involve neuroimaging, "brain scanning techniques that produce pictures of the structure or functioning of neurons."[9] Through neuroimaging techniques, researchers can directly observe people's brain activity while the individuals engage in various mental tasks.[10] These rapidly improving technologies promise to revolutionize the study of consumer behavior.[11]

Functional Magnetic Resonance Imaging (fMRI)

Functional magnetic resonance imaging (fMRI) methodology offers a noninvasive way to track changes in neural activity. The most common form of fMRI is the Blood Oxygen Level Dependent (BOLD) technique, which identifies brain areas with a high level of blood flow. The technique rests on the assumption that more blood flows to areas of high neural activity than to areas of low neural activity.

Standard fMRI procedure includes just a few steps. First, neuroimaging technicians take a series of baseline images of the brain region of interest, such as the area in the right hemisphere that acts up when processing metaphors. Second, they take another series of images while the subject performs a cognitive task, like "taking in" different advertisements that contain different metaphors to convey a concept. Third, they subtract the first set of images from the second set. They presume that the metaphors have successfully activated the brain areas most visible in the resulting image, and perhaps differentially if one metaphor is more engaging than another. Subjects might compare an ad conveying the same concept without use of a metaphor. At the same time, the technicians monitor other areas of the brain associated with positive and negative emotions or feelings as well as various memory processes to see whether the different ads activate them differentially. This research could lead to the conclusion that one particular ad more effectively elicits positive emotions and past memory and encodes new memory.

Functional Diffuse Optical Tomography (fDOT)

The fMRI approach has several disadvantages; specifically, participants must lie still within a noisy, cramped device. In addition, fMRI facilities are large and expensive. The fDOT technique has none of these drawbacks. It is described here simply as an example of the kinds of improvements occurring in brain imaging technologies. Indeed, subjects can move to some extent during the imaging process, allowing for on-site measurements in a nonlaboratory environment. Furthermore, the machine is quiet and relatively inexpensive to operate. Though fDOT can record neural activity only one centimeter beneath the surface of the brain, this coverage is often complete enough to reveal activity in many cortical areas of interest.

How does fDOT work? If you've ever shined a flashlight through your hand, you know that visible light can travel a significant distance through human tissue and still be detected. Biological tissues are especially transparent to near-infrared light, which when shined through the brain's surface can reveal variations in blood flow through particular areas. Differences in the absorption spectra for oxygenated and deoxygenated blood allow the researcher to acquire an indirect measure of neural activation. This technique uses laser sources and detectors, applied to the head right above the examined brain area. The principle is very similar to fMRI. Baseline measurements are compared with measurements during which the subjects are engaged in a cognitive task. For example, a possible exercise could instruct the participants to generate images of different icons, to which they were exposed before scanning. Brain activation could reveal how strongly visual areas are activated when people generate mental images of different icons. In particular, we could compare the depth of activation within each participant, then compare the alternative icons.

If we can validate new methods such as fDOT with more established techniques such as fMRI, their low cost and accessibility will allow researchers to test large numbers of subjects—which is desirable for a variety of marketing applications.

The Promise of Neuroimaging

Neuroimaging techniques can not only improve the content and application of standard market research techniques but also detect and measure consumer reactions to marketing stimuli. In the first case, neuroimaging can help managers determine the effectiveness of survey questionnaires (especially standardized tests or proprietary surveys) in gauging certain thoughts and feelings. Using the results of the neuroimaging studies, managers can design more effective paper-and-pencil tests, which can improve their understanding of consumers' thinking. Thus, neuroimaging can further improve established research tools.

Neuroimaging techniques can also isolate the important core metaphors or archetypes elicited for developing advertising or positioning strategy. Similarly, these techniques can assess which among alternative executions of the chosen core metaphor will get the most attention and be most memorable.

Stephen Kosslyn, a leading cognitive neuroscientist specializing in visual imagery and a professor of psychology at Harvard University, and I undertook a unique study to demonstrate the second promise of neuroimaging: detecting and measuring consumer reactions to marketing stimuli using brain imaging technology. The study examined consumer responses to three different versions of a specific retail setting as these settings were described in an audiotape. The results were compared to a far more exhaustive study on the same retail setting using multiple explicit methods. This allowed the two groups of researchers to compare results. The conclusions of the two studies were the same, although the nonneuroimaging study was far more detailed and comprehensive since it was also to be used to implement the most attractive scenario if one were found. Indeed, both studies selected the same scenario as being superior, and this scenario was implemented in several test sites.

The retail sites involved in the test increased their gross sales from 9 percent to 40 percent. This indicated that the brain imaging study produced results that were directionally valid, even if it did not provide the detail that was required for successful implementation. The imaging study showed increased activity in brain areas associated with positive and negative emotions, with storage and retrieval of information, and with predicted activity in the visual cortices, suggesting that consumers could readily visualize the proposed alternative retail scenarios. A conclusion that was reached with this and other work is that brain imaging studies might be a cost-effective way of evaluating alternative concepts, while other methods such as ethnographic studies, one-on-one interviews, and surveys would be appropriate for learning how to implement the chosen concept.

The Kosslyn team also used fMRI to evaluate consumers' response to advertisements. One study compared reactions to finished ads versus animatics; that is, the cartoon-like renditions of ads before their final production. This comparison is important, because the cost of going from an animatic to a finished ad can be very high. If companies discover that they can get reliable evaluations of an advertisement or other visual stimulus from consumers *before* creating the finished ad, they can realize considerable savings.

In a pilot test involving three pairs of animatics and finished ads, the researchers found that 95 percent of all areas of the brain activated by the finished ad were *also* activated by the animatic. Considerable work remains to better understand when such testing does and does not add value to the development and assessment of advertising. However, as this knowledge evolves, it will offer managers more constructive guidance as they develop and test new product ideas, alternative product positioning, and the design of products, packages, and retail experiences.

A Note of Caution

Caveats about using neuroimaging in psychological research, such as those pointed out by William Uttal, an industrial engineer and psychologist at Arizona State University, also apply to marketing.[12] And marketers must be mindful of the limitations of this approach.[13] For instance, the idea that we can accurately identify specific areas of the brain as responding to a particular stimulus is very alluring, but is reminiscent of phrenology. Marketers may be tempted to infer that a single active "spot" in the brain signals an effective ad, attractive package design, or engaging new product concept.

However, nothing about the brain is that simple. We cannot "read" specific thoughts; we can only tell that brain areas known to be associated with particular kinds of thoughts and feelings are being activated. Inferences can be made about the quality of those thoughts by knowing what other areas are coactive or active before and after another area, but this still does not identify the exact thought or feeling. In time, however, neuroimaging techniques will likely serve as helpful tools in bringing better and more meaningful goods and services to consumers.

Focus Group Folly

Many managers use focus groups to interview the mind/brain. While their usage has been declining, they remain the most popular method in marketing today, despite heavy criticism. Part of this criticism revolves around their inherent nature and part around their misapplication. For example, advertising executive Robert Morais cautions, "Never, never should focus groups be used as a basis for decision making."[14] John R. Hauser, Kirin Professor of Marketing at MIT's Sloan School of Management, recently noted, "If you have two hours to cover five to ten topics with eight people, then you have about one or two minutes on each topic with each person. You can't possibly get much beyond the surface given those constraints."[15] One-on-one interviews cost less than focus groups. In response to various criticisms, some focus group moderators are becoming more innovative in their approach, leading to better practice while also cautioning clients about inappropriate applications.[16]

Most managers and researchers agree that focus groups are misused and overused—but employ them anyway in conducting their market research. Why? The answer is simple: Focus groups are easy and affordable to implement. Like every research method, focus groups do have a place in the research toolbox.[17] For example, they can provide feedback on the attractiveness of an existing product design and ease of product use. Contrary to conventional wisdom, they are not effective when developing and evaluating new product ideas, testing ads, or evaluating brand images.[18] Nor do they get at deeper thoughts and feelings among consumers. In fact, focus groups fail an important test for any method: Is the method based on well-founded insights from the biological and social sciences and the humanities?

The most disturbing concern about focus groups is that little scientific foundation, from any discipline, supports their use. Group-therapy theory provides the closest thing to such grounding. However, group-therapy structure and techniques differ markedly from those employed in focus groups. Successful group therapy hinges on the same individuals meeting together multiple times, as well as in individual sessions with a highly trained therapist, something that doesn't happen with focus groups. According to Valerie J. Janesick, professor of educational leadership and policy studies at Florida International University, researchers can help groups of three or four individuals achieve more meaningful conversation by preceding the group meeting with extensive one-on-one interviews centering on the topic of concern.[19]

Herbert Rubin and Irene Rubin, two leaders in qualitative research, point out that focus groups do not allow moderators to build trust—a condition necessary for participants in any group to share highly personal thoughts and feelings.[20] Qualitative research experts Steven Taylor and Robert Bogdan suggest using focus groups only when the researcher "is not interested in the private aspects of people's lives."[21] Of course the private aspects of people's lives are often what matter most to marketers. To get to that deeper level, researchers need lengthy one-on-one interaction.[22]

Focus groups are actually *contraindicated* by important insights from several disciplines.

- Perhaps the most serious limitation of focus groups is that they are technically unable to identify the important connections between ideas and the development of socially shared mental models. At best they produce a list of ideas, but not the dynamics among them that make the ideas relevant in the first place.

- Robin Dunbar, professor of psychology at the University of Liverpool's School of Biological Sciences, presents strong evidence that the optimal number of individuals for any group interaction is three. Thus, ideal "group" interviews are best limited to one moderator and two or, at most, three participants. Dunbar says, "In fact, there appears to be a decisive upper limit of about four on the number of individuals who can be involved in a conversation."[23]

- Dunbar's position is supported by research performed on subject-matter experts. According to this research, no more than three experts are needed to identify all the factors relevant to solving a particular problem. Indeed, the contribution of the third expert will often prove minimal. This has been demonstrated in fields ranging from medicine to engineering. Individual consumers, of course, are experts on their own consumption experiences.

- The average length of speaking or "air time" for a focus group participant is about ten to twelve minutes. Research on narrative conversation among strangers suggests that participants struggle to achieve any depth of mutual understanding on a topic together within ten minutes. Thus, ten minutes from just one focus group participant doesn't facilitate deeper thinking among other participants, especially when issues of social dominance, eagerness to please, privacy, and so on are operating.[24]

- The ten-minute average individual air time in a focus group, with some people speaking much more than others, does not permit researchers to analyze much more than just the literal statements participants make, even if all ten minutes are devoted to a single issue.[25] Ten minutes of air time from several different focus group participants at best produces multiple versions of an idea but little depth of insight, which is the usual research objective.[26]

- Compelling evidence of the advantages of conventional one-on-one, hour-long interviews over focus groups is provided by Abbie Griffin and John R. Hauser, authors of "The Voice of the Customer."[27] Their empirical data clearly point out that several such interviews reveal as many consumer needs as several focus groups do. For instance, eight one-on-one interviews are as effective as eight focus groups (which may comprise between sixty-four and eighty consumers!). One-on-one interviews dramatically win out over focus groups in terms of cost effectiveness alone.
- Griffin and Hauser also found that to get the most out of focus group data, companies should employ multiple analysts to interpret transcripts or videotape. Having a group of people observe a session from behind a one-way mirror isn't enough: It doesn't stave off groupthink, nor does it enable observers to capture and reflect on participants' comments.

New Knowledge, New Power: The Need for Wisdom and Responsibility

The idea that we must learn about consumers' unconscious minds isn't new. Marketers, for instance, use statistical analyses to infer the relative value of different bundles of product attributes that consumers would otherwise have trouble articulating in response to direct questioning. Work-site observations by skilled researchers yield insights that customers do not otherwise provide about equipment needs. When marketers ask consumers exiting a supermarket if they handled competing brands and compared prices before making a choice, most consumers will say yes. This response suggests that they make their brand choices at the point of purchase. Yet observational techniques reveal that these same consumers spend only about five seconds at the category location in a store, and 90 percent of them handle only their chosen product.[28] In this case, direct observation demonstrates that the consumers made their brand choice *before* entering the store despite their belief that in-store activities were important.

Emerging research methods focus on the cognitive unconscious and its interactions with the conscious mind. These newer methods are based on knowledge about human thought and action from multiple disciplines and are providing richer insights than more surface-oriented approaches. Moreover, the same disciplines that inform the newer methods also provide knowledge that managers need in order to apply these insights.

One implication of these developments—of joining the knowledge society Peter Drucker describes—is that managers will know much more about consumers than they currently do. Moreover, this knowledge has implementable validity. That is, thoughtful managers can put it into action by changing the way they communicate with consumers through advertising and other means and the way they design and deliver products and services. Herein lies a potential trap—a trap probably best suggested by Sir Francis Bacon's oft-repeated phrase "Knowledge is power."[29] For most people, the phrase connotes the abuse of knowledge. Indeed, many consumers are already deeply suspicious of marketers and resentful of their attempts to influence consumers for their own ends.[30]

Fear of falling prey to the "knowledge is power" trap can discourage marketers from applying the new insights and methods described in this book. However, when Bacon made this statement, he was actually envisioning knowledge as a resource to be used for the benefit of humanity. And, like Bacon's understanding of knowledge, the intellectual products of the knowledge society that have implementable validity for marketing managers can also widely benefit individual consumers and society in general.

Yet these benefits accrue only when marketers synthesize knowledge from various fields and apply it responsibly, that is, in a way that respects consumers' best interests. This ability grows naturally from our sense of right and wrong and the courage to follow our conscience. As we learn more about consumers, our prime concern must be to make judicious and socially responsible use of our learning.

I believe that good or harm resides not in our knowledge or how we acquire it, but rather in how we use it. Indeed, *every idea in this book that disturbs the reader has significantly improved the health and well-being of people everywhere. This same positive potential exists when marketers use these insights.* Applied judiciously, they can help companies provide people with enduring value. The *possibility* of misuse shouldn't frighten us from discoveries, although it should heighten our vigilance. Avoidance only denies consumers the opportunity for higher-quality lives through improved goods and services and better ways of receiving them.

How do consumers see this question of knowledge abuse? We can best understand their perspective by considering their willingness to share information. As long as consumers have well-founded reasons to believe that marketers will use the information provided to benefit consumers, they feel quite comfortable sharing their deepest thoughts and feelings, of which they themselves are unaware. Research at the Harvard Business School's Mind of the Market Lab indicates that, to consumers, the most highly respected and trusted companies address their own *and* consumers' best interests in their marketing decisions. Moreover, consumers trust and respect companies that they believe genuinely want to understand the complexity of their thoughts and feelings, not just their surface qualities. One consumer expressed his frustration with what he perceives most companies are currently doing with their market research:

> *[Consumers] are giving these firms a wonderful, homemade cake as a gift. What do the companies go and do? They lick off the frosting without a clue or care about how much more they are missing. . . . They're saying they don't really care about me, or maybe that there's no more to me than the frosting they see.*

Consumers will clearly provide all kinds of data, whether through intensive one-on-one interviews, surveys, or brain-scanning sessions, as long as companies use what consumers reveal to provide more meaningful consumption-related experiences. For instance, the metaphor-elicitation processes I normally use invariably reveal many thoughts and feelings consumers didn't expect to share.[31] At times, these include very moving, personal stories.[32] Each interview begins with a variation of the following script: "If, at the end of the interview, you feel uncomfortable with anything you've shared or with the purpose of the research, you are free to take the tape, my notes, and your pictures. No explanation will be asked of you and, of course, you will still be paid."[33] At the end of the interview, the interviewer discloses the purpose and sponsor of the research. To my knowledge, in more than eight thousand interviews conducted globally in over two hundred projects, only two people have ever taken possession of their data at the end of the interview. One of them mailed the data back after a few days. I believe this behavior reflects not only the trust and general rapport that interviewers and participants have established but also consumers' desire to have companies understand who they are and a belief that this understanding can help companies develop and deliver better goods and services.

Finally, a distinction is to be drawn on the one hand between the acquiring and using of knowledge about unconscious processes to better understand and satisfy consumers and on the other hand using this information to influence them without their awareness. We can and do convey promises to others, both in ways that are conscious and unconscious to ourselves and to the audience. Fortunately, there is no evidence that promises conveyed but unkept are effective beyond the short term. For example, evidence involving the decay function of pure placebo effects suggests that the unconscious effects of belief and expectation are short-lived when not accompanied by an authentic treatment. As Raymond Bauer noted in his 1958 critique of Vance Packard's *The Hidden Persuaders* (itself a highly misleading book about deception), we must address a "primitive anxiety that we are on the verge of being able to establish complete control over human behavior to the extent that the victims of this control will not have a chance to resist it because they do not realize it is there."[34] This anxiety is as real—and as unfounded—today as it was in 1958 when Bauer spoke. Despite the advanced neuroimaging methods, metaphor-elicitation techniques, and other research approaches available today, managers cannot control people's minds, much less brainwash them unconsciously *or* consciously into making continued unwise or unwanted purchase decisions.[35]

The knowledge explosion now taking place promises only to deepen marketers' understanding of consumers' unconscious thoughts and feelings. Advances in physiological response technologies and in various social sciences such as those discussed in the next chapter provide consumers with more opportunity to express their "voice" and have it heard more reliably. This deeper understanding will permit marketers to influence consumers in the same way that a better understanding of learning processes enables educators to develop and deliver better educational experiences. Like the teacher, the marketer can offer only opportunity—and like the student, the consumer decides whether to embrace that opportunity and how to use it.

Chapter Six

Come to Think of It

What do you have, when you have a thought?

ARKETERS KNOW that consumers' thoughts shape their
preferences and product choices.[1] But, as we've seen,
most thoughts lie well below the surface and occur, exert their influence, and recede without the thinkers' awareness.[2] Moreover, much like
the person shown in figure 6-1, managers often fail to anticipate or
allow for their presence.

Metaphor elicitation can help managers tap into these critical but
elusive drivers of consumer behavior. Consensus maps, which build on
metaphor elicitation, also serve as valuable tools for peering into consumers' unconscious minds. In this chapter, we explore these maps.

The Nature of Thoughts

Consensus maps represent bundles of thoughts many consumers share
regarding specific problems and the products, services, and companies
that promise to address them. First, therefore, we should delve more
deeply into the nature of thoughts. What are thoughts, exactly? As central as they are to our lives, we often struggle to say what a thought
really is.[3] We might use the term *idea* or *concept* as a rough synonym, but
a more precise definition eludes us.

Managers must thoroughly understand what a thought is if they are
to comprehend and influence consumers' thinking and behavior and to
provide enduring value to customers. Most important, marketers must

FIGURE 6 - 1

Unsuspected Depth

REAL LIFE ADVENTURES

**Like icebergs, nine-tenths of the problem
is usually below the surface.**

know that a particular thought never stands alone. Individual thoughts
bundle together in the mind and work in partnership with behavior.[4]
In fact, we can imagine a thought as an instance of behavior, specifically
an electrochemical behavior that we can't see without a neuroimaging
device.

Many managers claim that they can discern a consumer's thinking
by observing that person's behavior. Such managers are using their own
system of interpretation to determine which thoughts each behavior
represents. Sometimes this works; often it does not.[5] For example, based

on their observations of consumers' in-store behavior, managers at a West Coast–based supermarket chain concluded that price was an important driver in selecting the chain's private labels over national brands of certain food items. However, when questioned after making purchases, most consumers didn't know the price paid for the items in question, and few could state which brand cost more. Managers' thinking proved an unreliable substitute for consumers' thinking, and the pricing policies that were put into effect based on this substitution led to lost profits until the company realized its mistake.

Although observing consumers can lead to important insights, we should use this approach in conjunction with one that accounts for the *consumer's* interpretation of his own behavior.[6] The tactic of a manager's substituting his thoughts for those of consumers can warp major marketing decisions.[7] William McComb, president of McNeil Consumer Healthcare, sums up this problem compellingly: "We slip from our obligation to know what consumers are thinking . . . into believing they are like us; and from there we slide further into believing we can think for them and understand their actions."

When managers understand how specific consumer thoughts partner with behaviors, they can shape the outcome of those partnerships through the use of more-creative marketing communications. For example, using metaphor elicitation, the dental referral service firm Futuredontics learned that many people don't visit their dentist every six months because they think that dentists invented the six-month checkup to secure enough business. The participants in this research project didn't understand that the six-month dental care regimen has sound medical reasons. By grasping the reasoning behind this patient behavior, Futuredontics could develop educational materials to explain the rationale behind the six-month schedule and could encourage dentists to underscore the importance of keeping appointments. Though the researchers have not kept statistical records of the project's outcome, participating dentists and office assistants report that these actions have been very effective.

Clearly, understanding the "why" behind the "what" of consumer thinking and behavior is the key to helping consumers make the right decisions for themselves. Iain Douglas, vice president for marketing at Gallo wines, develops maps showing how specific buyer thoughts and actions relate to one another. Gallo uses these maps as blueprints for building marketing strategy. Robert Summers, an Atlanta-based advertising consultant to many firms, points out that every element of strategy and every element of creative execution should contain a "why gene"—something that clearly explicates why consumers do what they do and how a company's advertising reflects this knowledge. Betty Hutchins of InnerViews, a Toronto-based research firm specializing in metaphor usage as a way of raising the curtains on the unconscious mind of both consumers and managers, calls consensus maps "the crystal ball of marketing strategy": If you don't look into it, then you can't anticipate consumer reactions to marketing decisions.

Constructs: Taming Thoughts with Labels

Thoughts arise from cognitive processes reflected in neurological activity.[8] They require concepts, which stand in for things other than themselves, according to Jesse J. Prinz of the Philosophy-Neuroscience-Psychology Program at Washington University.[9] This "stand-in" for quality is one reason why the use of metaphor (the representation of one thing in terms of another) is effective in eliciting hidden or deeply held thoughts and especially connections between thoughts.

Marketers often try to infer consumers' thoughts from their spoken or written statements (such as "I would never switch brands") or from their behavior (for example, going out of their way to find a particular brand or displaying an unconscious physiological reaction such as increased skin conductance upon seeing a familiar brand). Managers and researchers capture the supposed thoughts behind these statements or behaviors and give them a label or name, such as "brand loyalty." Cognitive scientists call such labels *constructs*. These constructs are not the *actual* thoughts or behaviors; rather, they represent marketers' *interpretation* of those thoughts or behaviors. Constructs enable people to talk about specific thoughts and behaviors; thus, they tame these elusive phenomena.

How do constructs look? We saw some of them in chapter 5, in reading about the metaphor-elicitation project in which consumers described how they picture companies that have consumers' best interests at heart. For example, constructs involving support, nurturing, and resources were identified. Other constructs from this study, inferred by researchers and managers from several companies analyzing the data, are shown in table 6-1.

For example, the thought labeled as dependability was inferred from quotes such as "I can rely on them because they know what's good for me is good for them" or "When things go wrong, they fix it right

TABLE 6 - 1

Companies That Care

SAMPLE OF CONSTRUCTS

Construct	Definition
Evolving	The continued development of the relationship between a consumer and a company. It involves believing that the relationship is enduring and dynamic as well as a "two-way street": The company and consumer learn from one another and adapt their behavior accordingly.
Care for Personnel	Consumers' perceptions of how a company treats its own employees, including wages, benefits, or general handling of employees.
Dependability	A company whose products and services can be counted on as reliable and consistent. A company that consumers can place their trust in in times of uncertainty. A company that is always there for the consumer and stands behind its product.
Honesty	Straightforward and truthful information about products is provided. Nothing is purposefully hidden from the consumer.
Innovation/Creativity	A company's attempt to continuously develop new products or services that improves its ability to satisfy consumer interests and needs. The ability to think differently, switch frameworks and function in diverse boxes, to fulfill its consumers. Openness to unconventional ideas instead of rigid adherence to the status quo.
Moral Character	Consideration of the ethical nature of a company's actions. Recognition of potential good and bad outcomes of business practices.
Proactive Orientation	A corporate attitude that attempts to preempt any problems by looking ahead, keeping in mind all possible outcomes and preparing accordingly.
Hospitality	A personable company that goes out of its way to make the consumer comfortable. The consumer feels wanted, warmly received, and cherished.

Source: Mind of the Market Laboratory, Harvard Business School.

then, no questions asked, no hassle." The construct of dependability also includes thoughts and feelings about a firm not being dependable: "This picture shows an abandoned house. That's how I feel about [a specific HMO]. I don't know if they're going to be there for me when I really, really need them. They weren't for my sister-in-law. She counted on them and they didn't do anything." Honesty is another important construct:

> *A company that has its customers' best interest in mind is going to be honest. If you expect a lot of problems and a rocky road, let me know at the start because I'll be more apt to accept errors if you are up front with me.*

Constructs are marketers and researchers' expressions of what they think is going on in a consumer's mind. Constructs are not the actual thoughts, but simply well-intentioned labels to capture and express them. They are short cuts summarizing others' ideas. However, these labels can influence the conclusions that marketers draw. Consider the construct "brand loyalty." It means one thing when it refers to a person's repeatedly buying a product—behavior that could simply reflect habit or passivity. It means something totally different when it refers to a person's going out of his way to find a specific brand or deferring a purchase until he finds it, a behavior that suggests dedication. For this reason, managers must closely examine the bases on which a construct was formulated. Others in the firm should also look at the raw data used to identify a construct. Creative staffs in advertising agencies and personnel in product R&D can gain additional insights into consumer thinking by seeing the images and language that consumers use. Someone in R&D or in an ad agency may pick up nuances that the brand manager missed.

As marketers conduct research, they often engage in lively discussion about the constructs that they see emerging in participants' responses. In particular, they debate whether a construct should be broad or narrow. Should the construct "moral responsibility" include a respondent's concern about both the physical and social environment, or do the two environments deserve separate constructs? Should the marketer lump the positive and negative qualities of dependability under one label, or separate them into dependable and undependable since the quality of experience in each instance differs? Marketers must address these issues before finalizing a consensus map.

The scope of a construct affects managers' subsequent interpretations of the evidence and shapes their decisions and actions. Harvard University's Jerome Kagan, one of today's most insightful psychologists, warns against too much abstraction or vagueness in defining constructs.[10] As we've seen, constructs such as "impulse buying," "fear," "customer satisfaction," and "brand loyalty" can mean different things in different settings and to different individuals. For example, consider the construct "fear." A fear that one may have body odor, that one will get into an accident, or that one will run out of crucial supplies during a party are all very different. Similarly, the meaning of "refreshing" changes when we use it to describe drinking bottled water, taking a shower after strenuous exercise, enjoying classical music in a park, or opening a window on a warm spring day. And finally, the "care" that consumers experience in a supermarket is not the same care they receive in an auto dealership or from a telephone help line. In fact, as we've noted earlier, one of the major points of convergence in recent thinking in philosophy, neuroscience, cognitive science, and sociology concerns the importance of the context in which thought and action occur.[11] The physical and social setting of experience gives very different meaning to the same terms—not just the differences in the settings in which a product is used, but in which research data are collected.

Kagan explains, "The biology of the brain provides the basis for an envelope of psychological outcomes, just as a large outdoor pen constrains the animals inside but does not determine any one arrangement of the animals."[12] The same construct, even in the same "pen," may take on different shades of meaning depending on context or situation. For example, the meaning of a "bargain" varies depending on the influence of a fellow shopper, which store or even which country one is in, and the mood of the shopper, not to mention the specific product or service and the nature of one's last purchase experience.[13] The basic thought may have different antecedents as well as different consequences in each setting and thus take on a different "persona" in each context. For example, the same consumers in a study in Europe described coffee and water using many of the same terms, such as balance, transformation, energizing, and rejuvenating. However, the imagery and metaphors associated with these thoughts revealed that the two beverages produced the thoughts captured by these labels in very different ways. Rejuvenation with coffee differs from rejuvenation with water. By better understanding the differences in the meanings that consumers attached to the very same terms, the coffee manufacturer effectively presented coffee consumption in a way that slowed the erosion of its market due to increased bottled water consumption.

Society Seeps into the Mind/Brain

Where do thoughts originate? At first, the answer seems obvious: in the mind, from thinking processes emerging from neural activities. Indeed, as cognitive neuroscientist Steven M. Kosslyn and many others suggest, our conscious and unconscious thoughts are the product of brain activity. However, that explanation stops short. The brain often produces what social settings condition it to do.[14]

Consider one's sense of self. Certainly a consumer's sense of self affects his thoughts about a product, company, or advertising campaign. But what is the self, precisely? One's sense of self is a private, personal quality. After all, what could we as individuals possess more than our self-image? What shapes who we are? The many influences include our biological makeup as well as our life experiences; our social world—that is, our parents, the casual social networks in which we circulate, our immediate community, and the social standards we learn as we mature; the larger culture around us; and the educational, governmental, occupational, and other institutions we encounter. Even our personal memories, as we shall see, have social origins.

The unique qualities of consumers tend to emerge through surface-level techniques. Companies that emphasize these unique qualities, especially by using sophisticated data-mining techniques, tend to generate multiple market segments that require greater product differentiation. Sure, they can tailor products and services to unique groups of consumers, but customization is a costly strategy and often results in competition based on unimportant differences. Fortunately, managers are learning that, at deeper levels of analysis, consumers share a similar "anatomy" of thought and behavior on a given topic. For example, one firm distributing its goods through retail settings around the globe discovered that the nature of the shopping experience in very different countries was actually quite similar in important ways. Another manufacturer with a global distribution channel found that consumers in very different cultures shared fundamental preferences for certain appliances, whereas the company had previously believed there were significant differences. This finding led to a more efficient and more effective product R&D process as well as better communications. The differing thoughts and actions that we observe at a surface level often rest on deeper, more common features. These deeper, shared features tend to drive consumer behavior most strongly and change little over time. Thus, their relative importance and stable nature make them better bases on which to segment markets and design goods and services. For example, Drake Stimson reports that, by shifting from a surface-level analysis of consumers using traditional methods and conducting deep analyses instead, P&G doubled its projected first-year sales of Febreze.[15]

The marketing community has made finer distinctions among consumers, resulting in more market segmentation. As with increasing specialization in scholarly disciplines, increasing market segmentation only worsens managers' tendency to focus on consumers' surface differences rather than their similarities. Of course, consumers are both similar to and different from one another in various ways. Their similarities hold the key to understanding their thinking and influencing their buying behavior. *The deeper we dig, the more we find that otherwise very different consumers share important thoughts and feelings about the same topic. These similarities powerfully drive consumer behavior and remain surprisingly stable over time.*

What explains the existence of shared, stable thoughts and feelings, or *human universals?* In part, they arise from the neurobiological structures we all share. But they also emerge because people across highly diverse cultures share many of the same problems and concerns, such as how to raise a family, how to find meaning in one's daily efforts, and many other challenges.

Box 6-1 provides more detail on human universals. While lengthy to identify the commonalities found across all cultures ever studied, it actually understates the incidence of shared features among diverse peoples.[16]

Box 6-1

Human Universals: The Myth of Diversity

People who study various cultures and societies do so for a good reason: Culture explains a considerable part of all behavior. Cross-cultural studies often focus on differences between groups, reflecting an inherent curiosity about our own uniqueness as well as what seems deviant about others. However, social scientists are giving more attention to traits and behaviors common to nearly all societies.

This focus has overturned widely held beliefs about the distinctiveness of different cultures. These beliefs include Margaret Mead's argument that adolescents in Samoa did not face the same challenges that their Western counterparts did, Benjamin Whorf's hypothesis that language shapes our perceptions of the world, and others' arguments that the meaning of facial expressions varies across cultures. These and many other supposed distinctions have been found wrong. Instead, evidence increasingly suggests that, at a deep level, various cultures display more commonalities than differences. Managers who are developing market-segmentation strategies within or across cultural boundaries should appreciate this news, because segmenting markets can be very expensive.

The following list of universal or near-universal human qualities, adapted from the work of Donald Brown, reveals how plentiful these shared traits are.[17] Anthropologists have identified hundreds of such qualities. Of course, cultures may differ markedly in how they express these shared traits, and marketers might attend to such differences. Fortunately, for any product or service category, the relevant list of universals for concept development, positioning, and other marketing decisions is only a small subset of those below.

• Use metaphors • Have a system of status and roles • Divide labor by sex and age • Regulate the expression of affect • Record numbers • Create art • Conceive of success and failure • Have standards for

measuring beauty and ugliness • Are ethnocentric • Choose pragmati-
cally • Believe in the supernatural • Have a range of temperaments •
Categorize color • Empathize • Dominate • Imagine • Personify • Create
solitary groups antagonistic to outsiders • Imitate outside influences •
Resist outside influences • Compete • Hold similar attitudes toward
supernatural occurrences, fear, hope, love, hate, good, bad, beauty,
ugliness, murder, theft, lying, and rape • Dance • Sing • Tell tales • Create literary art • Use figurative language • Symbolize • Establish rules
and leadership to govern the allocation of important resources • Trade
and transport goods • Establish rules and regulations • Develop similar
cognitive functions • Consider aspects of sexuality private • Adorn
themselves • Associate art with ritual • Establish etiquette • Need nov-
elty • Are curious • Express emotion with their faces • Interpret rather
than merely observe human behavior • Use symbolic means to cope
with envy • Reciprocate (in both positive and negative tit-for-tat ways) •
Give gifts • Use logic and the logical notions of relationship • Orient
in space and time • Recognize property rights • Associate music with
ritual • Are consciously aware of memory, emotions, experience of acting on the world and making decisions • Distinguish between public
and private • Experience being in control as opposed to under control •
Decide collectively • Have organizations distinct from the family • Follow rules about inheritance • Display personality apart from social
role • Recognize ascribed vs. achieved status • Use mood-altering
drugs • Prefer faces with average dimensions • Perform hairdressing
rituals • Give hair symbolic value • Overestimate the objectivity of
thought • Expect parental care and training of children • Provide for the
poor and unfortunate • Recognize economic obligations in exchanges
of goods and services • Demand truth in certain conditions • Cannot
transcend guilt • Are aggressive • Need privacy and silence occasionally • Need to explain the world • Sacrifice one's self for one's group •
Think men and women differ in more than only procreative ways • Lie •
Use and understand the concept of equity and most of the West's
other general legal concepts • Celebrate special occasions by looking
their best • Wish to allure • Desire to stand out from others • Feel pride,
shame, amusement, and shock • Forego present pleasure for a

(continued)

deferred good • Use same basic color categories • Identify the same geometric forms • Consider the relationship of nature to culture • Consider morally right and wrong methods of satisfying needs • Form a personality structure that integrates needs (id), values (superego), and executive-response processes (ego) • Attach meaning to the essentially meaningless • Provide for socialization of children and others • Control disruptive behaviors • Distinguishing between general and particular • Archetypal themes of love and hostility • Animism • Some degree of inequality and dominance • Play of imagination • Coordination • Subordination • Obscenity • Fear of the consequences of envy • Sentiments of affiliation • Sexual jealousy • The desire for children • Group regulation of individual actions • Supervision or leadership • Male predominance in public decision making • Mother–child tie • Families or households • Consultation in collective decision making • Informal versus formal consultation • Sexual modesty • Kinship • Succession • Moderator-type leader • Nonlocalized social groups • Intimate property vs. nonproperty • Loose property • Equation of social and physiological maternity • Dominant household dyad includes at least one adult • Interpersonal grooming • Problem solving by trial-and-error • Insight • Reasoning • Joking • More time and care spent on ritual or symbolic objects than on utilitarian objects • Sex differences in homicide • Revenge • The senses of duty and indebtedness • The concept of provocation • Resentment • Stages of cognitive development • Signals and sayings that convey erotic, reproductive, and gender meanings • Consciousness of birth and death • Mothers raising tonal frequency when speaking to children • Eyebrow flash • Expression of surprise • Facial expression of contempt • Imposing order on the universe • Reciprocity • Taboo • Anthropomorphizing • Identity • Religion that consists of an "ethos" and a "worldview" • Spatio-temporal orientation • Topographic and place names • Motivational orientation • Ideals • Symbolizing self in time and space • Conscious awareness of memory • Emotions • Self-responsibility • Social structure influenced by accumulated information • Mutual influence of personality and social role • Worldview involving entities not directly observed or observable • Curiosity about one's nature • Positive death customs • Care of ill or injured • Altruism • Denial of unwelcome facts • Distinction between good and bad, in-group and out-group, family and others • Some form of prohibition of rape, murder, and other violence • Regulation of relationships between family members • Concept of property • No economically egalitarian societies • Consuming substances to partake of their properties • Ornamentation • Rational thought • Psychological self-defense mechanisms • Psychological processes of projection, displacement, rationalization, sublimation • All languages employ thirteen semantic primes: I, you, someone, something, world, this, want, not want, think of, say, be a part of, become • Psychological language • Contrast between white-positive and black-negative • Concept of future and other "alternatives" • Relationships • Adultery • Courtship • Culture • Flirting • Homosexuality • Juvenile delinquency • Dominant individuals are a focus of attention • Games of skill and chance • Loyalty • Male activities that exclude females and/or are secret • Male dominance (in political arena) • Myths and legends • Persons who attempt (or pretend) to cure the ill • Psychoses and neuroses • Suicide • Taboos (and avoidances) • Traditional restraints on the rebelliousness of young men • Metered poetry • Association of poetry with ritual • Humans are inveterate predictors • Sounds as a medium of ritual communication or experience • Universal drive for altered states of consciousness • Play fighting • Fear of snakes

Source: Adapted from Donald E. Brown, *Human Universals* (New York: McGraw-Hill, Inc., 1991), 157–201.

Bundling Thoughts: Consensus Maps

As discussed above, the more deeply we dig into consumers' thoughts and feelings about a situation or context that these consumers have in common, the more likely we will find important constructs that they share as well. For example, in a study of how women picture their day, women from all walks of life, including those living in shelters as well highly successful professionals, displayed many of the same basic thoughts and feelings. To be sure, differences were apparent, including how they expressed those thoughts and feelings. But several constructs that captured the essence of how they picture their day were the same. Similarly, an OZA study found that shoppers in France, Japan, India, Egypt, the United States, and other countries displayed the same views of shopping as a journey; they perceived the same milestones, goals, frustrations, surprises, successes and failures, and personal achievements, even though the cultural settings varied substantially.

Not only do different consumers share many of the same deep thoughts and feelings about product or service needs or experiences, but the ways in which these constructs are related to one another are also shared by otherwise different people. This brings us to the important topic of "bundling" thoughts into meaningful systems.

If we gave constructs human qualities, then we might say that individual constructs become bored in the absence of communication with other constructs. In fact, an isolated construct has little meaning on its own. It has meaning only through its "conversations" with other constructs. Two analogies will help clarify this point.

Think of constructs as people. Every person changes in some way depending on each interaction. At work we have a professional demeanor; at home we may act more casually. We engage strangers in one way and longtime friends in another. Sometimes these differences are trivial, but often they are important. The more people we interact with and the more diverse they are, the more complex our own behavior becomes. The same is true of constructs. A construct becomes more multifaceted the more it interacts with other constructs. For example, by itself, the construct "escape" means little. But when it connects with other constructs, it conveys more meaning. Specifically, "escape" can represent something physical or emotional. When connected to "relief" and "work," it means avoiding stress, not physical danger. The construct "escape" becomes still more complex as we associate it with yet additional constructs such as home, poverty, embarrassment, and snack foods.[18]

Another analogy involves musical instruments. An instrument coordinates with others to yield distinct performances. A guitar can be a part of an orchestra and follow a pattern of associations with other instruments. It may be more or less active than other instruments, and its volume may differ over the course of the piece. There may even be a brief guitar solo. When played in a different musical piece, a guitar may follow a different pattern in its working relationship with other instruments. Moreover, the performance might vary (to the trained ear) according to the conductor or the acoustical properties of the performance setting. The guitar in a rock band would certainly have different interactions with the other band instruments than a classical guitar would have in an orchestra. Thus, the performance's context matters and extends to the mood and even prior experiences of listeners.[19]

The idea that constructs form networks with other constructs also has important managerial implications. *Associations among constructs, not constructs in isolation, drive consumer behavior.* For example, when an inexperienced customer walks into an automotive showroom, his feelings of uncertainty may activate and link the constructs "vulnerability" and "expertise" in his mind. (For convenience here, the term "vulnerability" takes on different values, such as "highly vulnerable" or "not at all vulnerable," just as "expertise" includes states where the consumer has lots of or little knowledge. Marketers must determine when to combine opposite states in a single construct and when to treat the opposite states as two different constructs.) A well-meaning friend might have heightened this association with a story of a bad experience at a car dealership. Thus the consumer may feel especially vulnerable and self-conscious about his lack of expertise.

As a result of this activation (recall our discussion of priming), the customer will notice certain things in the showroom and use them to confirm his assumptions about what the car-buying experience will be like. For example, as in most dealerships, he might see an aggressive salesperson, trophies displayed in a cubicle, leftover pizza, a Styrofoam coffee cup, and hints of a special offer. These objects may trigger vague images of predator and prey, which in turn may prime the innate "fight or flight" response that occurs when people feel threatened. If this response gets activated, the potential buyer will spend less time in the showroom—and therefore be less likely to buy a car.

The same two constructs working together may trigger other constructs in the shopper's mind, such as "need help." This new construct may lead the person to search for car-buying assistance from a trusted advisor, a helpful publication such as *Consumer Reports'* car-buying guide, or an online information source. *Thus, the associations among constructs start the journey toward actual behavior*. This doesn't mean that a simple list of constructs isn't helpful. Under the leadership of Tom Brailsford, head of knowledge management at Hallmark, that company has made impressive use of a list of more than twenty constructs reflecting consumers' thinking about companies that have their best interests at heart. Specifically, Hallmark has used the list to help retailers understand how they are perceived by their ultimate consumers.

To understand the associations among constructs that a particular group of consumers holds, marketers can develop a *consensus map*. A consensus map is a display showing how the thoughts and feelings a group of consumers share about a particular topic are also connected in similar ways.

Figure 6-2 is an example of a simple consensus map showing consumers' constructs about companies that would have their best interests at heart. (This map is a "submap" from a larger map of constructs on this topic.) The figure shows some of the major constructs and how they are connected with one another. Put differently, a consensus map shows most of the thinking of most consumers on a topic. Although the number of constructs varies from project to project, metaphor-elicitation techniques usually produce consensus maps that contain about 90 percent of all key ideas expressed by any individual consumer interviewed. (In validation studies conducted with several firms, including Eastman Kodak, DuPont, and General Motors, these techniques also basically double the number of ideas judged actionable and relevant to managers compared with other methods, which range from focus groups to surveys involving more than 30,000 respondents.) As noted in chapter 5, other researchers report that eight conventional one-hour, one-on-one personal interviews produce the same number of ideas as eight focus groups involving a total of sixty-five people.[20] Not surprisingly, more-thorough interviews based on recent advances in several disciplines can be unusually effective, producing a large number of important insights using a small number of people.[21]

In the diagram, lines connect the various constructs to show how consumers link them. For example, many firms study the construct "dignity" to understand consumers' thoughts about companies. Dignity

FIGURE 6 - 2

A Submap of Thoughts about a Company That Has Consumers' Best Interests at Heart

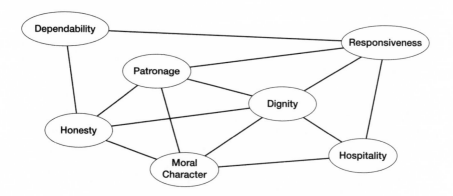

Source: Mind of the Market Laboratory/Harvard Business School.

is like an opinion leader: When activated in consumers' minds (for instance, through an advertisement, the behavior of a salesperson, or hearing an acquaintance describe an experience with a company), this construct in turn activates many other constructs (twelve of them, to be precise). By contrast, activating "hospitality" stimulates fewer constructs. While we know that constructs and associations are important, we can't exactly determine the relative importance among these constructs and the exact strength of their associations. For this information, we need a survey based on these constructs. Often managers focus on constructs that have many associations with other constructs. Or, based on certain strategic goals or a competitor's positioning, managers will study one construct in greater detail, independently of the other related constructs.

The data used to create figure 6-2 has enabled several firms to examine all the constructs that consumers in this study frequently associated with "dignity," whether directly or indirectly. They did this by further analyzing the data and then creating a submap around "dignity." A leading financial services firm used this submap (see figure 6-3) to strengthen its customers' already-positive judgments of the firm. The

FIGURE 6 - 3

A Submap for the Construct of Dignity

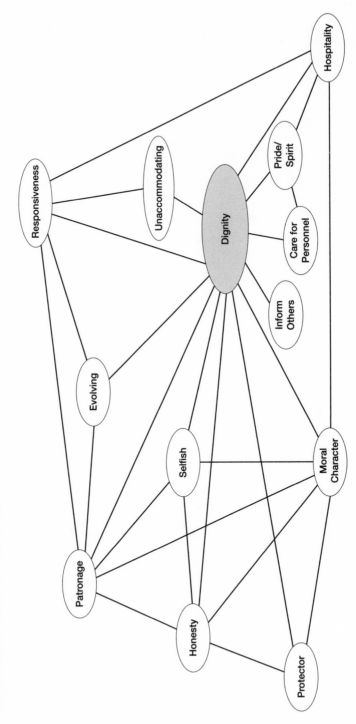

Source: Mind of the Market Laboratory/Harvard Business School.

insights gained from the submap resulted in even more effective communications about the firm's sense of pride and its evolving financial offerings. When "dignity" is activated in positive or negative ways, the other constructs shown in this figure will likely be activated as well. Likewise, the activation of one of these other constructs will probably activate "dignity." Thus, the influence of two constructs on one another flows in both directions.

This submap shows some additional interesting associations between "dignity" and other constructs. Consumers' judgments about how a company respects their dignity also relates to their perceptions of how the company treats its employees and whether the company appears to behave selfishly, has a sense of pride and spirit, and is evolving. When a major camera manufacturer originally conducted corporate-image surveys outside the United States, it overlooked the "care of personnel" construct. It later discovered that consumers questioned the firm's respect for employees. In its subsequent communications with consumers, the firm stressed its favorable treatment of its employees. The next time it conducted the survey, it saw a marked improvement not only in the "care of personnel" construct but also in assessments of "dignity" and "pride/spirit."

Our thoughts occur as activations among neurons. *Neurons that fire together wire together; thus particular groups of neurons come to represent a thought.* More important, different groups of neurons connect to form *systems* of thought. Constructs are names or labels that researchers and managers use to discuss consumers' thoughts as revealed through metaphor-elicitation and consensus-map interviews. While some thoughts seem to be hard-wired—that is, innate—many other thoughts are created by the social context in which we live.

Moreover, because our brain structure and functioning are similar (at least at birth) and we all grapple with similar problems and challenges in life, we develop many common qualities. These shared qualities may have different surface expressions, in the same way a language can have many different dialects. However, consumers from very different cultures share a great deal—and their commonalities outnumber their differences.

Understanding human universals is vital for companies that market to diverse audiences. It means first identifying what different market segments have in common and then asking, "What different expressions of these shared values, goals, or core behaviors must we respect and acknowledge?" Consensus maps can help marketers identify these commonalities and understand how they interact. Armed with these insights, managers can reengineer consumers' consensus maps to boost consumer satisfaction, strengthen brand loyalty, and enhance sales.

Reading the Mind of the Market

Using Consensus Maps

Customer frames of reference are the strategic

playing fields where innovative managers devise

and implement their creative leadership.

CONSENSUS MAPS are strategic playing fields for managers. Immunex used a consensus map about physician decision making as the basis for its very successful launch of Embrel; Schieffelin and Somerset used such maps to reposition several established beverage brands; Procter & Gamble, AT&T, IBM, and Samsung Electronics use consensus maps to develop new product concepts; and firms such as Coca-Cola, Bank of America, J. Walter Thompson, and Fidelity Investments use them to develop communication strategy. The construct associations illustrated in a consensus map represent how consumers currently think about a topic. The map thus captures the socially shared, connected constructs that are most prominent in the minds of those market-segment members relative to a specific topic. In this sense, a consensus map serves as an "anatomy" of the mind of the market.

As noted before, evidence suggests that when researchers use in-depth, one-on-one interviews to build a consensus map, they need only

a small number of consumers from a particular market segment to identify enough constructs and relevant associations to represent the larger
segment.[1] As Richard Wirthlin, CEO of the strategic research and consulting firm Wirthlin Worldwide, notes, "It never ceases to amaze me
how, when interviewed carefully, so few people can generate such
broadly representative ideas." Managers and researchers in several companies report independently that twelve to fifteen two-hour interviews
with representative consumers can yield a consensus map that accurately represents the larger population of that market segment.[2]

Once researchers have created a consensus map, managers must
interpret it very carefully. The map may reflect the impact of the company's prior or current marketing strategy. For example, a consensus
map developed for a leading software company revealed that the firm's
strategy succeeded in conveying "unparalleled expertise" to consumers
at the corporate brand level. Indeed, this construct affected consumers'
evaluation of the company's products and even its stock. Simultaneously, another important construct—"responsiveness to consumer problems"—didn't surface nearly as strongly in the consensus map. This
absence suggested that consumers didn't see the company as responsive
to them. Accordingly, the firm reexamined the "customer responsiveness" component of its strategy and changed several practices. Nine
months after the changes, the "responsive to consumer problems" construct surfaced in a new consensus map as a salient and positive feature
of consumer thinking. The firm credited the change as a force behind its
increased market share in certain product lines.

Key Strategic Questions

When working with consensus maps, managers must ask themselves
several questions:

- Which constructs should we analyze further?
- What do we convey to consumers relative to each construct?
- Do we activate these constructs in negative ways at certain
  points of contact with consumers? Do we plan the signals about
  each of these constructs or leave them to chance?

- How do we "score" on each of these constructs compared to our competitors?
- How do we score on the quality (positive or negative) and strength of associations between constructs?
- Who within the company is most responsible for each construct and construct association?
- What are we doing relative to one construct that adversely affects our desired position on another?

The answers to these questions can help managers evaluate their current marketing plans relative to consumer thinking and target areas of existing marketing strategy to reexamine.

Though researchers' interpretive summaries of raw data from the consensus-map interviews can help managers analyze and act on the map, the *original data*—in the form of metaphoric images and verbatim quotes—are even more vital. This raw material provides a fuller understanding of consumers' thoughts. It also enables managers to develop additional insights using their unique knowledge of the product or service in question.

Figures 7-1 through 7-4 show a sample consensus map and the raw data behind it, created for a study on privacy conducted by the Harvard Business School Mind of the Market Lab. Figure 7-1 shows the larger consensus map reflecting the key constructs and the important connections among them. In different ways, nearly all participants in the study mentioned each of these constructs *and* the connections between them. A subset of five constructs that firms such as Johnson & Johnson, American Century, General Motors, Hallmark, General Mills, the Coca-Cola Company, and others have found especially interesting is highlighted in the figure.

Figures 7-2 and 7-3 depict excerpts from the electronic version of the consensus map and the raw data behind the highlighted constructs. A user can click on a construct on a computer screen and access the construct definition, a set of sample quotations from which the construct emerged, and one or more visual metaphors that the study participants used to express their thoughts about the construct. Figures 7-2 and 7-3 show the data behind two constructs, "scrutiny" and "invasion."

However, as we saw earlier, the associations among constructs are far more meaningful than the constructs alone. The connections or "lines" in

FIGURE 7-1

Consensus Map for Consumer Thoughts about Privacy

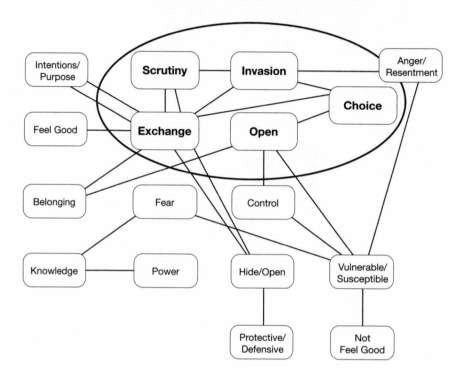

figures 7-2 and 7-3 represent consumers' reasoning processes that give texture and significance to their beliefs, feelings, and emotions. By clicking on a line, users see metaphors and quotations illustrating how the two constructs are related; that is, what "conversation" the two constructs are having with one another. Figure 7-4 provides an example.

Understanding these linkages is crucial, because they provide the best available basis for market segmentation. *That is, companies should define consumer segments on the basis of similarities* in their reasoning or thinking processes, *not on the constructs alone,* much less on other conventional criteria such as demographics or purchase volume, which are only proxy indicators of the thinking processes associated with buying behavior. For example, by defining consumer segments based on shared thinking about one of their products, a leading U.S.-based electronics firm developed a far more effective marketing strategy than its previous

FIGURE 7 - 2

The Meaning of Scrutiny

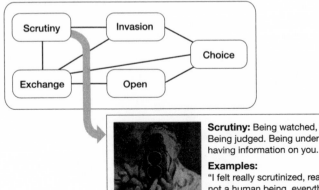

Scrutiny: Being watched, tracked, observed. Being judged. Being under a microscope, others having information on you. A sense of Big Brother.

Examples:

"I felt really scrutinized, really judged like you're not a human being, everything is just based on your numbers and they don't care what happened to you."

"I think that snapshot is something that can be examined. A snapshot is something that sort of freezes a moment in time and you can go back and you can look and you can examine those details. So, although there might be a lot of, a lot of detail, once you have the snapshot, once you have the photograph, you have all the time you want to go and pick through and comb through those details."

FIGURE 7 - 3

The Meaning of Invasion

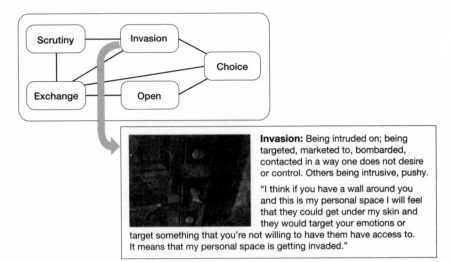

Invasion: Being intruded on; being targeted, marketed to, bombarded, contacted in a way one does not desire or control. Others being intrusive, pushy.

"I think if you have a wall around you and this is my personal space I will feel that they could get under my skin and they would target your emotions or target something that you're not willing to have them have access to. It means that my personal space is getting invaded."

FIGURE 7-4

The Reasoning Process Involving Scrutiny and Invasion

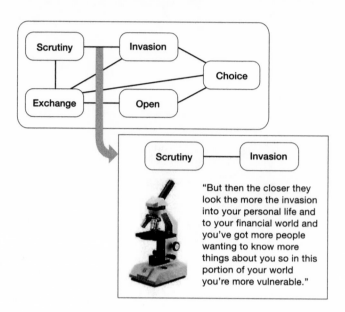

one, which was based only on a listing of variables developed in focus groups and surveys. Focus groups didn't identify associations among key thoughts. Though surveys provided valuable insights about associations among constructs, they didn't illuminate the actual reasoning that "glued" constructs together. The metaphor-elicitation approach enabled the company to define fewer meaningful segments. As a result, it achieved significant savings on its manufacturing and advertising budgets as well as exceeded projected annual sales by nearly 20 percent.

Reengineering the Mind of the Market

A consensus map is not necessarily "written in stone." However, maps representing fundamental issues such as what "feeling good" means are less changeable than is a submap reflecting a specific *way* of feeling good. Central human issues, such as the meaning of "home" (of relevance to Home Depot and IKEA), will not likely change over a few years in a given population, whereas subissues about "home" could. Such subissues might include the experience of keeping a home clean (of relevance to DuPont), exercise equipment for the home (of interest to Nautilus), and home appliance use (of interest to Samsung Electronics).

A consensus map can help managers "reengineer" the way in which they interact with customers and thereby encourage consumers to see their company's offerings in new ways. Since the human brain (and consequently the mind) retains plasticity far into adulthood, marketers can change these maps,[3] introduce new constructs into consumers' thinking, and help them form fresh associations among existing ideas. Through these changes, managers can reengineer the mind of the market.[4] Before making such shifts, managers must ask themselves the following questions:

- What do we want this map to look like six months or a year from now?
- What changes in this map would align it with our current consumer strategic vision?
- What constructs might we erase from current thinking? Which ones receive too much consumer attention and should we de-emphasize?
- Which constructs should we reinforce?
- What new constructs should we add, to distinguish us from our competitors?
- How might we introduce new constructs? To which existing constructs should we connect them?
- What associations among constructs should we reinforce? For example, how would we create a stronger link between "exchange" and "open" (in figure 7-1)?
- What new associations might we establish between constructs? For example, there is no direct association between "responsiveness" and "moral character," and "honesty" and "hospitality" in figure 6-2. Should we establish direct connections, or do indirect connections suffice?
- Which existing association might we eliminate or weaken?

A consensus map thus serves as a kind of road map for getting from one place in the mind of the market to another. From a manager's standpoint, having a consensus map is just as essential to strategic planning as having a regional atlas is to a traveler. Road maps show population centers (constructs) and existing major and minor routes from one center to another (that is, the neural pathways connecting neural clusters). A traveler might look at her regional atlas and consider how to avoid a city center, how long the trip will take, and what to bring along. Similarly, a consensus map helps managers identify opportunities for and obstacles to a successful marketing effort.

Using Consensus Maps: Perceptions of a Financial Services Firm

An East Coast–based financial services company used a somewhat more detailed version of the consensus map in figure 6-2 to evaluate how well it conveyed its respect for the dignity of its high-net-worth clients. (As noted earlier, clients feel that a company honors their dignity when it provides evidence that its customers are important.) An initial evaluation indicated that clients saw the firm positively in terms of "honesty" and "providing protection." However, they also viewed the company as unresponsive to their needs, as not evolving, as having little pride, and as treating its employees indifferently. These judgments were especially pronounced among accounts lost in the preceding fourteen months, the time period covered by the evaluation. Before the audit, key managers had predicted their "scores" on these constructs. Relative to clients' ratings, individual managers *overestimated* their performance on these constructs by 22 percent to almost 60 percent. Clearly, the managers' view of the company—and themselves—differed markedly from that of the firm's clients.

Some of the images clients used to describe the company drove this point home. For instance, one individual used a picture of Mount Everest to describe the firm's lack of responsiveness to clients. "No matter how many people climb it, no matter how bad conditions get, it doesn't budge. . . . Sure, it's strong and will last but it doesn't bend to special requests or needs. It treats all climbers the same: 'I dare you to change me.'" Another picture, this one of slaves rowing an ancient galley ship, reflected account managers' tendency, as judged by clients, to work intensively at the beginning of their relationship with high-net-worth clients. "Those guys," the client said in reference to the managers, "won't be around for you when you finish the voyage," reflecting a concern about long-term commitment from the managers.

The company explored how its own account managers experienced treatment by the company and how this experience was conveyed to clients. As one outcome of the in-depth follow-up, senior executives sent more congratulatory messages to account managers. Also, the account managers altered their behavior in certain ways and began using different words to describe the company to customers. As another outcome, the firm designed a special new brochure for clients and prospective hires. The brochure copy emphasized the unique opportunities that the company offered its employees, such as continuing professional-development assistance. By highlighting such programs, the firm demonstrated its commitment to treating account managers with respect.

All these changes in turn ensured that account managers treated clients with respect. A subsequent audit several months later showed dramatic improvement in all the areas targeted by the remedial effort. In addition to illustrating the power of a consensus map, this firm's experience also demonstrates how internal relations within a company can affect the corporate brand.

How did this company use its consensus map to implement needed change? After analyzing the map, the firm decided to establish a direct association between "dependability" and "dignity" in their clients' minds. The absence of this association became clear when managers examined the perception of the firm's competitors in the marketplace. Strengthening clients' association between "dependability" and "dignity," the managers realized, would help them differentiate the company from a major competitor. The firm set out to create other new connections in clients' minds as well. The second audit showed that the new associations were indeed taking hold and sharpening the company's competitive edge.

Using Consensus Maps: Achieving Financial Goals

Many men and women between the ages of thirty-five and forty-five are focused on achieving personal financial goals. As they strive toward these goals, they engage constructs that represent their experience during this journey. Table 7-1 shows some of these constructs identified in a study by another organization.

Figure 7-5, a submap of a larger consensus map for achieving financial goals, shows how the five constructs in table 7-1 relate to one another.

Although many people in this market segment share these constructs and their connecting paths, different people within the group might experience the system shown on the map differently. For instance, an independent person may feel quite confident about achieving his personal goals. He may acknowledge that life occasionally "throws you curve balls," but he doesn't worry about them. This same person may feel sufficiently well informed about personal finance that he does not want special assistance with financial decisions. Figure 7-5 suggests that the more knowledge people believe they have, the more confident they feel in making decisions. Furthermore, the more knowledgeable and confident they feel, the more likely they are to take chances, especially if their decisions won't strongly affect other people.

TABLE 7 - 1

Sample Personal Finance Constructs

Construct	Description
Confidence	The level of certainty (or uncertainty) about reaching one's goal.
Discipline	How steadfast one is in following an established course of action for achieving one's goals.
Chance	The role and salience of things one has little or no control over, such as winning a lottery or suffering a major, uninsured property loss.
Knowledge	The expertise to develop and implement a financial plan.
Beneficiaries	Other people directly affected by one's success or failure in achieving one's goals.

FIGURE 7 - 5

A Submap for Achieving Financial Goals

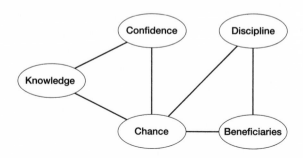

On the other hand, those who believe that they lack knowledge feel less confident and vulnerable to the vagaries of chance—a situation that, in their view, requires more financial planning discipline. As one consumer explained:

> *Because I don't have much control over what happens to me or even to the economy, I must be extra careful to make sure I put enough money away to protect my children no matter what happens. But I sometimes feel guilty about that, since I have less to spend making their experiences better now. And, well, I'll say it, why can't I enjoy some of the fruits of my labor too?*

The more confident person engages with chance differently:

> *I think chance is there, but I also think you make your own luck, so I don't worry a whole lot about putting money away on a routine basis. After all, how often does it really rain, and so what if it does? It's just me now.*

Both people expressed thoughts about chance, discipline, and beneficiaries and made the same connections among them even while engaging with these constructs differently. The financial services firm sponsoring this study understood that its clients filter the information the company provides through the "lens" represented in figure 7-5, even though the filter, in effect, has different colors for different groups of "viewers." An individual who wavers about her ability to achieve her personal financial goals might see the firm's financial planner as a surrogate knowledge bank. The company could craft its marketing information to communicate this option, demonstrating that the company's financial planners are skilled at managing balanced portfolios. To more financially experienced individuals, the firm could characterize its financial planners as additional knowledge resources to help clients assess risk and gain even greater confidence in their financial decisions. After all, even experts share knowledge and seek guidance from one another.

How could the firm reengineer the mind of the market in this situation? It could find ways to make uncertain individuals feel more comfortable about managing risk. Or induce a greater sense of risk and vulnerability among those individuals who currently feel quite confident by, for instance, emphasizing that one can never have enough knowledge about personal finance. Or present its financial planning service as a helpful option for those who feel they lack self-discipline.

Managers can generate ideas for reengineering a consensus map by analyzing the map and its supporting data or for forming hypotheses to test further. For example, the financial services firm noticed that the construct of "fun" was missing from the consensus map. The company hypothesized that, with the proper coach or guide, consumers might view financial planning as an engaging, interesting, and enjoyable activity rather than an intimidating chore. Indeed, this company decided to experiment with this construct. By creating a game-oriented software package for planning, it helped consumers associate the construct "fun" with the constructs "confidence" and "discipline." The experiment proved a resounding success. A new consensus map developed more than a year later showed "fun" as a key feature of clients' thinking.

When Consensus Maps Interact

Consumers have thousands of constructs—and hence thousands of consensus maps—in their minds. Some are broad, such as "what is an innovation?" Others may be quite specific, such as "what I think of detergentless washing machines." Also, just as hearing one story reminds us of another, activating one consensus map (which itself is a kind of story) may activate another map. This "domino effect" happens because different consensus maps often share constructs. Shared constructs are like doorbells at different homes that are wired together. Pressing a doorbell at one home stimulates activity in that home and may cause the doorbell at a neighboring home or another one even farther away to ring. Activity then increases in those homes as well. With consensus maps, when a single "button" is pressed, activity erupts in several locations—including in other maps.

For example, the construct "anticipation" may crop up in numerous consensus maps. Consensus maps of consumers' thinking about exercise include the anticipation of working out with friends and of feeling relaxed and accomplished afterward. Yet "anticipation" also shows up as a construct in consumers' consensus maps about eating snack foods. For instance, an individual may anticipate eating a candy bar as a reward for completing a difficult task (such as exercising). Sometimes people highly prize just the *idea* of indulging in a snack food. The anticipation is an important part of the snack-food consumption experience.

Of course, the *experience* of anticipation differs depending on whether anticipation is associated with exercise or with a snack-food feast. These differences stem from the influence of the other constructs in the respective maps. Still, maps that share "anticipation" as a construct are theoretically capable of "ringing" one another whenever the anticipation "bell" is pressed. Nobel laureate and neuroscientist Gerald Edelman calls this process "reentrant mapping."[5] In our case, the thought of engaging in a workout activates "anticipation" and other constructs in the working-out map. Once the neural cluster represented by "anticipation" has been triggered, it may trigger other maps where "anticipation" also appears. (See figure 7-6.)

Figure 7-6 shows two consensus maps. Since the two maps share a common construct, "anticipation," each has the potential to activate the other, represented by the dotted line in the figure. When the map for working out is activated, as shown in figure 7-7, the "anticipation" construct in that map may activate the same construct in the snack-bar map, as shown in figure 7-8. The different shades highlighting "anticipation" in both maps indicate that this construct differs in the two maps

FIGURE 7 - 6

Reentrant Mapping (Step 1)

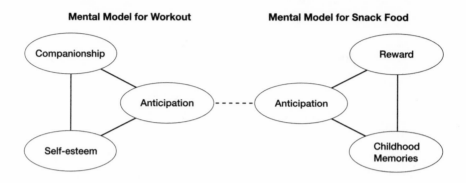

FIGURE 7 - 7

Reentrant Mapping (Step 2)

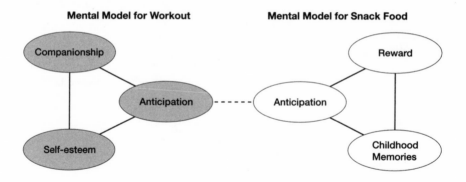

because of its association with different constructs in each. If the activation of "anticipation" in the snack-food map is strong enough or if the two maps share other constructs, then the entire snack-food map *and* working-out map may become active, as shown in figure 7-9. For example, the two maps may share constructs such as "reward," "indulgence," "energy," and perhaps "guilt."

Consensus maps reflect the shared frame of reference or viewing lens among those in a target market about a particular topic or issue. These

FIGURE 7 - 8

Reentrant Mapping (Step 3)

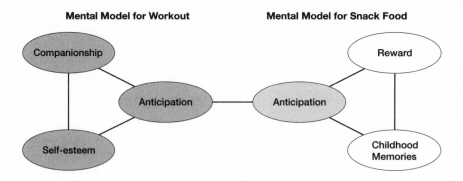

Mental Model for Workout   Mental Model for Snack Food

FIGURE 7 - 9

Reentrant Mapping (Step 4)

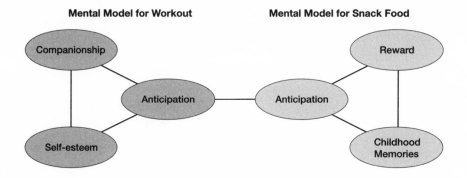

Mental Model for Workout   Mental Model for Snack Food

maps change as consumer experiences change, and marketing actions are one source of change. Thus, whenever managers tinker with a construct in a particular consensus map, they must think about how those changes might activate other bundles of thought in that map or in other maps that may seem unrelated but in fact influence the purchase and use of a product or service. To be proactive in reengineering consensus maps—consumers' shared mental models—marketers need to have a clear understanding of them and a clear vision of how they would like consumer consensus maps to look. Then they must evaluate the feasibility of marketing actions to bring those changes about.

Chapter Eight

Memory's Fragile Power

Life needs the mythmaking of memory.

ALL OF US ASSUME that our memories inherently belong to us, accurately reflect reality, remain under our conscious control, and influence us only when we "call them up" or "bring them to mind." Yet recent research in psychology, biology, sociology, and neuroscience reveals that our assumptions about memory are tenuous at best. Memories are malleable: Not only do they fade or disappear over time, they change every time they come to mind, with every new human experience.

"Memories don't sit in one place, waiting patiently to be retrieved" like snapshots, write Elizabeth F. Loftus, professor of psychology at the University of Washington, and Katherine Ketchum, author of *The Spirituality of Imperfection*. "They drift through the brain, more like clouds or vapor than something we can put our hands on."[1]

So what are memories? They are the "fragile but powerful products of what we recall from the past, believe about the present, and imagine about the future," says Harvard University psychology professor Daniel Schacter, a leading authority in memory research.[2] Although memories can distort and inaccurately represent our experiences, they still influence us considerably. "Even when memories are vivid and subjectively

---

This chapter title is based on a phrase suggested by Daniel Schacter.

compelling," Schacter continues, "there is still no guarantee that they are accurate. Even though vivid memories are often veridical, it is striking that a variety of conditions exist in which subjectively compelling memories are grossly inaccurate."[3]

Research on what Schacter calls the "sin of suggestibility" shows that the very research methods—surveys, personal interviews, and group discussions—used to understand consumers' memories can alter those memories. Marketing managers thus must understand *how* memories are produced if they hope to influence *what* consumers will remember about their products or services. *Consumers' memories are shaped by the social and cultural world in which consumers live and in which they seek to define themselves.*[4] Society and culture therefore play a leading role in the malleability of memory. As Jeffrey Prager, professor of sociology at UCLA and a faculty member at the Southern California Psychoanalytic Institute, explains, "The memories consumers create are narrative fragments intended to account for one's feelings and bodily sensations."[5] They are a new "photo" creating a new picture to explain a current experience under the disguise of simply retrieving a preexisting photo.

Marketers do strive to create powerful memories for consumers about a product or service. Ad campaigns aim to facilitate a consumer's storage and recall of the feelings and thoughts associated with the product. For example, managers hope that providing a free sample or an advertisement will etch the image of the product in a consumer's memory—an image that he will remember later, when it comes time to decide whether to buy.

Of course, this kind of technique is well known to most marketers. What's more startling is marketers' ability to influence far more than what people recall from an ad or sample. Specifically, marketing strategies can affect the shape, texture, and accuracy of a memory.[6] *In essence, marketers play a central role in creating consumers' memories, thanks to memory's intricate association with metaphor.* Yet many managers remain unaware of just how much impact they have in this area.

A marketing research study in Brazil also exemplified the notion that memory can be distorted by newer experiences. In this unpublished, proprietary study of supplier relationships, researchers led purchasing agents loyal to a particular supplier to recall poor service after they'd claimed to be satisfied by the service. By asking particular questions, raising an eyebrow in response to positive comments about the supplier, and showing other surprised reactions to expressions of satisfaction, the researchers subtly discouraged the purchasing agents from making positive comments about the supplier. Indeed, the positive comments tapered off and gave way to new, more negative feelings. Through their exposure to subtle verbal and nonverbal feedback, the purchasing agents created a new, more troubling memory of their longstanding relationship with the supplier. They were unconscious of any change in their memory of this relationship, but their confidence in that relationship slipped.[7]

How Memory Works

To grasp the nature of memory, managers must familiarize themselves with three cognitive elements that work together to create the experience called "memory." They must also understand the different *types* of memory that exist and the ways in which consumers encode and retrieve memories.

The Three Elements of Memory

Memories manifest themselves physically as electrochemical etchings in our brain cells. Neuroscientists call these etchings *engrams*. As we encounter and absorb information, that information enters neurons that represent *short-term* memory. There it may evaporate in seconds or be passed on and etched into other neurons that represent *long-term* memory. Of course, not everything we encounter is recorded for later retrieval. But if a fact or event has emotional significance to us, we'll be more likely to store it in long-term memory. As we'll see, other factors also increase the likelihood that a fact or event will be stored.

Once stored, engrams are activated by *cues* or *stimuli*—such as an insert for a seasonal sale at your favorite clothing store that falls out of your newspaper, your best friend's suggestion to see a particular film, or a point-of-purchase display for batteries that you see at the drugstore checkout. The seasonal-sale ad may cue a memory of a stylish pair of shoes or a briefcase you bought at a great price last year at the store. Your friend's film recommendation cues you to remember another film you enjoyed that this same friend recommended. The battery display reminds you that your camera battery ran out at the wedding you attended last weekend.

Some cues are obvious. Others are quite subtle, working their magic in the shadows of the unconscious mind. Typically, we're not consciously aware of most cues. Yet these stimuli count among the most influential tools that marketing managers can use to incite the memories that will inspire consumers to buy.

As we'll see in the next chapter, a metaphor is a relationship between two memory structures.[8] That's why metaphors are a powerful way of eliciting hidden thoughts and feelings, and why the choice of metaphor matters so much in product design and market communications.

Experience Engineering, Inc., practices effective "cue management." Led by Lou Carbone, Experience Engineering designs sales and service-delivery environments intended to create positive memories in the minds of consumers. Box 8-1 describes an example of their work involving a hospital emergency room. As you might imagine, few experiences are more memorable than being admitted to a hospital. Patients' hospital experiences, quite aside from the technical quality of the medical care they receive, can strongly affect their recovery. For these and other reasons, careful management of patients' *total* experience in a medical setting can have enormous social value, not to mention raising the reputation of the hospital in the public's eye.

In addition to engrams and cues, consumers' *goals* or *purposes* affect the memories that they create. In particular, goals and purposes influence which cues people notice, and therefore which engrams become activated in their minds. A year-long study in Great Britain showed that, when women brought a child to shop for food, specifically to teach the child about wise shopping behaviors, these women

Box 8-1

Customer-Experience Management at University Hospital

Business Issue

In 1997 University Hospital (UH) in Augusta, Georgia, implemented an experience-management design for its Emergency Services Department. Patient satisfaction scores had slowly declined, and competition was increasing from urgent-care outlets throughout the city.

Implementation

The emergency room's (ER) experience-management initiatives began by assigning a cross-functional task force from the hospital and the ER. Representatives from management, medical staff, housekeeping, and security participated in experience-awareness exercises, defining the emotional connection that would anchor the creation of all experience cues. The subsequent experience design focused on connecting patients and their families with the hospital in a more reassuring and empathetic way.

The group identified more than one hundred cues that could strengthen these connections, including the following:

- **Directional road signs.** The hospital placed additional signs farther out in all directions from the campus. Signs reading "Hospital 3 miles" reassured newcomers to the area.

- **Reconfigured furniture.** Patients and families viewed chairs arranged in traditional straight rows as big "waiting" cues. The hospital rearranged the chairs in small circles with tables to moderate the perception of a long wait, to promote conversation and privacy, and to open up the area.

- **Security guard turned greeter.** A stationary security guard, previously posted behind an imposing desk, became a roving ambassador to help people navigate the registration process.

(continued)

- **User-friendly language.** The hospital created "Care Points" to help patients find their way around. For example, it changed the puzzling "Triage Station" sign over the emergency room reception desk to "Care Point 1—Reception." "Pediatric Emergency" became Care Point 3, denoted by a popsicle icon.

- **"Emergency room air-traffic controller."** In the past, once patients were admitted, registration staff and waiting family had been cut off from patients' progress "inside." The hospital created a new position to track patient charts and inform family regularly.

No one set of cues transformed the patient experience at this hospital. Rather, the benefit eliminated the negatives, followed by the cumulative design and building of positive cues—all of which helped the hospital to better reassure and empathize with patients.

The Power of Eliminating Negative Clues

An experience-management system should move an organization beyond a commodity experience to a palette of preferential clues that engender greater loyalty to the organization. Firms usually create and implement such a design in stages over several months. But organizations can benefit immediately by simply attending to and eliminating negative clues in consumers' experience.

Once the UH experience task force began looking through the lens of experience management, "a huge revelation and transformation took place," according to George Ann Phillips, director of emergency services at University Hospital. "It was impossible to look at the world the same way again."

For example, the initial scanning for clues so motivated some members of the experience project team—doctors, nurses, and administrative staff—that they devoted part of a weekend to changing the morgue experience for the surviving family. How might this be done? Normal procedure had involved simply wheeling the body on a gurney into a storage room, where the family spent time with each other and their loved one. In a day's time, the group put up curtains for privacy, replaced harsh fluorescent lighting with incandescent lamps, furnished the area with chairs, repainted the room, and even hung a wallpaper border.

Results

Within one month of reducing negative cues, the ER experienced a one-third decline in customer complaints. After implementing the experience design, the facility's "overall quality of care" rating increased 13 percent, and it earned recognition from medical staff as the most improved department in the hospital complex. Ultimately, the hospital implemented key specifications of the experience design in the form of $5 million in renovations, to be completed in 2003.

Source: Courtesy of Experience Engineering, Minneapolis, MN, and University Hospital, Augusta, GA.

remembered fewer bad experiences and described them less negatively than when shopping with children for other reasons. In one study, researchers discovered that consumers described their most recent experience at a bar differently depending on the reason they were given for being interviewed. The different reasons for asking them to share this experience constituted different goals as well as different stimuli. When a goal is to quench thirst, consumers usually recall prior experiences with cold beverages rather than warm beverages. When the goal is to spend casual time with friends, consumers may recall a broader array of beverage experiences.

Types of Memory

Learning and memory are closely connected processes. Through *learning,* we acquire new information. Through *memory,* we can retain that new information in a form that we retrieve later. Like a complex database, the human brain stores and retrieves memories as bits of data. To understand memory, psychologists commonly organize it into three categories: semantic, episodic, and procedural. While all three memory types are important, we emphasize semantic and episodic memory in this discussion.

Semantic memory occurs when we recall the meaning of the words and symbols that surround us. How many American consumers can see a swoosh mark and not think "Nike"? Or hear the soundtrack from the movie *Jaws* and not imagine a shark's fin breaking the surface of the ocean? Semantic memory enables us to recognize our favorite brand of orange juice, name a type of automobile or handbag, tell time, and identify a jingle from an advertisement.

Episodic memories involve the time, place, and situational aspects of events. For instance, many of us vividly remember dressing up in costumes as children and touring our neighborhoods on Halloween, or meeting our first love at age sixteen. Even a trip to Disney World with the kids can remain etched in a parent's mind for decades. As adults, we remember all the major transitions in our children's lives, such as their first day of school or the death of a pet.

Whereas semantic memory is the "what" and "how" of our experiences, episodic memory is the "where," "when," and "with whom." Episodic memory fosters our sense of self in that our experiences with other people in varying circumstances contribute to our self-identity. Consumers express their self-identities through their choices in the marketplace. Yet marketers rarely evaluate this aspect of memory when testing advertisements or new-product names.

Procedural memory involves learned skills. As children, we learn how to use the toilet, tie our shoes, and ride a bicycle. As adults, we learn how to drive a car, vote in elections, and complete our income tax forms. Procedural memory preserves process steps, the "how-to" instructions needed to manage our lives. For consumers, memories of this type include "scripts" explaining what constitutes wise shopping behavior. For example, a script might contain rules, such as when to haggle over price, where to get the freshest produce, and whom to ask for sales assistance.

The Unconsciousness of Memory

Memory may also be explicit or implicit. *Explicit* memories are those that we can voluntarily bring to mind. Surveys and focus groups tap into explicit memory by asking consumers to recall aspects of their experiences (such as quality of service, friendliness of staff, and so forth). *Implicit* memories are those that we cannot readily or voluntarily recall, even though they strongly influence our conscious thoughts and our actions. Implicit memory depends on structures in the brain that are older in evolutionary terms.

Until recently, researchers focused on explicit memory, because they assumed that this form of memory enabled *implicit* memory to occur. But memory researchers have begun differentiating memory based on the consciousness of the process. As it turns out, our most powerful memories, those that most sway consumer behavior, are often buried deep in our unconscious.[9] Processes that activate those memories, such as priming, often work without our awareness.

As we saw in earlier chapters, priming significantly influences the unconscious mind. Through priming, one cue or stimulus facilitates the recognition of, or attention to, another cue. You may recall the well-known drawing in which viewers see the image of either a young woman or much older woman. However, we can influence what the person sees by first showing words that describe being young or old.

Consider the following lists of words:

noble	princess	court
castle	regal	prince
crown	subjects	purple
tiara	king	carriage
reign	jester	jewels
servant	monarch	joust
throne	royal	

Now close this book and write down as many words as you can remember. Or read the list to somebody else and ask him to write down the words that he can remember. That's what researchers did in a study. One researcher read the list aloud to the participants, asked them to write down all the words that they could remember from the list, and then asked them how certain they were of their answers.

They claimed to be just as sure about their correct answers as they were about a particular incorrect answer—the word *queen*. Though *queen* doesn't appear on the list, two-thirds of the study's participants wrote down "queen" as a word "heard." In effect, the presence of other related words like king, prince, and princess suggested that *queen* also appeared; that is, the related words primed people to think unconsciously about queens.

A particular product name or an image in an advertisement can also prime consumers' recollections of what they consider important in a product or service. Something as simple as a wall clock included in a magazine-ad photo can exert a powerful impact on what consumers retain about the ad. For example, a picture of someone being helped at a service counter in a setting where a wall clock is displayed is more than twice as likely to evoke the notion of speedy service than the same image without the wall clock. The wall clock primes unconscious thoughts about time and hence speed of service. A consumer is more likely to retrieve and use the criterion of speed when evaluating this service provider, even though the ad makes no explicit reference to speed of service. To borrow an analogy from Mark Twain, the difference between the right marketing stimulus and almost the right stimulus is the difference between lightning and a lightning bug.

Memory Storage and Retrieval

Remembering and forgetting are like Siamese twins: One doesn't go far without the other.[10] We simply can't hold every important thought in our conscious mind. If we tried to do so, then we'd soon become distracted and unproductive. Imagine that while you were shopping for a car, memories about a recent trip to the grocery store, your cousin's birthday party, or your Aunt Esther's famous apple pies kept flooding your mind. Without memory, we cannot afford to forget, but without forgetting we cannot focus our attention on the decision at hand.

Memory storage, or encoding, along with memory retrieval are also virtually inseparable. *Encoding* involves transferring what we see, hear, smell, taste, touch, think, and feel into our brain cells as engrams. *How* we encode an event or fact strongly determines *whether* we will recall it later. The intention to recall it won't ensure our doing so. For information to move to long-term memory, we must encode it thoroughly and deeply. This process occurs at various levels in the brain—many of them deep in the unconscious.

One of the most influential theories about encoding is the "levels of processing" approach. According to this theory, we analyze stimuli at many different levels. At shallow levels, we notice physical or sensory characteristics, such as the color of autumn leaves. At deeper levels, we analyze the meaning of those physical or sensory characteristics. For example, if you live in New England, then seeing bright orange leaves might remind you that summer is coming to an end. If we process a cue at a shallow level, then the resulting engram won't last long. If we process a stimulus deeply, then the engram will endure longer and we'll remember it more easily.

Table 8-1 describes various factors that influence whether information will reach long-term memory. For example, memories strengthen when we weave them into existing and new memories about our experiences.[11] Compared to a novice, an expert on home power tools will more likely remember a particular detail about a tool because the product has greater personal significance.

Once a memory is encoded, *retrieval* processes help us pull it from memory. The brain uses several kinds of retrieval processes. For example, when you see an image of a home-baked apple pie, perhaps you remember a favorite aunt who baked pies for Sunday dinner. The cue of the pie triggers your memory of your aunt. This *associative retrieval* occurs involuntarily as a stimulus triggers a related memory. When you try to remember the last time that you went to the dry cleaners, attended a wine tasting, or ate a banana, you *consciously* work to retrieve a memory. This *strategic retrieval* is voluntary—akin to searching for a file on your computer's hard drive.

Context—including cues—is critical in both associative and strategic retrieval. The Encoding Specificity Hypothesis suggests that the degree to which a current experience resembles the original context in which we *encoded* a memory determines how easily we can *retrieve* the same memory later.

Research also shows that the more information provided during retrieval (for example, an image of a smiling, elderly woman serving an

TABLE 8 - 1

Elements Affecting Recall

Element	Description	Consumer Thought
Has personal significance	The product or service fits a consumer's sense of self.	"That dress is so me!"
Is compatible with current mood	Happy (or sad) feelings foster encoding and retrieval of happy (or sad) product experiences.	"My grandmother always made us cookies with Nestlé chocolate chips."
Is tagged by an emotion	The person associates an intense emotion with the event or product.	"It wasn't just my first car; it was a symbol of my dad's recognition that I was growing up."
Is action-oriented	The product or event enables the person to take some desired action.	"It promises immediate relief from heartburn."
Is consistent with existing concepts	The product or event fits into an existing consensus map.	"When I use Downy, I'm taking better care of my children because I am caring for their clothes."
Has important consequences	Misreading directions on a label could cause harm.	"I'm in deep trouble if I've connected these wires incorrectly."
Is distinct	The product or event creates a first-time experience.	"This soda feels 'like fireworks on my tongue.'"
Is surprising	The product or event falls outside the person's comfort zone or expectations.	"Their chef's definition of mild is my definition of unbearably hot."
Can spawn a story	The product or event triggers other important associations in memory.	"PG&E provided the light that enabled me to read so that I could escape thinking about being abused."
Is frequently rehearsed	The product or event is repetitive.	"My kids are always singing their jingles."

apple pie—not just an apple pie sitting all by itself), the more likely you'll be to retrieve additional details from the original memory. For instance, you might remember not just your aunt and her pies, but the fact that she made them for you every Sunday.

Sensory cues can play a particularly powerful role in reinstating the context of an earlier experience—thereby facilitating retrieval of memories. For instance, the smell of a pie baking in the oven may cause you to remember additional details about your Sunday gatherings. The more sensory cues you notice, the more the original context of a particular experience becomes reinstated in your mind. Olfactory and other sensory cues are hardwired into the brain's limbic system, the seat of emotion, and stimulate vivid recollections.[12]

In fact, sensory images involving sight, sound, smell, and bodily sensations add so much realism to a recollection that the memory-retrieval experience can be surprisingly intense.[13] A TV commercial showing a person savoring the aroma of freshly brewed coffee can trigger these same olfactory sensations in viewers. The colors burgundy and hunter green, which evoke memories of tradition and belonging in many consumers, have helped one clothing manufacturer sell business suits made of fabrics in these colors.

What happens between encoding and retrieval? During encoding, the brain's hippocampal region becomes active and helps integrate new information with our existing knowledge. Research in neurobiology indicates that a consolidation period occurs after encoding. During this consolidation process, newly learned information transforms from its vulnerable form in short-term memory to a more enduring form in long-term memory. During this transition, memories become particularly susceptible to distortion. The length of this interval depends on the nature of the learned material; that is, more complex information takes longer to process. This time period may consist of seconds, minutes, hours, or even days. The information is then stored in the neocortex and distributed throughout the brain.

Managers can increase the likelihood of creating enduring memories by emphasizing unique product qualities that have personal significance for consumers. However, managers must also consider the mood of consumers at the time of encoding and retrieval. Television programming or magazine content that surrounds an advertisement can prime a viewer to respond to the ad in a particular way through the mood induced by the programming or content.

If an advertisement sets a mood for the consumer, then a company can reinstate that same frame of mind by creating store environments consistent with that mood, designing corresponding future ads, and ensuring that product packaging or point-of-purchase displays reinforce the mood. Additionally, managers can set up the context for consumers' later retrieval of the original ad. For example, they can:

- Focus consumers' attention on contextual cues such as the fresh smell of clothes as they come out of the dryer.
- Link the drinking of champagne to landmark events, such as a graduation, and to recurring occasions like wedding anniversaries or birthdays.
- "Remind" consumers of past experiences through autobiographical referencing, such as "Remember your first Buick. . . ."
- Implement general cues versus specific ones. "Remember family picnics" is more inclusive—and therefore more effective—than "Remember the family picnics you went on when you were eleven years old."

Anne Thistleton, a marketing consultant, envisions the encoding and retrieval of memory as a journey punctuated by special moments. She has used figures 8-1 and 8-2 to help management at the Coca-Cola Company better understand how to make use of memory and create enduring, memorable experiences with the brand. As figure 8-1 suggests, remembering an earlier experience does more than retrieve the

FIGURE 8 - 1

The Journey of Memory

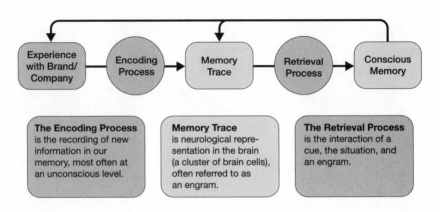

Source: Anne Thistleton.

FIGURE 8 - 2

Influences on the Encoding of a Memory

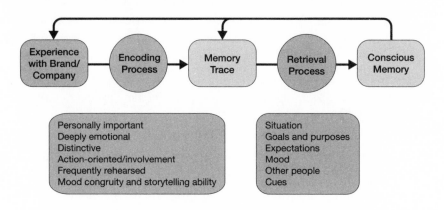

Personally important
Deeply emotional
Distinctive
Action-oriented/involvement
Frequently rehearsed
Mood congruity and storytelling ability

Situation
Goals and purposes
Expectations
Mood
Other people
Cues

Source: Anne Thistleton.

past; it also influences our current experience—which in turn becomes the starting point for the next memory "journey." When all the points along this journey occur smoothly, consumers are more likely to buy a product or service. In effect, figure 8-1 describes the manufacture of desire. Positive recall of a positive past experience can enhance a person's current experience of consumption, which in turn becomes a "future" memory. This process increases the likelihood that the person will want to buy and use the same product in the future. However, this likelihood is influenced by several factors that determine how well particular experiences are encoded. This is shown in figure 8-2.

Memory Reconstruction

Research in the last decade has changed how we think about memory. We often think of memory as a photo stored in a photo album, like a lollipop in a bowl of individually wrapped treats—something that we can just reach for and retrieve whenever we want. Based on such traditional metaphors for memory, many companies have designed their marketing communications and other touch points with consumers as if they can recall these messages as originally received. However, memory experts now view memory as a malleable *process,* not as a single, unchanging structure within the brain.

We store many different pieces, or chunks, of a memory throughout the brain and reassemble them later during the retrieval process. During retrieval and reassembly, a memory changes. Thus memories are not perfect replicas of an earlier event, but are impressions that shift in response to cues and to our reasons for noticing those cues. *Memory, then, is a current perception shaped by specific contexts, including the consumer's past and current moods and sense of identity.*[14] Daniel Schacter clarifies:

> It was once believed that remembering a past experience is merely a matter of bringing to mind a stored record of the event, but recent research has overturned this persisting myth. We will see how even the simple act of calling to mind a memory of a particular past experience—what you did last Saturday night or where you went on your first date—is constructed from influences operating in the present as well as from information you have stored about the past.[15]

Likewise, how we remember an experience with a customer-service representative hinges on whether the triggering cue for that memory is positive or negative. If a friend describes a positive customer-service experience at the same store, then we may recall our own experience as less offensive than it might actually have been. If our friend describes a negative experience, then we may recall worse treatment than we actually received. If we have an uneventful dinner at a restaurant, then hear that a friend had an awful experience at the same place, then we may recall our dining experience as "below average." If, instead, our friend told us that she had the best meal of her life there, then we might recall our experience as "above average."

Not only do we recall an experience differently depending on the triggering cue; *we are unaware of the change.* What we recall about a particular experience now seems to be exactly what we recalled about that same experience last week or last year. A report by Linda Levine and her colleagues on a longitudinal study of memory changes during the O. J. Simpson murder trial aptly illustrates this phenomenon. When the jury announced its verdict in 1995, various participants in this study had reported feeling happiness, anger, or surprise. Five years later, when the researchers asked these same individuals to describe their feelings after the verdict, the participants reported very different ones. The changes were in line with their current feelings of happiness, anger, or surprise. The participants were unaware that their initial feelings reported at the time of the verdict had been different.[16]

So every time we remember a particular experience, we're responding to different cues and goals. Thus a different bundle of neurons is activated with every recall of a single experience. The difference between neurons activated the first time and those activated the twentieth time can be trivial. In such cases, for all practical purposes, the memory remains "true" and unchanged. This relative stability occurs mostly with matters that have high personal relevance and that we frequently rehearse, such as remembering our own name.

In addition to cues and goals, imagination plays a big part in the reconstruction of our memories. Indeed, memory and imagination together create what we know and think.[17] Marketers actively participate in this partnering of consumers' memory and imagination—sometimes with powerful consequences. For example, what consumers *recall* about prior product or shopping experiences will differ from their *actual* experiences if marketers refer to those past experiences in positive ways. This phenomenon is known as *backward framing*. By using *forward framing,* marketers can influence consumers' expectations about a *future* experience. These expectations, in turn, alter their actual future experiences—and their memories of those experiences.

Most marketing communications focus on forward framing, for example, in the form of magazine advertisements, advice from knowledgeable salespeople, or word-of-mouth recommendations. Such framing conditions consumers to look for and even expect specific qualities in a product or shopping experience. For instance, if you've seen an ad for a new cellular phone and several of your friends are raving about the phone's superior technical features, you may be more likely to notice those features when you encounter that same phone in a store.

Forward framing thus makes presumably positive qualities more salient, or noticeable, for consumers. (Marketers can also use forward framing in comparative ads to highlight the negative qualities of a competitor's product.) When a quality is salient, it is at the forefront of a consumer's mind. Hence, the person better appreciates that quality when he or she encounters it. As a result of this greater appreciation, the consumer has a better experience with the product than he or she would have otherwise (unless, of course, the product blatantly fails to deliver). With better product experiences, consumers are more likely to buy that same product again.

Backward framing is distinct from information that causes consumers to *consciously* reassess a prior experience based on new information. For instance, if you purchased a lawnmower and couldn't get it to work properly, you might initially be unhappy with the manufacturer. However, you might rethink your evaluation of the product if you learned that you hadn't read the instructions carefully or that the mower wasn't intended to mulch all the dead leaves that fell on your lawn in October. Additional information about the mower (for example, that you can buy attachments to improve its mulching effectiveness) or unexpected benefits of using it might cause you to reappraise your experience with the product.

Sometimes the malleable nature of the memory process can prompt us to remember events that could not have occurred. The impact of suggestion and biased beliefs in the creation of false memories has been well documented.[18] However, until recently, false memory's impact on consumer decision making remained unclear. For example, could marketers influence the memory reconstruction process in such a way as to create false memories in consumers' minds?

Kathryn Braun-LaTour suggests that, yes, marketers *can* exert such influence. In a series of careful studies, Braun-LaTour explored whether exposure to advertising *after* a product experience could alter consumers' memories of that experience.[19] Participants in this study were given candy in a green wrapper. After they ate the candy, they were shown an advertisement of a candy wrapped in blue. When asked what color the wrapper on the real candy was, about half of the participants answered "blue." This memory distortion occurred even when the participants had been warned that the advertisement was printed with bad ink and that the colors in the ad were not reliable. In another study, participants were served a vinegar-tinged, salty orange drink (not the tastiest beverage!). However, after seeing an ad suggesting that the drink was "refreshing," the participants remembered their tasting experience as "refreshing."[20]

Though these findings powerfully demonstrate that advertising can infiltrate memory, they do not address whether an ad can create a memory of something that never happened. To explore that question, Braun-LaTour showed people an advertisement for Disney suggesting that all kids who visit Disneyland have the opportunity to shake hands with Bugs Bunny during their visit. Bugs Bunny is actually a Warner Bros. character and thus would never be seen in a Disney resort. However, about 16 percent of those who saw the ad later reported that they remembered meeting Bugs during a childhood visit to Disneyland. A control group had no such recollections. Apparently, advertising—if constructed properly—*can* lead to the creation of false memories.[21] When asked, many consumers insist that they rely primarily on their own first-hand experiences with products—not advertising—in making purchasing decisions. Yet, clearly, advertising can strongly alter what consumers remember about their past, and thus influence their behaviors.

Recently, neuropsychologists and neurobiologists have provided exciting new evidence supporting memory-reconstruction theory. Technologies such as PET scanning and functional magnetic resonance imaging (fMRI) provide visual evidence of this reconstruction process. Strikingly similar areas of the brain often become activated during both "false" and "true" memories, although some differences may occur as well.[22]

The Role of Mood in Memory

Fundamental biological processes involved in emotions and mood states also affect the encoding and retrieval of memories, as described in box 8-2. The impact of these processes has important implications for the context in which a product or ad is placed (for example, what appears in the pages before and after a magazine ad, or what's on TV before and after a commercial). The context of a marketing communication can establish emotions and moods that in turn affect how consumers process and recall the communication.

Box 8-2

Mood and Memory

Moods are subtle and general feelings.[23] Though people are often unaware of their mood, it can profoundly affect their explicit thinking. Mood often stems from the interaction of external events with the body's electrochemical systems and contributes to the malleable nature of memory.

Considerable research has examined the impact of mood on memory. One dominant theory suggests that a mood activates a network of associations in our memory that surrounds that mood or emotion.[24] If we are in a "happy" mood, then a network of associations with feeling happy will be activated. Our good mood primes our thoughts about feeling well. A recent theory proposing a neuropsychological mechanism underlying the effect of positive mood on cognition has interesting implications for memory.[25] This theory suggests that the effect of positive mood on problem solving and memory is associated with the release of the neurotransmitter dopamine in the brain. When a reward induces a positive mood, the amount of dopamine in the brain increases. That increase in turn leads to more flexible and creative thinking and enhances the recall of certain memories.

Most research on mood and memory has focused on two phenomena: mood-dependent memory and mood-congruent memory. Both processes speak to mood's impact on memory reconstruction.

Mood-Dependent Memory

When consumers are in the same mood at the time of both encoding and recall, they retrieve memories more easily. For example, if consumers are in a good mood when they first hear about a product's attributes, they will more accurately recall those attributes later if they are again in a good mood. However, recall improves only if consumers consciously attribute the *cause* of their good mood to the event that they associate with the mood. The simultaneous emergence of the mood and presentation of the associated cue is not sufficient on its own to improve recall.

Showing happy people staying at a particular motel chain won't establish the connection unless viewers of the image see the motel chain as contributing to that happy mood.

Mood-Congruent Memory

Consumers' mood also sensitizes them to information congruent with that mood. For instance, consumers in a good mood will be more aware of positive qualities in products or experiences that they encounter. People who feel happy will notice and remember happy events more than events that provoke sadness or anger.

What accounts for this association? The answer is surprisingly simple: It requires too much mental effort to shift from a negative mood to appreciate something positive. This exertion explains why we can't cheer up an unhappy customer simply by addressing her complaint.

Mood congruence also affects retrieval. Regardless of a consumer's mood at the time a memory is encoded, congruence between her current mood and the things she needs to remember enhances recall. For example, you can probably remember the name of a comedy when you're in a good mood—even if you weren't in a good mood when you first heard about the comedy. The mood-congruence effect seems stronger for implicit memory.

The impact of mood dependence and mood congruence is especially noticeable in retail contexts. In one study, consumers viewed a restaurant review that contained an equal number of positive and negative statements. Those who read the review while in a happy state of mind evaluated the restaurant more positively than those who read it while in a sour mood. This outcome suggests that the TV programming flanking a TV ad influences brand recall significantly. Positive programming will support memory encoding and retrieval more than negative programming. Thus marketers should think carefully about the surrounding context of the time slots that they buy.

In another study, researchers tried to induce a happy mood in mall shoppers by giving each a small gift. Later, in what they thought was an unrelated survey, consumers who had received the gift (that is, supposedly happy people) more likely reported satisfaction with

(continued)

their cars or televisions than did people who had not received a gift (that is, supposedly unhappy people).

Consistent with neuropsychological theory, recent empirical evidence suggests that positive mood does in fact enhance recall of brand names.[26] Thus, a positive mood may also lead consumers to engage in more "relational elaboration"; that is, thinking more about the ways a given brand may relate to other brands. This relational elaboration leads consumers to cluster or categorize brands, and the resulting multiple associations facilitate future recollection of the brands. The more consumers remember brands, the more likely they are to buy them.

Source: Professor Nancy Puccinelli of Emerson College contributed to this box.

Before continuing, one word of caution: Not all memories get reconstructed during the retrieval process. Consumers need some stability in their memory. After all, this stability saves consumers the trouble of having to consciously retrieve and evaluate memories of products and then make new decisions with every purchase. Yet some memory changes can be significant. Marketers can unknowingly—or knowingly—enhance the brain's proclivity for reconstituting memory.

Memory research over the last decade has yielded important developments. The metaphor of the unchanging photograph no longer fits what we know of consumer memory. Past and current circumstances, environment, and mood all shape what consumers recall about their experiences with a product, service, or company. As consumers create memories through their interactions with marketers, those memories in turn influence what new memories they will create. Market researchers and the professionals who design marketing communications should keep these findings in mind:

- Memories don't simply record consumers' pasts; they link their pasts, presents, and futures.

- Memories are malleable.
- Memory is selective; what consumers already know shapes what they encode and retrieve.
- Memory systems can contain only so much information; consumers recall only what suits the moment.
- Memory stores both generic and specific information.

Managers can design memory-shaping environments that will ultimately alter what consumers recall about a company's brand or product. Memory research has now provided managers with a new lens through which to interpret and analyze the memories that consumers describe in market research studies.

Chapter Nine

Memory, Metaphor, and Stories

Memory is another source of fiction.

—*Paul John Eakin, in* Memory, Brain and Belief

A S WE'VE SEEN in the preceding chapters, consumers' meta-phors and memories involve re-presentation, as do stories. A metaphor re-presents one thing in terms of another and influences thought. A memory re-presents an experience encountered in the past. A story narrates a past, present, or future event. All three contain truths and fictions, thoughts and emotions, and all three overlap. Memories are stories, stories consist of memories, and both are often expressed through metaphors. Most important, the fusion of memory, metaphor, and story enables consumers to create meaning around, or to see personal relevance in, a company or a specific brand.

In this chapter, we explore the social contexts for memory and the nature of the fusion of memory, metaphor, and story. Through the metaphors marketers use, they are able to alter prior memories and create new meanings or stories about their brands. Metaphors, as we saw in the last chapter, bridge two different sets of memories.[1] That bridge has two-way traffic, and both sets of memories are changed as a result of the interaction between them. Shared social contexts facilitate the use of metaphors that have common meaning for consumers.

Memories have a deep association with storytelling, according to Roger C. Schank and R. P. Abelson, authors of the article, "Knowledge and Memory: The Real Story." *To tell a story,* they maintain, *is to remember,* an important idea explored in chapter 7: "We remember by telling stories. Storytelling is not something we just happen to do. It is something we virtually have to do if we want to remember anything. . . . [T]he stories we create are the memories we have."[2]

Through these narratives, consumers tell stories about themselves. Like a partially improvised stage play, a particular story changes depending on the stimuli of the moment and the goals of the actors. The props and costumes for such a play are the goods and services consumers desire, purchase, and use. The stage consists of the boundaries of what society values.[3] Marketing managers provide the props and costumes and, as agents of the larger society, help consumers create memories and hence define their self-identities. Indeed, marketing's intimate role in the creation of self-identity is possibly one reason behind consumers' ambivalence toward the marketing profession.

Through marketing, companies re-present events to consumers and tell a new story about those events. In this way, marketers partner with consumers in creating consumers' memories. This partnership shapes memories *as* consumers record and recall them—another example of how the conscious and unconscious minds of managers and consumers interact. Marketing efforts alter not only how easily consumers recollect a product experience but also whether they remember the experience as satisfying or dissatisfying.

For example, in a study conducted by Dr. Kathryn Braun-LaTour of Marketing Memories, moviegoers who initially expressed negative opinions about a film were later shown a favorable review and asked to describe their initial evaluation of the film, the one to which they had testified earlier. The researchers asked the study participants only to indicate what their *initial* opinion was—not what they thought of the film *after* reading the review. They even told the participants that they were taking part in a memory test!

The moviegoers remembered initially judging the film in much more positive terms *after* they read the favorable review. Yet they remained completely unaware that they had distorted their memory of their original opinion. These consumers believed that they were repeating the exact same sentiments they had expressed the first time around. The reverse also occurred when consumers who initially expressed a positive opinion subsequently read a negative review of the film.

Memory and the Mind-Body-Brain-Society Paradigm

In many ways, memory is a private matter. Memory emerges from our imagination through the synergistic interactions of the engrams, cues, and goals operating at the moment. However, memory is highly social as well.[4] The childhood treats we recall so fondly were made possible by a long chain of other people, starting with growers or bakers and concluding with the people handing them to us. We are reminded of them now by advertising, which is the product of yet another string of people. Shaking hands with Mickey Mouse is made possible through social conventions such as the notion of a family vacation and a parent who wants his child to have this memory. Thus, *memory is ultimately a social event.* Susan Engel, author of *Context Is Everything: The Nature of Memory,* explains this social aspect of memory in these words:

> [T]he process of remembering can only be understood in an appropriately rich and dynamic way if it is understood as a kind of chemistry between inner processes and outer settings. It is the dynamic interplay between inner and outer that gives rise to the thing we know as memory.[5]

The Co-evolution of Biology and Culture

As we saw in chapter 2, the mind, brain, body, and society have a symbiotic relationship with one another. E. O. Wilson used the phrase "gene-culture co-evolution" to express this notion.[6] *How we remember and what we deem important to remember are functions of both our biology and our culture.* Our biological makeup and cultural ways both evolve through natural selection, and each influences the other.[7] Sometimes one leads and one lags, but they always remain close and coordinated. Though genetic changes unfold slowly, they have evolved in a way that permits considerable flexibility in how our learning and memory respond to cultural or social forces. As we've seen, the culture a person grows up in strongly influences his or her brain's "wiring," or neural pathways, in the early years of life. The stories we hear starting in early childhood become important frames of reference or mental models that later influence the products and brands we buy, especially if stories about those brands resonate with deep cultural meanings embedded in our memories.

Social Memory

As you may have concluded, cultural artifacts, events, and rituals facilitate our encoding, retrieval, and reconstruction of memory. We'll use the term "social memory" to refer to these factors. Put differently, we can think about certain important memories as being stored externally as well as internally. These externally stored memories reside in:

- social norms
- rituals and rites
- vocal and instrumental music
- icons
- language
- bodily movements, posture, and gestures
- architecture
- social structures
- objects
- sensory stimuli
- formal archival records

Yes, social memories are everywhere.[8] But these repositories do more than just "contain" our shared understandings. They also shape those understandings. The information stored in them also may be misplaced or lost, or may undergo change owing to extensive use or neglect.

For example, consider Coke advertisements as social containers. A Coke ad depicting teens dancing at a party to a particular style of music activates one neuron cluster, thus producing a particular experience of Coca-Cola. Another ad showing a baby polar bear and baby seal sharing a Coke activates a different neuron cluster, thus producing yet another experience. The two social settings depicted in the ads have different meanings for an individual viewer and thus are likely to activate different internally stored Coke associations.

The Unity of Internal and External Memory

Social-memory containers are not only repositories for shared understandings within a culture; they also can serve as engrams, retrieval cues, and purposes or goals themselves. Thus they can *produce* the experience of memory. Indeed, our internal memory would be impoverished without these external phenomena—and visa versa. For instance, children who have no social contact suffer serious and irreversible deficiencies in their brain development and functioning. Likewise, individuals who suffer damage to brain areas essential to memory lose the ability to maintain meaningful social relationships. So as with other artificial distinctions that we human beings have made, our convenient separation of internal and social memory simply does not reflect reality. Each kind of memory shapes and is shaped by the other; neither means much by itself.

Let's take a closer look at some of the social-memory containers we listed earlier.

Social Norms

Norms serve as guidelines governing our *aspirations,* such as our desire for world harmony, and our *behaviors,* such as how we relate to our children.

Norms on nutritional practices influence how mothers temper their children's consumption of cola drinks. These norms are transmitted and reinforced among mothers and across generations from mother to child. Similarly, children have their own norms governing their requests for colas. Families have norms for resolving clashes of norms between mothers and children. Nutritional norms exert a major influence on consumers' shopping behavior. They affect whether shoppers will notice particular food products; how much time, if any, they devote to the consideration of a purchase; how much they purchase; and which brands they buy. These norms, which include when and what to provide as a treat and what constitutes moderation, also determine whether a consumer will buy the product in the first place. For example, if a nutritional norm triggers prior memories of Coca-Cola, including semantic recollections of its contents and episodic memories of sharing a Coke with friends, a mom may more likely buy Coke for her household.

Sensory Systems

Our various senses help us understand our external world and represent it internally in the form of memories. Thus our sensory systems play a critical role in our encoding, retrieval, and reconstruction of those memories. The way in which the senses interact with memory varies from one social setting to another.[9] For example, what a people knows of the world through the sense of touch or smell changes from one culture to another.

Odor, as an external cue, has inspired extensive research on memory.[10] For instance, scientists have discovered that a pleasant scent stimulates consumers to encode and later recall unfamiliar brands more than familiar brands.[11] The pleasant scent serves as a special "memory marker" that gives that memory distinctiveness. Moreover, certain odors, such as the scent of lemon, make us more alert and enhance our ability to process information. Such odors might therefore be especially important when marketers are introducing a brand that is new to a particular market segment. Finally, men and women differ in their behavioral responses to odors and in the way they encode and retrieve memories involving odor.[12] Odor can also operate outside of our awareness, a situation called "blind smell."

Sound, and more specifically music, can also serve as a powerful social-memory container.[13] Certain music can activate communal memories of family, places, and things.[14] Kay Shelemay, an ethnomusicologist at Harvard University, argues that sound creates a sense of community and of belonging to past or future generations:

[Music] brings the past into the present through both its content and the act of performance, while also serving as a device through which long-forgotten aspects of the past and information unconsciously carried can be evoked, accessed, and remembered.[15]

Like other forms of art, music is biologically adaptive. That is, it enables people of similar minds to transmit information to one another, to find shared meaning, and to respond to specific events in common ways. Music can activate memories of specific concepts as well as recollections of fundamental emotions. Though music has been widely employed in advertising, marketers have not yet systematically studied the use of music as a way of helping consumers encode and retrieve concepts and emotions.

Rituals and Rites

Through rituals and rites, we honor national and religious holidays, celebrate birthdays and wedding anniversaries, and participate in ceremonies.[16] Advertising for diamonds, jewelry, and graduation gifts is designed to evoke these social memories. A shopper's experience in a supermarket aisle is her expression of the values embodied in her norms about raising children. Point-of-purchase cues can activate memories of social norms and influence how shoppers interpret those cues. For example, the shopper's anticipation of how her children will respond if she does or doesn't bring home a box of Cocoa Puffs will activate norms governing how much sugar intake she allows her children, as well as when she allows them a special treat. Though marketers focus their attention on the individual shopper's "performance" in the cereal aisle, the script for that performance, as well as the degree and type of improvisation the shopper demonstrates, are lodged in social relationships that reach far beyond the store.

Icons

Brand names, packages, logos, and other symbols can become icons. An icon is a symbolic image. Rooted in the consumers' external world, icons not only take on meaning based on people's experiences in that external world, but also can convey private meanings.[17] For example, a young woman in Belgium shared a personal story about Coca-Cola with others at her grandfather's funeral. The grandfather, a diabetic who had always been under the watchful eye of his spouse, would enter into a secret conspiracy with his granddaughter when she visited him as a young girl. When the grandmother was busy, grandfather and granddaughter would go off to a café and share a forbidden Coca-Cola. As this young girl grew into a woman, Coca-Cola became an icon, a symbolic image of her relationship with her grandfather—a relationship that was made special through the surreptitious quality of sharing the Coke. For her, the Coke brand became an icon that "contained" a unique memory of togetherness and conspiracy.

The Power of Social Memory

We acquire much semantic knowledge (the "what" and "how" of our experiences) through unconscious observation and imitation of other people (which is one reason celebrity advertising works so well). We also build our semantic knowledge through formal instruction and work experience. Thus other people and institutions are the gatekeepers influencing the kinds of semantic and episodic memories we create. Learning how to ride a bike, blow bubbles with gum, sing, split an atom, launch a rocket, and sail a ship all require a social order that makes such things possible and worth remembering. Similarly, attaching memorable significance to a surprise birthday party, religious ceremony, first rock concert, or that time when your child used a toilet in the display section of Home Depot calls for a social world that makes the event salient and relevant to you. Souvenirs ranging from T-shirts to photographs become obvious social markers of memory.

Once we establish memories, other people, institutions, and our culture reshape them and store them in external repositories, including language, dance, music, myths, stories, rituals, holidays, art, commemorative stamps, films, and educational institutions. These repositories are dedicated to the creation and maintenance of shared semantic and episodic memories. Through shared values and beliefs, societies define what is proper and what we must remember. Therefore, as societies change, so do the memories they impart.

One major implication of the social origin of memory relates to customer relationship management (CRM). The literature on CRM often ignores the centrality of memory and the ways in which relationships between marketers and consumers constantly cocreate consumers' memories. Without an understanding of what memory really is and how to manage it, CRM can't fulfill its promise of enduring customer loyalty and soaring profits. People who manage customer relationships must grasp how consumers store, retrieve, and reconstruct memories of every interaction with a firm. These interactions may be direct, as when customers deal with a global account manager. They may also be indirect, as through word-of-mouth. And every new encounter alters a customer's recall of a prior encounter—often in trivial ways, but sometimes in significant ways. Thus *every* consumer interaction can make—or break—a brand.

Memory as Metaphor

Often, we come to understand something new by relating it to past experience. When we venture forth, we use what we already know to grasp the unfamiliar. In fact, our brains automatically retrieve existing information and weave it into the emerging thoughts about our new experience. For instance, after tasting a new food, you might say, "It tastes like chicken!" This remark crops up so often it has become a joke. Even if the new food is entirely unrelated to chicken (rattlesnake, frog's legs, certain insects), you use the relevant information most readily available in your memory—the familiar taste of chicken—to capture and describe the novel experience.

In this sense, memory and metaphor have a lot in common: They both represent one thing in terms of another. As we saw in chapter 8, the memory process emerges from the interaction of an engram and a cue under the influence of the remembering person's goal or purpose. Memory can also be creative, as when we unconsciously represent a prior experience differently with each recall. We can think of these changes as *unconscious metaphors;* that is, re-creations of the past. We mistake these as accurate reflections of past realities, because we usually remain unaware that our memories have changed.

Some people's memories represent *kinds* of things that occurred in the past, even though the *specific* episodes never happened. Such memories are literally false but figuratively accurate; they are metaphors representing the shared essence that may characterize a number of individual, seemingly unrelated events.[18]

A study of consumer deception exemplifies this kind of memory in the realm of marketing. The researchers asked consumers to describe the most upsetting experience they had ever had with a store or product. The study participants had all filed formal complaints with local or state consumer protection agencies in the past. However, in recalling the most upsetting experience, they often named stores or brands that did not exist at the time of the supposed episode. Through telling their stories, the participants translated several different experiences that *had* happened to them into a specific event that had *not* happened. The researchers concluded that the consumers telling these stories fully believed them in all their details.[19]

Marketers' actions, intentional or not, *help consumers re-present a particular past experience in new and different terms.* Thus, marketers and consumers cocreate metaphors of experience. Marketers influence how consumers recreate their experience—their memory—of various touchpoints along their shopping journey.

Now the plot thickens even more.

Memory as Story

As we've seen, memory is story based; that is, it involves the use of prior events stored as engrams to help explain or interpret new events involving cues and goals.[20] A story is an accounting of one or more experiences involving both episodic and semantic memory. Marketers help consumers create stories about brands through the kinds of information and the types of experience they provide prior to, during, and after the shopping experience. Recent studies on the brain, memory, and belief make this idea more compelling than ever.[21] As Indiana University professor of English Paul John Eakin wrote in his article "Autobiography, Identity, and the Fictions of Memory":

> Looking back, I suspect that I have always regarded memory as autobiography's anchor, the source of that core factual truth that enables us to distinguish autobiography's fiction from the kind we more commonly call fiction. Recent research on memory, however, has radically destabilized such a notion; memory, whether we like it or not, is one more source of fiction. . . .[22]

Part of the power of stories is that we are seldom aware that we are engaged in storytelling.[23] As psychoanalyst and New York University faculty member Donnel B. Stern notes, "The process of telling one's own life story . . . is not volutional in any simple way, any more than is our construction of dreams, or, for that matter, our construction of the next moment's experience . . . our life stories are simply there."[24]

Stories contain both our beliefs and our knowledge about the world.[25] The similarity of the words *store* and *story* is not a coincidence, after all. Most research on memory draws a clear distinction between belief and knowledge, although both constitute parts of memory and therefore story.[26] A *belief* is something we recall and consider true; for example, that we got a good deal on the vehicle we purchased. Remember, most market research, perhaps 80 percent or more, is confirmatory, designed to reinforce an existing belief or what we already consider true rather than to uncover new insights.[27] Not surprisingly, when the results of a study contradict a key assumption, managers blame the methodology. Instead of considering *whether* something is wrong, managers look for *what* is wrong; that is, they allow, at least initially, for the possibility that their belief could be wrong. Unlike beliefs, *knowledge* is the information—such as the price offered by a competing auto dealer—on which truth is based. Captured in story form, knowledge enables us to recognize and respond appropriately to new, unfamiliar events and situations.

Screenwriter Robert McKee notes, "What happens is fact, not truth. Truth is what we *think about* what happens."[28] According to the facts, the generic brand of a product or the less well known service provider is every bit as good as the national brand or more prominent service provider. But for many consumers who have these facts, the "truth"—that is, what they actually believe as revealed by how they respond to the facts—differs dramatically: The national brand *is* better and they will buy it instead.

Successful brands help consumers create stories full of promise. For example, Coca-Cola inspires consumers to create stories about refreshment. Malibu rum stimulates the idea of escape from the small annoyances of life. Fidelity Investments promises quality financial advice. Other brands, such as Tanqueray gin or BMW, are badge brands; that is, they inspire consumers to create *aspirational* stories about who they are and who they believe they can become. Whether brand stories are about who one is or what one can experience, the actual product usually factors less in the story than do the imaginative processes of the consumer. In other words, the story exceeds the brand's physical features. Greg Clarke, president of Traditional Yachts, captures this idea nicely: "People prefer the American Tug over other alternatives because it offers the best way for them to fulfill a dream. The boat is great, of course, but their dream makes it better. It is like the two things together make the American Tug something no boat builder could ever design or make."

Similarly, a Corvette owner does not just own a car or a brand. His legal ownership of the vehicle may matter under some circumstances, like when the police stop him. However, legal possession of the car is not essential to the experience of *driving* it. People buy Corvettes because, in one owner's words, "driving around in a shiny red sports car makes me feel cool and sexy. I enjoy being the focus of attention and having strangers ask about the car." The real or anticipated experience of *driving* the car forms a Corvette owner's beliefs about the value of owning the car and shapes the stories he creates about it. His beliefs provide emotional color to the otherwise bland state of simply owning a vehicle.

The Buick Retail Experience offers an excellent example of how Buick is considering creating a new story about a brand (see box 9-1). Through this project, General Motors set out to explore how customers feel about automobile dealerships, why they feel the way they do, and what they *want* to feel. The company then used the insights gained from the research to improve consumers' experience of shopping for a car at a Buick dealership.

Box 9-1

Customer-Experience Management at Buick

Business Issue

In 1995 General Motors (GM) embarked on a corporate-wide brand-management review. For several years, the Buick retail brand had struggled to expand its customer base and sustain margin contribution to the GM organization. Both Buick corporate and GM recognized the need to evolve the brand image in order to appeal to a new, broader market.

The Buick Division applied experience-management techniques with the goal of experientially defining brand attributes and embedding them into a prototype Buick customer experience. Senior management, wholesale managers, and top-producing retail dealers comprised the task force that led the two-year initiative focused on retail innovation and the Buick Retail Experience.

Implementation

Dubbed the Buick Flagship Experience, the program had a clearly defined goal: to create a highly distinctive "single-point" retail customer-experience strategy where only Buick cars were sold—not Oldsmobile or Chevy or any other GM brand. That is, the goal was to create a place where consumers would want to buy Buicks and bring them in for service—a place that was exclusively and experientially Buick. In order to do this, the task force needed a clearer understanding of the emotional underpinnings that went along with buying and owning a Buick.

Working with Experience Engineering, Inc., the task force members conducted an exhaustive and comprehensive review of multiple dealer environments and processes. They accomplished this through numerous field trips to various dealerships, videotaped observation of customers using stationary cameras and pinhole cameras embedded in a task force member's necktie and wristwatch, and in-depth customer

(continued)

interviews that helped the team members see and feel the car-buying experience from the customer's perspective. The task force then compared its findings to Buick brand-recognition criteria and numerous research studies. The objective of this phase was to define what the most influential and differentiating *emotional* outcome of the Buick experience *should be,* given the brand's attributes and in-depth customer-experience observation and input. Research revealed that the Buick Flagship brand experience should focus on making customers feel a sense of *belonging, recognition* as valued individuals, and *comfort.*

According to Larry Hice, general sales and service manager of the Buick Motor Division of GM, "Managing experiences is brand positioning at its absolute pinnacle, because brand is so much more than just the metal that sits on the showroom floor. It's about how you display that piece of metal, how you treat that person when they walk in the front door. When those things are aligned with the brand, it is powerful."

The Flagship Experience Design

In order to make their findings actionable, the task force members designed a holistic customer experience that aimed to reinforce consumers' sense of belonging, recognition, and comfort. Specifically, they implemented several hundred cues, ranging from complex building and façade changes to tweaking of small process details, at top-producing, independent Buick dealerships that elected to participate in the program.

Cues in the experience design included the following:

- A carillon bell tower (the universal symbol for community and welcome) was installed at every Flagship location to convey a sense of *belonging*. A twenty-four-hour computer was housed on the ground floor of the tower to help consumers access community information as well as Buick product information.

- Parklike settings on dealership grounds, complete with the smell of freshly cut grass and the sound of chirping birds, reinforced *comfort* and *recognition*.

- A uniformed greeter, coached to *recognize* customers when possible, patrolled the winding brick drive-up paths and directed customers to the desired area of the dealership.

- In the showrooms, the salesmen's "bullpen" was replaced with *comfortable* living-room settings, fireplaces, and overstuffed chairs.

- Through a "stealth" sales process, experientially coached salesmen entered the showroom only when a customer paged. Unobtrusive computer information bays placed among the showroom cars provided information of interest to customers.

- A silent paging system summoned personnel so that customers throughout the complex did not have to hear the page.

- A community room was made available for members of the public to book community and group meetings and events.

In addition to incorporating more than one hundred environmental cues, the experience-management task force recast many "front stage" roles in the dealership by teaching salesmen new behaviors and language designed to give customers a sense of *recognition* and *belonging*.

Results

The Flagship Experience Design was implemented in six independent Buick dealerships. Upon completion, all six dealers posted increased gross sales in the first year, ranging from 9 percent to 40 percent. Customer satisfaction scores increased unilaterally.

According to Larry Hice, "The Flagship Experience truly created new opportunities for dealers to be something different in the marketplace. This is not a touchy-feely, feel-good kind of thing that can't be tracked. It is revenue-producing strategy. When done right, customers will refer and repeat on that alone. That's revenue."

Source: Courtesy of Experience Engineering, Inc., Minneapolis, MN, and the Buick Motor Division, General Motors.

Belief and knowledge interact at both conscious and unconscious levels. However, somewhat different neural activities are involved in each. Howard Eichenbaum and J. Alexander Bodkin explained this notion in their article, "Belief and Knowledge as Forms of Memory":

> *Knowledge-driven memory processing is "bottom up," in that new experiences are paramount in forcing novel bits of information together to build or modify a memory scheme. . . . By contrast, belief-driven memory processing is "top down," in that the general schema is paramount in guiding the interpretation of new experience to confirm convictions and to specify actions consistent with those convictions.*[29]

The partnership between knowledge and belief as forms of memory, with their top-down *and* bottom-up processing, further supports the claim that consumers think in nonlinear as well as linear ways. That is, when consumers consider whether to buy a product or service, they take into account both the potential functional benefits of the product, such as the risk potential of an investment plan, *and* the deep emotional benefits, such as providing security for one's loved ones.

Moreover, for all practical purposes, consumers analyze both kinds of benefits simultaneously, rather than considering first one and then the other. This phenomenon reflects the little-understood neural process whereby neural clusters both exchange and respond simultaneously to information. By analogy, the process resembles a phone conversation in which two people speak at the same time while still hearing and responding meaningfully to what each is saying. Traditional laddering techniques are valuable in identifying associations between the attributes of a product or service, the functional consequences of those attributes, and the psychological and other emotional reasons why those consequences are or are not valued. However, the conventional way of presenting these associations often misses the more complex, nonlinear, and powerful ways that attributes, values, and consequences interact. Furthermore, what may be a simple attribute for one person could be a deep value for another. What for one consumer is merely a pleasant scent might be experienced as fear (or joy) by another consumer.

To leverage these processes, marketers should always present a product's functional and emotional benefits closely together in their communications to consumers, even if they do so in highly subtle ways. The idea of extra traction made possible by the design of a tire's tread, when coupled with a picture of an infant, will trigger feelings or thoughts of safety in a more powerful way than showing an adult or simply documenting the benefits of the tread. Some people will notice the tire and the infant at the same time, and the connections (tread and safety) between them are activated from both directions. In other cases, someone may notice the tire or the infant first, but once the tread-to-safety connection is made, further thoughts and feelings about safety will cause more thinking about tread. Thus the design of any communication, including store features, packaging, and even billing information received in the mail, should be attentive to the partnership between function and emotion.

Memory and the Familiar

People remember new information more easily when it has some connection to what they already know and has personal relevance for them. New information becomes even more memorable if we "tag" it (that is, associate it) with an emotion.[30] Thus the familiar strongly influences what people notice, remember, and feel. Even when we encounter a contradiction or a surprise, we compare the familiar with the unfamiliar in order to figure out what's going on.[31] For example, most humor involves a violation of assumptions or expectations. It's that violation of the familiar that makes us smile or laugh and remember the joke later. The theories or ideas that most cause us to say, "That's interesting!" are those that challenge our longest-held assumptions.[32] It's no coincidence that the very factors that influence the memorableness of an experience are the same criteria by which we judge whether a story is engaging.

Box 9-2 describes an exercise that reveals how automatically we use the "old" to understand the "new."

The statement that memory is "story based" doesn't mean that memories take the form of "Once upon a time." Instead, we remember

Box 9-2

An Animal on Another Planet

On the first day of class in my Customer Behavior Laboratory course at the Harvard Business School, I invite students to imagine that scientists have discovered a new planet. I ask the students to draw a picture of an animal that would live there, assuming any atmospheric considerations. After the students have all drawn something in their notebooks, I ask for volunteers to share their creations. Usually about twenty people draw their creatures on the blackboard. The animals range in complexity from squiggly lines to elaborate six-eyed beings. At first glance, these creatures have no resemblance to any animal on Earth.

However, as students begin to describe what they see, they quickly establish that these creations do resemble earthly animals in certain respects. Even squiggly lines can be bisected lengthwise into symmetrical shapes. The alien creatures have sensing devices resembling eyes, ears, noses, tongues, antennae, and other familiar parts. Their features usually come in pairs; eyes are located near mouths and noses; limbs appear in even numbers and as extensions for locomotion; and so on.

experiences and images as integrated bundles of information. In the process of remembering, we often add information. Recall the picture of the two creatures running in a hallway from chapter 3. People's tendency to believe that the creatures differ in size, that one is angry and the other frightened, and that one is chasing the other demonstrates our human ability to add or subtract information as we create and recall stories. Figure 9-1 shows the same two creatures without the simple cue of visual depth (a hallway); figure 9-2 shows them in the hallway. Notice that figure 9-1 wouldn't generate a story as easily as figure 9-2 would. The simple cue of a hallway encourages us to add size, anger, fright, a chase, and escape to an image, and we get a much more vivid story. In marketing, the firm adds the cues corresponding to the hallway while

At this point, students usually point out that I asked them specifically to draw an "animal," not a "living creature." This observation usually leads to a discussion of how the students might have represented "living creature." The new ideas demonstrate the diversity of possibilities that a higher level of abstraction may have generated. But even in the latter case, "living" (as we know it) still constrains our thinking. Few students indicate that they first considered what conditions on another planet might be like and how these circumstances would dictate the bodily structure of beings who lived on that planet. Seldom does a student consider drawing creatures that resemble shoes, elbows, or raisins. This exercise serves as a reference point throughout the course. It demonstrates:

- How quickly we refer to what we already know when we encounter a new challenge

- How unaware we are of the influence of the familiar

- How easily we represent one thing in terms of another

- How we struggle to create a new idea that doesn't relate to what we already know

the consumer adds the other elements just mentioned to explain or account for what is going on.

Significantly, *what we know and remember constitutes the ingredients for storytelling, the re-presentation of our beliefs.* Storytelling can be verbal, pictorial (as in the preceding example), or take many other forms, such as music and dance. Marketers must learn the ingredients—the relevant thoughts and feelings—that consumers use to create a story involving the brand or other issue that the marketer is addressing. The marketer should carefully select and design additional cues encouraging consumers to construct favorable stories. The two creatures in figure 9-1 elicit a much less engaging story when placed on a seesaw instead of in a hallway. The cues that marketers can add, of course, can be a product's

FIGURE 9 - 1

Two Creatures without a Hallway

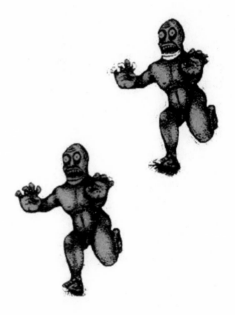

Adapted from *Mind Sights* by Roger N. Shepard, © 1990 by W. H. Freeman.
Reprinted by permission of Henry Holt and Company, LLC.

ingredients, a simple statement of purported benefits, the elements of package design, the background music in a store, the store personnel's attire, the look and feel of a Web site, and so on. By adding distinctive as well as familiar elements, the marketer and the consumer jointly create a story that will more likely result in a purchase.

• • •

FIGURE 9 - 2

Two Creatures within a Hallway

From *Mind Sights* by Roger N. Shepard, © 1990 by W. H. Freeman.
Reprinted by permission of Henry Holt and Company, LLC.

Memories, we've seen, are both personal and social. We experience them individually, and yet their content is also stored all around us in the form of social norms, icons, and so on. What we remember is a re-presentation, a metaphor, for social or cultural events and meanings that are personally relevant. These are communicated and stored in the form of stories. As noted earlier, the closeness of *store* and *story* is not accidental.

Metaphor brings together different stories or sets of memories. For example, the metaphor that Chevy trucks are like a rock brings to mind for U.S. consumers the meaning of Chevy trucks and of a rock. When these are brought together, a new meaning or story—a new memory—is created.

Chapter Ten

Stories and Brands

Story is metaphor for life.

T HE IDEA that brands are a form of storytelling is not new.[1] In fact, as psychologist Sidney J. Levy of Northwestern University and the University of Arizona explains:

> *The largest activity in marketing is the provision and consumption of stories. This fact is so general and pervasive that it commonly escapes notice or it is so prominent and noticeable that it interpenetrates all experience. . . . Stories are bought and sold, they are part of the media of exchange, and they are the vehicles for all other goods and services.*[2]

Because storytelling is so central to memory and metaphor, we should fully understand the process. Consensus maps (chapters 6 and 7) are the filters that consumers use when attending to, processing, and responding to marketing stimuli; stories simply embellish these maps. When managers tell a brand story, they engage or activate their consumers' consensus maps. When managers tell new stories, they are trying to reengineer those maps.

However, consumers don't passively receive these brand stories. To the contrary, managers and consumers cocreate the meanings of brands, as Susan Fournier of the Harvard Business School has demonstrated in her work on brand relationships and brand meaning.[3] Wendy Gordon of the Fourth Room based in London also cautions managers: "Most importantly we need to remember that *brands only exist in the minds of others*. The brand in my mind is not the same as the one in yours."[4] [Italics in original.]

Storytelling and Brand Building

Larry Huston, a senior vice president and lead creative director at Procter & Gamble and a leading marketing authority on storytelling in brand building, points out this relationship:

> *All brands have a story, a story that consumers tell themselves when they reach for the product in the store to buy it. The story will likely be subconscious if the person is already a loyal buyer or conscious in the case of a new trial experience. For example, when Mom reaches for a juice drink, her story might be, "My kids love this and it's good for them." There are many story moments in a brand's daily life. That same Mom may tell a friend a word-of-mouth story: "I have weaned my kids away from soft drinks. This new juice drink? They love it and it's good for them. I always have it in the refrigerator, and I let them drink all they want. This stuff is vitamin fortified."*
>
> *In addition to word-of-mouth stories and purchase stories, many brands have creation stories. We have all heard the creation stories of HP, Apple, Microsoft, Coca-Cola, and on and on. Often the main character, or protagonist, in a brand-creation story is an individual—and these characters all have their stories. The stories of Walt Disney, Ralph Lauren, or Coco Chanel enrich the brand and make it more human and approachable. In nearly all cases, these individuals have hero journey stories. These are stories of adversity, rejection, renewal, and triumph. Hero stories are fundamental human archetypes that resonate across all cultures. And, of course, one of the classic approaches in advertising is to create hero advertising. The challenge, of course, is to do this in a fresh way, not in a clichéd way. Authenticity and voice are keys to successful brand storytelling.*[5]

Huston has created the Boot Camp operation at P&G, whereby brand managers create brand stories, including films portraying the stories.

This training helps the managers develop more meaningful connections between consumers and P&G brands.

Others have also explored the power of storytelling. Recently, Roland Kulen launched the Story Development Studio to develop and evaluate film scripts, television programs, and novels in various stages. His developers explore the deep metaphors in the writers', directors', and producers' work, as well as moviegoers', TV viewers', and readers' metaphors about the materials. Kulen and his colleagues use the metaphor-elicitation technique to help writers express their goals and explore how well their stories achieve those goals. Then, using the same methodology, the studio gauges the intended audience's reactions, which it factors into the script development process.

Storytelling and Archetypes

Many consumer memories are *archetypes,* defined as images that capture essential, universal commonalities across a variety of experiences. For example, read the sentence below and respond quickly:

Think of a vegetable.

For many North Americans, the vegetable that comes to mind immediately is "carrot." Regardless of whether people enjoy or eat carrots regularly, carrots are the archetypal vegetable for many people. Carrots represent all vegetables. All societies share many archetypes, such as "hero," "villain," "sage," and "pauper," although the specific stories featuring these archetypes may vary.[6] These archetypes appear in fables, fairy tales, novels, and, most important, in everyday life—including people's experiences as consumers. Archetypes help us make sense of life's challenges, behave properly, and understand who we are. Not surprisingly, advertisers often use archetypes to represent the kinds of experiences that consumers have with a product, even though each consumer has his own version of that experience.[7] A financial services ad may present a grandparent as the sage, although different grandparents may relate to the sage role in different ways, depending on their personal situations.

Marketers who wish to influence the stories that consumers create must *build stories around archetypes, not stereotypes*. A story built around an archetype involves a *universal theme,* that is, a core or deep metaphor simultaneously embedded in a unique setting.[8] The stereotypical story stresses a setting and not a deeper, more universal quality to be found in many settings. Consumers in different situations can still relate to an ad or a message about a brand conveyed through an unfamiliar setting if it involves a clear archetype or core metaphor. Product stories that involve archetypes can span cultures or subcultures, whereas those that stress functional attributes and perhaps immediate, surface psychological or social benefits usually misfire. Showing a homemaker's pleasure when using a certain household product is stereotypical, even though it accurately portrays what many people experience using the product. However, showing the homemaker's major *faux pas* and subsequent redemption by selecting the brand in question taps into a deeper, more relevant experience expressed universally as the hero's journey.

Box 10-1 looks more closely at archetypes and how societies use them. Developed by Dr. Canan Habib, a specialist in literature and a research associate with Olson Zaltman Associates, this box focuses on the use of archetypes in literature.

Archetypes as Core Metaphors

Often archetypes and core metaphors are one and the same.[9] As we saw in chapter 4, a core metaphor contains the common, underlying elements of otherwise different and more surface-level metaphors. For example, the idea of (im)balance is present in each of the following expressions: "I'm back on track again"; "That puts me off"; "If I eat this now, then I'll pay for it later"; "That offer is awfully one-sided." Thus (im)balance is the deep metaphor uniting these seemingly unrelated surface metaphors.

Box 10-1

Archetypes in Literature

An *archetype* is an idea, character, action, object, situation, event, or setting containing essential characteristics that are primitive, general, and universal rather than sophisticated and unique. Theories about archetypes draw from a diverse range of fields, including anthropology, psychology, and literary analysis.

Anthropologists have developed the following two "monomyths"—overall patterns that contain diverse archetypal symbols.

- **Seasonal myths** involve cycles of human life that follow the patterns of the seasons. Birth and youth are represented by spring; growth, by summer; fruition or maturity, by autumn; and death, by winter. Like the seasons of the year, the cycle of life is continuous. Death is followed by rebirth, as winter is followed by spring.

- **Hero myths** often depict the hero as having an unusual birth, a great man or god as a father, and qualities of greatness himself. Many heroes are sent into exile or put in dangerous situations; must pass a test or a trial to prove themselves; have achieved great deeds, thus "saving the day"; and suffer a mysterious death. Many hero myths suggest that a supposedly deceased hero is not really dead, or that he might be reborn.

One scholar organizes archetypal patterns under the following five headings.

1. **Subjects:** Birth, coming of age, love, guilt, redemption, death; that is, big, universal issues.

2. **Themes:** The conflict between reason and imagination, free will and destiny, appearance and reality, individual and society—with a focus on how individuals deal with universal subjects.

3. **Situations:** The tension between parents and children, the rivalry between brothers, the problems of incestuous desire, the search for a father, the ambivalence of the male-female relationship, the young

(continued)

man from the country first arriving in the city—with an emphasis on how individuals address universal subjects *with one another.*

4. **Characters:** The braggart, buffoon, hero, devil, rebel, wanderer, enchantress, maiden, witch, and so on. Includes man and woman in general.

5. **Images:** Certain animals, birds, and natural phenomena and settings. Includes fire, sky, earth, rain, water, direction (such as up/down), colors, and shades (such as light/dark). Colors may represent other ideas, such as life/death, memory/forgetfulness, growth/decline, happiness/fear, wakefulness/sleep, and so forth.

Other scholars divide archetypal patterns into two main groups, the cycle of life and archetypal images.

The Cycle of Life

The Divine Family: Sky Father—Earth Mother

The Divine Family: Mating with a mortal

Becoming: Initiation

Becoming: The fall from innocence to experience

Becoming: The task

Becoming: The journey and the quest

Becoming: The search for the father

Becoming: Death and rebirth

Archetypal characters, such as heroes and antiheroes, the wise fool, the devil, the outcast, the double, the scapegoat, and the temptress, repeatedly appear in the cycle of life.

Archetypal Images

Archetypal images are more complicated than stereotypes because they stand for things other than themselves. Yet even without referring to anthropology or psychology, we can grasp why certain images have come to represent certain ideas, as shown in the following examples.

- **Up/Down:** The law of gravity governs everyone. As you might expect, going *up* is normally more difficult than going *down;* therefore, the idea of going up should convey achievement and excellence. Images associated with the idea of *up,* such as a flying bird, flying arrow, star, mountain, growing tree, and tower, represent what we want to reach or attain; in short, something good. *Down* connotes the opposite idea. We "fall" into bad habits or bankruptcy. An abyss symbolizes downfall, emptiness, and chaos.

- **Blood:** This fluid represents life, strength, dignity of inheritance, magic, death (if too much blood is spilled), and the making of an oath. Blood is associated with moments of death, birth, puberty, and the more general ideas of health.

- **Field/Earth** and **Sky/Rain:** These images represent woman and man. Sky (male) sends rain as a fertilizer. Earth (female) receives the fertilizer and gives birth to crops and babies.

- **Light/Dark:** These symbolize certain mental and spiritual qualities. For example, metaphors involving *light* convey the following: illumination, clarification, illustration, brightening, and emotional relief. Darkness is associated not only with corpses, ghosts, unhappiness, the unknown, and evil, but also with possibility and the furtherance of new life (the darkness of the womb). At times, physical darkness or blindness may symbolize inner light or vision.

- **Fire:** Fire constantly moves and changes. Fire links with the ideas of *up, sun, sky,* and the gods, and with the male.

- **Woman:** This archetype historically portrayed women as either nurturing mothers, witches, or prostitutes. In recent literary tradition, more variety has emerged, and images of female identity have softer edges. For example, we can depict a woman simultaneously as the object of desire and as a nurturer.

- **The Double, or the Second Self:** The double can appear in many shapes: a friend, a twin brother, a pursuer, a tempter, a beloved, a fragmented mind, or opposite images such as the fair maid and the femme fatale. The double reflects a simultaneous duality and unity. It can be a complementary identity, a total opposite, or a seeming opposite to the self.

Source: Dr. Canan Habib, Olson Zaltman Associates.

Two concepts—"journey" and "transformation"—aptly illustrate the overlap of deep metaphors and archetypes.

- *The Shopper's Journey.* Consumers describe their shopping experiences in terms of an archetypal journey, complete with many side roads that entice the shopper to digress and find surprise, excitement, and even trouble. In taking this journey, a consumer may experience numerous archetypal events, such as succumbing to temptation (the hero's fall from grace), confronting a store manager (the power of danger and challenge to build character), overcoming resource constraints (additional character building), and arriving home triumphant—with a bargain in hand or a treat for the family (the return of the conquering hero). When a consumer repeatedly experiences such events along the shopper's journey, he or she then becomes a trusted advisor for more naïve consumers. (The hero assumes community leadership and receives well-earned admiration.) For example, General Motors is using the Internet to create positive memories in which the company assumes the character of the archetypal trusted advisor. Fidelity Investments presents the journey of financial planning as one full of opportunity and yet one where danger lurks. In both cases the discreet services of a trusted guide can help the investor become a hero.
- *Childhood Transformation.* Transformation involves moving from one state of being to another, with each state having both desirable and undesirable qualities. For example, children undergo transformation as they reach certain milestones, such as taking their first steps, realizing they can manipulate others, losing their first tooth, going to the first day of school, and so on. In archetypal terms, these transformations may involve struggle, defeat, and victory for the child and the parent. The childhood transformation journey has many touchpoints. One, food, is a central factor in young people's daily lives and overall development. Certain meals, such as breakfast and snacks, and specific food products and brands, such as Cheerios, are quietly relevant to the various milestones children reach. Breakfast becomes a setting and Cheerios a prop for the enactment of certain transfor-

mations. The challenge for a brand like Cheerios is to develop a story in which it becomes a reassuring "constant" for mothers as they experience the bittersweet feelings associated with the changes their children are experiencing—some of which are played out at mealtimes.

Like all core metaphors, archetypes are deeply embedded in every culture's social memory. They are imprinted in the minds of its individual members in multiple ways.[10] Moreover, they contain important cultural information that people retrieve in the form of stories. For example, the story of Little Red Riding Hood involves an archetypal journey. At least forty-eight different versions of this story exist around the world, each conveying a different twist appropriate to a particular time period, social setting, and goal of the storyteller. But all the versions tell the story of a nice person who ignores sage advice, gives in to temptation, suffers a near-fatal disaster, and is rescued through the intervention of an unexpected party.[11] In many accounts of their shopping experiences, consumers in France, Japan, and the United States described themselves in terms of Little Red Riding Hood's experiences without ever explicitly referencing this story. Companies can tell this powerful story, or various parts of it, in many ways. For example, General Motors' OnStar communication system assumes the part of the woodsman in Little Red Riding Hood as a rescuer in diverse but dangerous situations, some of which are brought on by the folly of the driver. For some adults, Mickey Mouse is described in emotional, metaphoric terms as a savior that helped them get through very trying times as a child.

Hallmark provides a good example of managers bringing memory, metaphor, and story together to help build more positive consumer experiences and a clearer statement of the firm's corporate vision. To serve certain consumer segments better, Hallmark's managers set out to understand more deeply how thoughts and feelings about motherhood are retrieved from memory and affect women's lives. Obviously, such a complex issue would inspire many accounts. In fact, each mother participating in the study told stories that were uniquely individual at one level and yet, at a deeper level, were in some way shared by other mothers. We can title one of these stories "Mother as a Role Model," a prominent archetype in leadership stories.

Table 10-1 describes some of the visual images that the interviewees brought to their metaphor-elicitation interview as initial metaphors expressing their thoughts and feelings about being a mom. The table contains comments that the mothers made as they explained their interpretation of the images. Through the use of visual images, the interviews enabled study participants to retrieve episodic, semantic, and procedural memories to express their thoughts and feelings. As you'll see, a particular picture may have initially represented one idea, but in

TABLE 10 - 1

The Mother as a Role Model Story

Initial Visual Metaphor	Verbatim Example
A colorful photograph of crudités and condiments—neatly arranged plates of fruits, vegetables, and spreads.	"[Kids] learn everything from you. They imitate how you talk, your facial expressions, your language. You're thrilled when they do something positive, but when they say something snotty, you go, 'Oh my God, they said that just the way I do.' You realize how much you impact their thoughts and feelings."
A simple photograph of five Lincoln pennies floating, seemingly rotating, against a white background.	"I'm very committed to racial integration and equality. My children have been very indoctrinated. My children are both fairly color blind. It's one of the things I'm very proud of. [It's a priority] that my children can walk through the world and know all different kinds of people and can communicate and there's not discrimination."
A small boy lying on his belly in the grass and examining several blades through a large magnifying glass, so that his eye appears larger than the rest of his face.	"You aim high in your own behavior because you are a role model for them. Being a good person is such a huge thing. It's made me a much better person because I want them to be that kind of person . . . that's the kind of stamp of quality I want to pass on to them."
Two young girls at school. One with blond hair and a light complexion sits cross-legged with a book in her lap and a smile on her face. She is listening to the other girl, who has two long dark braids and a darker complexion and is kneeling as she whispers into the first girl's ear.	"My kids are always watching me. I must be really cognizant of the choices I make and the manner in which I choose to conduct myself in every moment of my waking hours, because I'm under the microscope." "Say I'm in the car and I'm driving and somebody has just cut me off and chosen to flip me off. I could do the exact same thing. Or I can just take a big, deep breath and I can turn to my kids and say, boy, it seems like that person really has something on their mind that they're choosing to be really angry."

response to probing from the interviewers, participants uncovered other meanings that were not evident during a simple inspection of the picture.

Hallmark's managers and researchers, using their prior experience along with insights from the outside research team, identified several basic stories in the participants' comments. Each story generated several ideas for new products and services that Hallmark is developing to better address the realities of being a mother.

Memory, Story, and the Self

What we remember, *how* we remember, and *why* we remember depend largely on our sense of self, of who we are as individuals. We have many selves, which gives the opportunity to remember different things, in different ways, and for different reasons. These many differences connected with different selves provide managers with enormous opportunities for helping consumers create personally relevant stories about a brand or company.[12]

Ulric Neisser, a leader in cognitive psychology and memory research, offers a well-known illustration.[13] According to Neisser, we have an *ecological self;* that is, who we are in a particular physical setting. For example, the statement, "This is where I always shop . . ." expresses a person's ecological self from a marketing standpoint. We also have an *interpersonal self*—who we are when we interact with other people. "I always demand good service" expresses the person's interpersonal self. These two selves can differ markedly, and are present in all individuals from infancy onward.

But we have other selves as well. For example, through our *extended self,* we experience events in the present by remembering the past and anticipating the future. For example, we might express our extended self when we think about reliving a childhood experience through our own children, such as planning a trip to Disney World so that they can enjoy the same experience we did. Moreover, we have a *private self,* which responds to events and experiences in uniquely personal ways. We express this self when we tell others, for example, "You can't even begin to imagine how I. . . ."

Finally, we have a *conceptual self*. Perhaps the most introspective of our selves, our conceptual self is aware of our other selves. It recognizes itself in products and services as if these were inner mirrors. Consumers will more likely accept offerings that are consonant with their conceptual selves than those that are incongruous. Our conceptual self causes us to reject a chintzy piece of furniture because it doesn't want to associate itself with such a symbol of cheapness. This self also reflects and regenerates itself in the sense that it wants other people's selves to resemble it. This is why mothers say things like, "I take my children shopping now and then to teach them the value of things," or why we actively give advice: "If I were you, then I'd go for the pink one."

All of our selves—ecological, interpersonal, extended, private, and conceptual—combine to provide a kind of container for our many different memories. Memories with different products and services involve one or more of these selves. Marketers must understand which self is likely involved in particular situations for their offerings. The story crafted for using a product or service in a particular situation must reflect the appropriate self. Alternatively, the portrayal of a product must accommodate multiple selves. A Nestlé advertisement for confectionary in Europe represents an upscale box of chocolates as a gift to one's self to leverage the indulgent dimension of our conceptual self and also a gift to give others, appealing to the social norms relevant to the ecological self as well as expressing the interpersonal self.

Implications for Advertising

We discussed in chapter 3 that the human brain spends most of its time communicating with itself. One of these "conversations" involves the construction of stories—the bringing together of thought and emotion through various brain structures.[14] To build stories, the brain distributes stimuli (such as product designs, purchase settings, marketing communications, and other cues) from the thalamus to the cortex and the amygdala. Whereas the cortex is associated with thought, the amygdala (in partnership with the thalamus) is associated with emotion and unconscious processes in the brain. (See figure 10-1.)

FIGURE 10-1

The Limbic Pathway

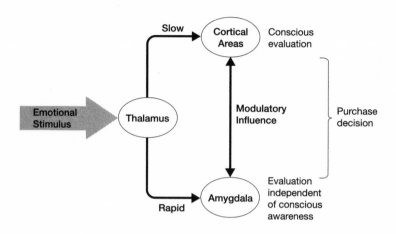

The cortex modulates emotional responses from the amygdala. However, in the case of storytelling, feelings arising in the amygdala also further influence the cortex. Thus emotions and thoughts stimulate and shape one another much as children sitting around a campfire do when they tell "true" stories about frightening events that allegedly happened nearby. The crackling fire, deepening darkness, and mysterious night noises strengthen the drama of the stories, just as marketing cues can strengthen the meaning and impact of a brand's stories created by consumers. However, there is something important missing from figure 10-1 that requires us to revisit the topic of consensus maps.

Consensus maps such as that shown in figure 10-2 involving Nestlé Crunch Bars tell a story about a brand, company, or situation that is shared by consumers in a market segment.

The map in figure 10-2 contains just a few of the overall thoughts about the role that Nestlé Crunch Bars play in certain consumers' lives. These thoughts involve valued memories, physical locations, and sensory qualities, among other things. Such consensus maps represent diagrams of stories that consumers create. The constructs, or thoughts, in a map represent the key "characters" or players in the story, with some more influential than others. The associations *among* these constructs

FIGURE 10-2

Nestlé Crunch Bar Submap

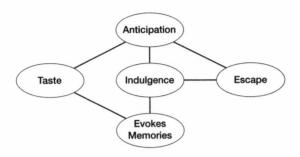

become the story consumers tell—that is, the memory they retain—about Nestlé Crunch Bars. As we've seen, researchers can learn of these stories by helping consumers generate metaphor-rich narratives. The true *character* of a thought emerges through its connections with other thoughts. Clusters of directly connected constructs are often embodied in deep metaphors or archetypes. For example, in the Nestlé consensus map, the "true" character of all the constructs—"anticipation," "memories," and "escape"—is captured by the deep metaphor of time. That is, "anticipation" is forward looking, "memory" is backward looking, and "escape" focuses on the present. Simple definitions of the constructs provide their characterization.

Consensus maps play a special role, as shown in figure 10-3. Before marketing stimuli travel to the thalamus and from there to the cortex and amygdala, they are filtered through a consensus map.

As discussed elsewhere, consensus maps are filters and routers; they cause us to attend to information relevant to the constructs they contain. Moreover, as one construct, or thought, within a consensus map is activated, it can stimulate another thought within that same map, or even in a related map. Whenever a new thought is activated, it primes yet additional thoughts. Thus information engaged by one thought, such as "anticipation," is routed to "indulgence" for further assessment. In this way, the brain activates an entire story. An individual may be aware of some parts of the resulting story, but other parts of the story will remain buried in the unconscious mind. The metaphor-elicitation

FIGURE 10-3

Consensus Maps Filter Marketing Stimuli

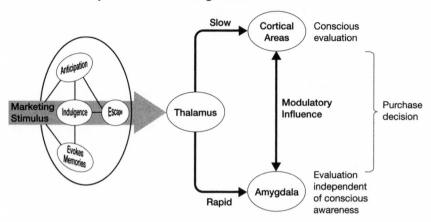

process described in the appendix (to chapter 4) is a way of surfacing the conscious and unconscious elements of consumers' stories and representing them diagrammatically as a consensus map.

The neurological processes behind storytelling have major implications for marketers. Traditionally, marketers who want to understand consumers' responses to advertising ask questions such as:

- What do people like (or dislike) about the ad?
- What are consumers' attitudes toward the ad?
- What do they remember about the ad?
- What did consumers learn about the brand from the ad?
- What are consumers' attitudes toward the brand?
- Did the ad influence consumers' intention to buy the brand?

These questions may generate valuable information. However, they reflect the belief that marketers can "inject" stories about a brand into consumers through advertising. None of these questions would reveal the stories that *consumers create in response* to an ad. Nor do they examine whether consumers' stories match the meaning that the advertiser *intended* to convey. Furthermore, an accurate replay of an ad's message doesn't mean that the consumer feels it is relevant, believes it, or even understands it.

In creating stories about brands based on advertising, consumers draw on the very elements that constitute memory: past experiences with the brand, existing thoughts and feelings about it, the reasons for having an interest in the brand, and the cues available about the brand from nonmarketing sources. All of these factors are present in the consensus map that is activated when a consumer is exposed to an ad or thinks of the brand for other reasons. Thus, marketers must ask questions that shed light on how those factors are working *together* to form the bundle of connected thoughts and feelings in a consensus map. (Recall from the preface that a consensus map is simply a way of showing the connections among bundles of neurons that constitute human thought and feelings.)

John Grant, author of *After Image,* provides an insightful view of the role of storytelling in today's consumers' lives, described in box 10-2.

So how can marketers leverage the power of storytelling in their efforts to understand and better serve consumers? Jerry Olson, the Strong Professor of Marketing at Pennsylvania State University and managing partner of Olson Zaltman Associates, has designed a way to use storytelling and metaphor to evaluate the effectiveness of an advertisement and make any necessary changes. In contrast to typical methods, Olson's metaphor-based approach includes asking such questions as:

- What meanings about the brand do consumers acquire *and* generate?
- What meanings do consumers form about the product category?
- How much of the resulting meaning can we attribute to the ad content and how much to consumers' own frames of reference?
- Do consumers form the same meanings specified in the marketing strategy?
- Does the ad permit different consumer segments to create different stories with the same underlying, deep metaphor?
- Are these multiple stories consistent or inconsistent with the strategy's intended message?
- How readily do consumers form the meanings and stories? How much effort do they expend to do so?

Box 10-2

Myth and Story and Marketing

Stories compress information into readily useable forms. They deal with the most typical dilemmas in human life. Contrast this format with the book of instructions required for a video player—a small fragment of daily life—and you can see, by contrast, how economical stories are in passing information.

The word *myth* suggests the passing down of the wisdom of ancestors—wisdom being simply "knowing how to act" in any given situation. But not all myths are archaic. Modern myths include safe sex, political correctness, and the "New Man." These are spontaneous modern forms that tell us how to act—spontaneous because they have formed in reaction to new social contexts.

Our current time is unique in that the majority of memes (culturally transmitted ideas) come from our peers and not our ancestors; we live in a "post-tradition and custom" society. Many factors drive this sudden imbalance toward the new: education and the explosion of available information; the pace of technological, social, and commercial change; the rapid intermingling of regional cultures; and many other twenty-first-century influences.

The net result? We wake up every day in a world where we aren't quite sure how to live. This fundamental uncertainty embraces trivial lifestyle decisions such as what to eat for breakfast and what to wear, as well as important issues like how to be a man (or woman). Indeed, the "little" issues are in many senses more fundamental, as anthropologists often find. Once you have decided to eat fruit for breakfast and groom yourself in soft modern casuals, you are on the way to being a "New Man"!

These uncertainties, great and small, create the ideal conditions for building brands. Brands are units of social consumption. We've known for some time that we mostly buy the "how to live" component, with the actual object or service thrown in. Brands that exploit this

(continued)

ambiguity create packets of meaning—in the form of stories—which we can apply to our lives. But that is a 180-degree shift in the role of brands. This about-face is one of the central battlegrounds between traditional and new marketing practices.

The old view of brand marketing, developed in the 1950s and still widely practiced and believed, concerns attaching existing social meanings to products and services. *This cigarette makes you rugged and individual "like a cowboy." That newspaper makes you educated, liberal, and a little "bohemian."* The following diagram shows this flow of cultural logic:

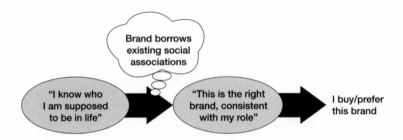

Stories in this marketing context have less potential to carry the social meanings in an engaging form; they are merely advertising devices. As John Grant says:

> Most of the advertising that I did in the 1980s and early 1990s followed this formula. For example, our Volkswagen advertising used cameos: *the guy who lost his shirt at the casino, the woman who stormed out on her sugar daddy.* All to carry the idea of the heroic underdog; the VW GTi as a poor man's Porsche.

Increasingly, people are no longer in the luxurious position of being certain about their life, role, and identity. We change careers five times in a lifetime and change social relationships, homes, and social roles

perhaps even more often. We are constantly struggling to find meaningful ways to live. *Brands can now affect consumers as surrogate tra-
ditions*. (See the following diagram.)

The role of stories, including myths, then becomes central. They
are not mere advertising devices to carry fixed meanings. They are
the meaning itself. They are *real*. That's why approaches like the
metaphor-elicitation technique are so valuable. To *act* at a deeper level
of cultural meaning, you first must *look* at the world on that level.

For example, consider the Volkswagen Bug—one of the most
successful product launches (or, to be more accurate, relaunches) of
the 1990s. The story of this car is that it's what open-collar workers
in the United States drove—the geek-mobile. That's not an advertising confection. It really was the car of choice in places like San Francisco and Seattle. If that's the life you chose, then this VW was the car
for you.

Sometimes an actual story establishes the brand. For example:

- Tourism in Scotland got a considerable boost following the success of the movie *Trainspotting*.

- IBM's Deep Blue established credentials for personal (yet powerful) computing.

- Bulgari watches were popularized by Fay Weldon's novel, *The Bulgari Connection*.

Source: Used by permission of John Grant.

Different firms implement Olson's approach differently, depending on the goal of the advertising. However, analysis of the answers to the above questions usually focuses on:

- the richness and diversity of the stories consumers generate based on the ad
- the stories' fit with the ad's intended message or strategic goal
- the ease with which consumers generate their stories
- the uniqueness of the stories relative to the particular brand
- the degree to which the stories are more related to product category or to the brand

We can use this approach in developing advertising and in evaluating alternative executions. For example, exploring consumers' stories in the *advertising conceptualization* stage (prior to preparation of the creative brief) can later help creative staffs anticipate consumers' reactions to the ideas and concepts that may appear in the ad. Consumers' stories are also valuable during the *ad-building stage,* when advertisers are considering potential content such as tag lines or particular symbols. Storytelling has also proven useful during the *ad-production* phase, when creative staffs develop partially completed communications such as print mock-ups, rough cuts, storyboards, or animatics. Finally, storytelling is valuable when evaluating competitors' efforts.

Several assumptions underlie this approach, all of which have solid grounding in literary studies and in neuroscience, and two of them merit special attention. First, as we discussed in chapter 9, the meaning of a brand resides in the minds of *consumers,* not in the physical brand itself or in advertising about the brand. That is, consumers—not managers—ultimately create brand meaning. This meaning emerges from the interaction between consumers' consensus maps and their brand experiences—including exposure to brand attributes, product performance, and advertising. Marketers can influence the meaning that consumers create by providing critical raw materials in the form of icons, metaphors, and phrases. However, they cannot *control* consumers' manufacture of meaning.

Second, a brand's meaning exists in several forms in consumers' memories. Some of the meaning is "at the surface"; that is, consumers can easily bring it to their consciousness. Such surface meaning may include the physical attributes of the brand ("Cummins marine engines are designed for accessibility during routine maintenance") or the functional consequences of using the product ("These engines are less expensive to repair"). But further brand meaning exists at deeper, more personal levels. This deeper meaning includes knowledge about the psychological consequences of a brand ("These engines make me feel more secure in bad seas") or the social consequences ("The engine noise doesn't intrude into our conversations"). Finally, even deeper meanings involve consumers' core values and life goals ("This engine will take me anywhere; it gives me a sense of independence and freedom").

Box 10-3 depicts a possible story that may underly the world's leading brand, Coca-Cola. The story introduces and illustrates the terms *characterization, character, events, archetype,* and *controlling idea*—all of which marketers must understand to create effective stories.

Consumers develop coherent stories about brands, and those stories are encoded in their memories. These stories may change owing to actions taken by managers, influences from other consumers, and, of course, consumers' new experiences or reassessments of prior experiences.

Consumers use a variety of "data" to develop their stories, including—but hardly limited to—the product and promotional cues provided by marketers. Consumers' stories also serve as metaphors for their experiences. These metaphors may be deep; for example, they may reflect universal themes such as balance, journey, and transformation. They may also be specific and expressed by references such as "got ripped off," "received a helping hand," or "it lit a fire under me."

Consumers often share the same *basic* story, though with individual variations. A consensus map depicts the essential thoughts and feelings in a story and how they are stitched together in memory. These common elements represent the *archetypal* story of a brand. Marketers can understand these stories by eliciting surface-level and core metaphors from consumers—thereby shining a light into consumers' unconscious, but essential, thoughts held deep in memory.

Box 10-3

A Possible Brand Story of Coca-Cola

Characterizations are how a product or brand is described in coherent ways, such as through formal marketing communications or word-of-mouth, and in the consumer's own mind. Consumers in several countries describe Coca-Cola in ways that suggest several consistent dualities. For instance, people characterize the beverage as both American and universal, as providing both energy and calm, as old but somehow contemporary, as appropriate for young people as well as older people, as ideal for enjoying alone or with friends, and so on. Strategy consultant Jack Carew suggests that brands grow even more powerful when consumers characterize them through qualities that, although they appear to conflict, are in fact resolved by some higher order of thought. For example, the higher-order notion that Coke is "worldly" brings together the seemingly contrasting constructs "American" and "universal."

But a characterization is not the same as *character*. The characterization is a *description* of the brand, while *character* is what a brand *does*. For example, Coca-Cola's character is revealed when it seemingly "chooses" to do one or another thing for us, such as quench our thirst or refresh us. In effect, a brand's character senses our needs. It expresses the element of a duality that is most appropriate for the moment, such as "relax alone" versus "be energized with friends." Character, then, emerges during the moment of consumption. A complex brand, one that has many dualities, has a multifaceted character. Thus the same consumer may experience it in very different ways at different times, and different consumers may experience it in the same way. Of course, brands don't actively "choose" how to best please consumers. Rather, the "choice" is a function of the salient desire of the consumer, *as if* the brand reads their mind and provides the appropriate satisfaction. The more complex the brand, the greater the range of choices that a manager can communicate about that brand.

Deep character is revealed when a "choice" conflicts with a brand's characterization. Traditional marketing communications characterized Coca-Cola as refreshing, energizing, and social, qualities that align with the way many consumers experience the beverage. Yet on the surface, these characterizations also conflict with other qualities that are equally important and appealing to frequent Coke drinkers.

Characterization and character are only two parts of a brand's story. *Events* constitute key moments in the life of a brand's character. By selecting key events and portraying them in an ad, a firm provides the framework for the story that it wants consumers to create about the brand.

Finally, all stories have a *controlling idea,* which communicates the value of the brand and a reason for that value. The controlling idea becomes more powerful when the brand has many different kinds of value at different times. The controlling idea behind Coke may be that it transforms. It replenishes energy (a change in value) when a consumer's energy diminishes; it rehydrates when the consumer is dehydrated; it relaxes and calms when the person feels tense; it makes consumers feel more comfortable with other people; it helps people to escape within themselves while remaining in the presence of others. Again, these changes in value stem from the combination of the product's qualities and consumers' immediate needs or desires.

Source: Used with permission of The Coca-Cola Company.

Part III

Thinking Differently and Deeply

Chapter Eleven

Crowbars for Creative Thinking

The difference between creating an idea and imitating someone else's is the difference between a Picasso and graffiti.

The difference between a Picasso and graffiti is the difference between disciplined imagination and vacuous thought.

TAPPING INTO CONSUMERS' unconscious thinking is only the first step to designing more effective marketing communications, products, and services. Managers must also understand *their own* unconscious thoughts about consumers and marketing—and think in entirely new, interdisciplinary ways. To that end, we shift our focus from consumers' thinking to that of marketing professionals and managers.

Managers who want to consider new ideas or reshape their own thinking face four challenges. Specifically, they must:

- create or identify new ideas themselves
- understand new ideas that they encounter
- critically examine those ideas
- leverage them imaginatively in their own work

Can you meet those four challenges? If so, congratulations: You possess the curiosity, the capacity to wonder, and the willingness to modify your current mental inventory, all vital to breakthrough thinking. Since ideas are the "coin of the marketing realm," these abilities distinguish exceptional managers from the merely good ones. Several mental exercises can help managers kick some old habits and think in new ways. Alone, however, they won't ensure the highest-quality thinking. Managers must also draw on the leading-edge knowledge from other disciplines.

Four Assumptions

How many times have we heard that "managers must think out of the box to excel in business today"? How often have we nodded in agreement? But consider the following four propositions.

Imaginative Thought and Routine Thought Involve the Same Cognitive Processes

Many people believe that creative thinking requires a special, almost magical cognitive process. But little evidence supports this belief.[1] Almost everyone can think more imaginatively by relying on visual imagery and metaphor, which are central to all thought.[2] Indeed, we all possess the mental tools for creative thought, even if we don't use them effectively. That's not to say that everyone can think imaginatively in any endeavor, and that we're equally creative. We aren't. People who have accumulated many diverse experiences have the highest capacity for creativity. Likewise, exposure to a wealth of ideas enables people to surface, test, and (if useful) change their existing thought processes more easily.

Organizational Environments Are Critical Elements in Managers' Creative Capacities

Organizational climates and workplace attitudes can strengthen or hinder a marketer's creative thinking. In fact, the organizational climate within which our imaginations operate matters more than our individual imaginations. That climate largely determines whether or not we can form, surface, and pursue creative ideas that can be put into practice effectively. Special programs or books designed to encourage innovative thought can't succeed unless a company explicitly values originality. Yet too few companies genuinely welcome creativity. It challenges the comfort zones of established thought and threatens the security of familiar practices. When asked whether they'd send their child to a school that supported creative thinking to the same degree their company does, 80 percent of managers answered no.

The good news is that companies *can* implement specific practices to stimulate creative thinking among managers. For example:

- For its internal consulting group, the J. Walter Thompson advertising agency deliberately hires people with graduate degrees in disciplines as diverse as molecular biology, mathematics, engineering, and nineteenth-century French literature. New hires also have broad work experience ranging from investment banking and brand management to strategic planning and advertising. The crosscurrents of these perspectives enable employees to address client issues in fresh ways. All that creativity pays big dividends: The agency's billings doubled in less than three years after it formed this group.

- Every month, Larry Huston, a Procter & Gamble vice president and lead creative director, deliberately introduces his staff to at least one new idea from nonbusiness sources to encourage unfamiliar perspectives on the firm's current best practices. Huston poses a vital question whenever he introduces a new idea: "What would change if we acted on this idea?" The question often generates useful answers. Most important, it encourages his staff to see the world differently, open themselves to change, and consider even more new ideas.

- William McComb, president of McNeil Consumer Healthcare, periodically bans the "business as usual" ideas that crop up in business-plan review meetings. His approach stimulates his colleagues to break from routine quickly when they encounter situations where "the usual" doesn't help. This quick, fresh thinking enables these managers to find better solutions *and* save considerable time and money.

In addition to generating breakthrough ideas, these practices engender a positive climate of *eager restlessness* among key personnel. According to Vincent P. Barabba, head of Corporate Planning and Knowledge

Development at General Motors, this quality rouses managers to wonder each day where the next opportunity to improve will emerge. It also stimulates people to think differently and to enrich existing ideas with new ones. Even when eager restlessness doesn't yield a tangible outcome, it transforms managers' state of mind. People begin expecting more, and "good enough" no longer is.

Managers Can Find More Knowledge about Consumers *outside* the Marketing Discipline

By any measure, traditional market research provides only a small part of available knowledge about consumers. The social and biological sciences and humanities devote appreciably more human and financial resources to knowledge development than the marketing profession does. Fortunately for marketers, much of the work in the nonmarketing areas relates directly to marketing, and managers with both the curiosity and the time to explore it can do so for free. Thus, another crowbar is the willingness to tour other fields and the ability to find relevance where others see triviality.

Shared Themes Connect Highly Diverse Areas of Study

Pulitzer Prize–winning author and scientist E. O. Wilson introduced the term "consilience" to describe the unity of knowledge that connects seemingly unrelated disciplines.[3] For example, many topics that interest visual artists also engage neuroscientists; problems that attract sociologists also pique linguists and evolutionary biologists; and certain matters of theological significance captivate mathematicians and physicists alike. Likewise, mathematical models of physical events shed light on many sociological phenomena. Particularly exciting is that, the more overlap among multiple disciplines, the more valuable those disciplines become for marketing managers. Rob Scalea, chief strategy officer at the J. Walter Thompson advertising agency, calls the application of ideas from these overlapping fields "combination therapy," or the orchestration of multiple but well-coordinated attacks on a problem.

To spur creative thinking, managers must dare to differ and play constructively with ideas. They must blend knowledge from seemingly unrelated disciplines with knowledge accumulated through market research and their everyday professional experience. Only then can they free themselves from conventional habits of thought.

Breaking Out of the Box

The *breaking-out-of-the-box* metaphor suggests freedom and escape but ignores the reality that *we inevitably break from one cubicle into another one*. Change-minded managers must become "honest cat burglars," not simply abandoning their ways of thinking and slinking aimlessly about the world of ideas, but clawing different boxes, gleaning new knowledge, and playing with it.

As Stephan Haeckel notes, "People in highly unpredictable environments can survive if they are skilled at invoking metaphors and experience to impose pattern on signals that make no sense in the current context. These kinds of people excel in high-performance teams, not on continuous improvement projects." Box 11-1 describes one of these creative thinkers.

Even managers who value new boxes may want to return to old ones. This recidivism sometimes makes good sense. After all, our established ways of thought have brought us a long way. However, we tend to flounder in familiarity and fail to venture out frequently and extensively enough to collect worthwhile ideas. We can't redecorate our primary cognitive lodging. So, to escape this box, we must wander often but acknowledge that not every expedition will prove valuable.

How to Think Creatively

How we think is more personal than *what* we think. That's why most managers spend considerable money to validate an existing idea and even more money before changing what and how they think about it. After observing some of the most imaginative executives, I've distilled the following ten theories-in-use to pry us loose of conventional thinking when it proves ineffective.

Box 11-1

Meaning from Apparent Noise

In the 1960s, IBM sales rep Bob Hippe became a legend by closing an order for IBM's largest scientific computer *without* using the company's fabled "sales cycle" process that was drilled into all IBM sales trainees during their first eighteen months with the firm.

When Hippe showed up at Boeing in Wichita to meet with the company's chief engineer, he found his customer's office in turmoil. Engineers and scientists scurried in and out of the chief engineer's office, shouting and waving designs, brandishing yellow pads covered by partial differential equations. The secretary told Hippe that the chief engineer couldn't see him that day because of a major crisis: The mechanism for weighing airplanes had broken down, meaning that no B-52s at Wichita could take off. (Federal regulations required that planes be weighed before every flight.)

Without hesitation, Hippe asked the secretary for thirty minutes—plus some string, a ruler, and a tire gauge—to show the chief engineer another method to weigh a B-52. The secretary immediately ushered him in. Hippe took these tools to the first B-52 on the tarmac. He wrapped the string around one of the tire pods, used the tire gauge to determine the pressure in each tire in the pod, calculated the average pressure of the tires in that pod, and multiplied the pressure times the width and length of the rectangle formed by the string. He repeated this procedure for all the pods and totaled the results to arrive at the bomber's weight.

Like everyone who took high school physics, Hippe knew that weight is a force, and that force equals pressure times area. But only Hippe applied that knowledge successfully to the challenge at hand without state-of-the-art technology. He identified a pattern in an abstraction learned years earlier in school and saw a new way to apply it—during a sales call. He quickly converted apparent "noise" (seemingly irrelevant information) into new, valuable meaning, an essential information-management and marketing function.

People like Bob Hippe can mitigate efforts fraught with uncertainty. Indeed, the U.S. armed services use extensive screening processes to identify individuals with this kind of creative aptitude. Fighter pilots and recruits in high-performance teams can turn apparent noise into meaning more usefully than other people.

Source: Courtesy of Stephan Haeckel, the IBM Corporation. See also Stephan Haeckel, "Managing Knowledge in Adaptive Enterprises," in Charles Despres and Daniele Chauvel, eds., *Knowledge Horizons: The Present and Promise of Knowledge Management* (New York: Butterworth-Heinemann, 2000).

Unlike the abundance of books, twelve-step programs, and consultants offering formulae for fleeing our worn cognitive hampers, these practices result from intense, conscious effort and experimentation.

1. Favor restlessness over contentment.
2. Wonder about the cow's crumpled horn.
3. Play with accidental data.
4. View conclusions as beginnings.
5. Get outdated.
6. Stop squeezing the same baby chicken.
7. Nurture cool passion.
8. Have the courage of *your* convictions, not someone else's.
9. Ask generic questions.
10. Avoid premature dismissal.

Set any initial skepticism aside, but don't follow these practices blindly. Rather, as Harvard Business School professor Max Bazerman suggests, evaluate each one's appropriateness to your own situation and adapt the rules to your own style.[4]

Favor Restlessness Over Contentment

Contentment feels good but fosters little innovation. It doesn't motivate us to adjust techniques or spot cracks in the status quo. Consider the companies that favor restlessness over contentment.

- Motorola, for example, realized that its device designed to allow business travelers to summon help in isolated parking lots or hotel corridors could benefit its employees working late at night. If Motorola hadn't worried about its employees' safety, then it wouldn't have applied its consumer research findings to its internal safety concerns. Thus its eager restiveness led it to discover important new uses for existing technologies.

- Procter & Gamble, through metaphor-elicitation research, discovered not only what consumers need in household and personal care products, but also how they want those needs met. By developing detailed consensus maps (see chapter 7) from interviews with individual consumers and then finding similarities among these maps, P&G has honed its product-development skills and significantly increased its success in new-product development.

- To cultivate restlessness, a senior manager in a global electronics and home-appliance firm occasionally asks her staff to replace terms such as "loyalty," "brand equity," or "consumer need" in business plans, memos, and other reports with alternative terms. In their search for alternatives, managers frequently reexamine the very meaning of the forbidden term, thereby discovering its limitations as well as its possible new meanings. For example, in rewriting a memo without the word "incentive" (the memo's central subject!), one manager discovered that the company's consumer-incentive programs had ignored intrinsic rewards, such as shoppers' feelings of heroism, when exploiting an incentive.

- A senior vice president at Hallmark requires her staff to summarize research by citing the single most important question left unanswered. This policy, she believes, keeps people from developing the false sense of security that large volumes of statistical data often engender. The strategy also enables her staff to pose important questions without criticizing the researchers and opens them more to the unknown, where tomorrow's answers await.

These efforts inspire managers to reexamine patterns of thought and frequently used meanings and underlying assumptions. Without induced restlessness, Starbucks would probably never have developed the concept of a caffeine-induced oasis that has contributed so much to the chain's growth and success.

Wonder about the Cow's Crumpled Horn

Have you ever read *This Is the House That Jack Built,* the story of the cow with the crumpled horn that tossed the dog, that worried the cat, that ate the rat, and so on? If so, you may have wondered, Who crumpled the cow's horn? Why? How did it happen? Does the cow know about it? Why just that one horn? How would *I* crumple a cow's horn? What will the cow think? Does it hurt?

Our second crowbar is a variation on these musings. The key question is: What irregularity can we create in a standard way of thinking or in a standard practice to wrinkle the issue at hand? Our brains are wired to perceive irregularities and to wonder about their origins, so this question is powerful.[5] Managers automatically develop causal explanations for irregularities.[6] Let's face it: A crushed can (or a crumpled horn) catches our eye more than the undamaged one next to it. Irregularities interest us. Their mysterious past begs an explanation or the creation of stories to answer the question, What transformed the object from one state to another?

An irregular or aberrant datum—a high sales statistic for a particular year or a bizarre reason for enjoying Cheerios—can generate valuable new product ideas, advertising campaigns, and marketing-mix strategies. For example, while examining scanner data, a Home Depot executive noticed an unusually high response to a sales promotion in a store that ordinarily performed like other stores in the same region. Rather than dismiss the response as a random event, she visited the store during the promotion and searched for clues to the aberrance. She noticed that the featured product—a home-plumbing tool kit—was displayed next to certain bathroom fixtures also on sale. Further study revealed that when both products were on sale and placed next to one another in the store, customers snapped up significantly more of them than when the two were displayed separately. Because noncompeting manufacturers offered the two products, the companies coordinated their respective sales promotions—to everyone's benefit.

The ability to detect anomalies evolved early in our species for survival.[7] It allowed early hunters to spot weak or vulnerable prey and spared them from becoming prey themselves. We still watch for anomalies in people's facial expressions to detect their emotions and predict their actions. However, managers rarely exercise this ability in consumer research. Instead, they engage in the questionable practice of discarding or discounting so-called outlier information—data that fall outside an established pattern. Why? Because researchers consider outlier data distracting. By deleting it, they can more easily focus on the established pattern. Thus, they miss outlying information that could help them design new products or attention-getting advertising messages.

Managers must detect both anomalies and patterns. For example, Budget Rent a Car analyzed its fleet diversity, the variety in its models of rental cars. Managers and researchers alike assumed that consumers didn't value fleet diversity. At the same time, the consumer vehicle market revealed a strong attraction to vehicle diversity. Budget's executives ignored this inconsistency until their advertising agency pointed it out. Budget then redefined its concept of fleet diversity, and in just five weeks, saw an uptick in sales for the first time in a decade.

Play with Accidental Data

Look at the following image. What do you see?

The answer appears at the end of this chapter. Even if you guessed correctly, you would likely have identified the answer more quickly with the same amount of information as above, but in the form shown in the middle image at the end of the chapter. Both incomplete images of the object contain the same total length of lines, that is, the same exact amount of information. But the incomplete information in the middle version is *nonaccidental, that is, it is configured in a way that favors a correct interpretation* whereas the information in the image shown earlier is *accidental* or random. The nonaccidental form of information enables us to close the spaces in the figure and recognize the object.

Unfortunately, consumers present data to marketers in the accidental form. That is, they haven't conveniently arranged cues about their innermost thoughts and feelings so that managers can easily "fill in the blanks." When managers encounter information in accidental form, they must ask: "How can I add new 'lines' or rearrange those already there to surface new meanings from these data?" This creative thinking requires active play with the data.

At an East Coast U.S. hospital, a staff member engaged in such play by collecting accidental data—and finding magic medicine in it. She noted that patients on one side of a floor were discharged earlier than those on the opposite side, even though room assignments were random. Staffers had observed this pattern for years. But this staff member became curious—and playful. She searched available hospital data to explain the mysterious pattern. Her curiosity intensified when she failed to find any explanation. She then looked beyond the hospital. By observing the grounds outside, she discovered that the rooms of patients with shorter hospital stays overlooked an attractive park—while patients with longer stays overlooked an immense parking lot. This observation led her to the idea of "therapeutic imaging," viewing appealing scenes to aid patients' recovery. A major company specializing in imagery explored this idea further and developed a new business.

View Conclusions as Beginnings

Managers and researchers often think of themselves as detectives solving "crimes"; that is, drawing conclusions about marketplace mysteries. This orientation offers some benefits but also has serious limitations. Specifically, to formulate new questions and think outside the box, managers must not only solve "crimes" but also commit them— that is, create entirely new mysteries. They must treat conclusions as beginnings.

This attitude doesn't come naturally to everyone. Real detectives prefer closing cases, not opening new ones, and they hate reopening closed ones. In fact, "getting closure" has more positive connotations than "starting over" or "back to the beginning." This propensity to conclude can severely damage a marketer's ability to think differently.

Like young readers who wonder about the cow's crumpled horn, managers must actively seek new questions rather than answer existing ones. Research findings—solved crimes—are great for formulating new interrogations. For example, marketers can ask some simple preliminary questions:

- What additional information would make me mistrust this conclusion?
- Am I sure that this information isn't relevant to my work? How might it apply?
- What question (and subsequent answer) would disrupt or corrupt these results?
- What do these findings lack or miss altogether? How should I further interrogate the data?
- Have I questioned the results deeply enough to unearth all their secrets?

How does this crowbar work? Suppose some new evidence suggests that a consumer incentive program sparks repeat patronage. In such a case, the program manager could simply continue the program. However, by treating the evidence as a *starting* point, that same manager could create questions to reveal what the program is concealing. Answers to those questions might lead to insights for generating greater profits or better incentive plans.

This form of creative thinking can lead to significant benefits. Christine Smith, former director of marketing for Futuredontics, noticed a lack of data in focus groups about the dental office waiting-room experience. She wondered about the data's silence on this topic and decided to use metaphor-elicitation interviews to explore the topic more deeply. As it turned out, the waiting-room experience—with its scary, behind-closed-doors noises and odors—powerfully discouraged people from visiting their dentists. Because of the additional study, several dentists added extra insulation to their doors and placed fresh flowers in the waiting room to improve the waiting experience. The result? Patients visited them more frequently.

Get Outdated

Children practice a principle that (to them) seems to make perfect sense: "If it ain't broke, then break it." This attitude is such an intrinsic part of being a kid that there's probably a special gene for it. However, as children develop, powerful socialization processes and organizational routines convert that rule to "If it ain't broke, then don't monkey with it." Besides, busy marketing managers usually have enough broken things to fix in a day's work. But sometimes breaking something makes sense, like challenging a prevailing idea or overhauling an existing process—even if that something functions adequately.

If you simply can't break something that's working fine, then consider this compromise: Outdate the existing (and functional) idea or process. That is, ask yourself, "How can I make what I currently know and do look out of date or old-fashioned as soon as possible?" The question focuses on making progress rather than celebrating the status quo. It encourages insightful connections among seemingly irrelevant ideas and current practices.

The inspiration to outdate or break a current effort sometimes comes from unlikely sources, as the following examples illustrate.

- At Ford Motor Company, a manager responsible for a customer-loyalty program used an article that she'd read in a doctor's waiting room to improve her already successful program. The article described social bonding among nonhuman primates, a subject that most managers might ignore. How would the loyalty program look if it leveraged the idea about nonhuman primate grooming? This question eventually inspired the company to experiment with grooming concepts relative to consumer car care. Early results suggest that consumer loyalty to Ford's vehicles has begun to intensify.
- Jeffrey Hartley of the design staff at General Motors leads a similar program, which has helped the company find new ways to get designers and consumers working together much earlier in the vehicle-design process. See box 11-2.

Box 11-2

Getting Close to Customers at General Motors

Dr. Jeffrey Hartley, a psychologist and manager of Brand Character and Theme Research at General Motors, has established local panels of customers to ensure that GM designers and marketers get to know customers deeply through repeated, direct interactions. In this way, he says:

> We avoid the trap of a one-way mirror in which someone else asks our questions. [Instead,] we visit with panel members on several occasions, asking some questions that are obvious and some that are quite relevant but have only occurred to us by our having observed consumers' choices over a period of a year. These important questions and resulting insights would otherwise have been missed if we had only brief and shallow encounters with customers.
>
> At first glance the goal of knowing your customers—seeing the world through their eyes—seems daunting. After all, how well can you see through your spouse's eyes? But through repeated interactions between our personnel and our customers, we build trust and understanding—not possible in focus groups, especially for tacit information. We don't just try to find out what customers want; we try to impress upon them what our world is like, and what decisions we must make. Then they are better equipped to help us delight them.

GM has established such a panel for its Saturn Brand Character Studio. To qualify for the panel, people participate in multiple face-to-face interviews in which researchers explore their values and their emotional connections with their vehicle. As it turns out, Saturn owners have a sense of community and care greatly about the common good and needs of others. They reflect these values in their concern for the safety and comfort of their passengers—as important to them as their own safety and comfort. Saturn owners tend to have an optimistic outlook yet realize that life also brings hardship and challenge. They are emotionally stable, secure within themselves, and face life with a positive attitude. They are also self-confident and feel in control. They want to lead a well-balanced, happy life.

Understanding such values and characteristics helps GM explore its customers' vehicle-ownership experiences more deeply. Panel members become wellsprings of valuable insight. For example, recounts Hartley:

> We paired panel members up with Saturn design and marketing people and sent them to the Detroit auto show to talk about what vehicles caught their eye and why. Again, this was informal, and the dialogue [notice the use of *dialogue,* not *interrogation*] was fluid and two way, with our people explaining why a certain feature was put on a vehicle, even if it was not a GM car. In another event, we had panel members select products which communicated optimism (since this was a key customer and Saturn value). Consumers discussed these images and products with our people one on one. Designers and marketers then understood—directly from customers—what makes a product seem optimistic.

The design and marketing staffs who work with panel members become privy to Saturn customers' most emotional memories. The more they get to know these customers by listening to their recollections, the more committed they are to serving customer needs. As one manager explains:

> It is easy to forget or ignore a meeting you had from 9:00 to 10:00 A.M. on Monday where you receive a debrief about what your customers are like. But you can't ignore dozens of emotionally saturated episodes with real people—people you know personally and can easily picture in your mind's eye and hear in your mind's ear. Sitting back at your desk at work, you might feel discomfort if you decide against what John or Elizabeth would want.

(continued)

It is also interesting that different designers and managers tender different interpretations of what panel members express, which they explore before arriving at a common understanding. When they can't agree, they examine the bases for the continued disagreement, and, if possible, resolve them. This approach uses disagreement productively, surfaces the unconscious thinking among managers, and sheds light on how that thinking influences their interactions with consumers.

Source: Courtesy of Dr. Jeffrey Hartley, the General Motors Corporation.

Stop Squeezing the Same Baby Chicken

Ideas aren't quite like diamonds: They don't last forever (although good ones have long lives). Therefore, a manager must commit to the *process of improving* ideas and practices as much as to the ideas and practices themselves. Nancy Cox, the lead manager for creative processes at Hallmark, addresses the underlying problem by asking this provocative question: "Are you still squeezing the same baby chicken?" We often become overly attached to a new idea and hold on to it very tightly, as children do to baby chickens. It's not healthy for the chickens.

Commitments to particular ideas often block the path to improvement, because of a tendency to defend them when challenged. That's why face-to-face interactions between managers and consumers work well. Such exchanges can produce forceful emotional experiences that push managers into new modes of thinking.[8] Dismissing a challenge from a colleague is easier than dismissing one from live consumers. For example, a cross-functional management team in a sporting goods company had a preconception of a novel engineering design that it wanted to incorporate into a new product. Some managers expressed concerns about negative consumer reactions but were ignored. They eventually held a prelaunch trial in which several consumers used the product for a month. The entire team watched the personal interviews with these consumers following the trial period. In nearly all instances, the consumers reacted negatively to this particular design feature. The vividness of consumers' negative reactions promptly produced a significant change. The product itself proved very successful. If the design engineers on the team had committed less to the particular feature and more to the development of an appealing product, then they'd have tested the feature at issue much earlier and saved considerable R&D money, not to mention launched the product sooner.

Nurture Cool Passion

Passion (or emotion) for new ideas fuels creative thinking, while coolness (reason) harnesses its energy. Imaginative thinking integrates both without censuring the process. A manager at Eastman Kodak notes, "My model for retaining an idea is simple: Only those with high combustion quotients move forward. If an idea does not light a fire for me, it is unlikely to do so with my colleagues."

Heat serves as an essential catalyst for burning through the box. But managers must contain and focus that heat with a cool detachment. Communications consultant and marketing strategist Mary Jarman call this talent for cool passion "di-stance": the knack of being both *part* of your ideas and *separate* from them. Cool passion requires a delicate balance between the nurturing attitude of a parent and the dampening mind-set of a skeptic. To practice cool passion, a manager must simultaneously explore the conditions under which an idea *will* and *will not* work—and then ensure the presence of the former conditions and absence of the latter. As Stephan Haeckel at IBM's Advanced Business Institute suggests, creating good ideas requires "active tinkering and occasional serious surgery" to overcome our cognitive limitations.

Have the Courage of *Your* Convictions

Breaking out of the box requires courage to stand alone or wade into tomorrow's mainstream before others know where it is (or even that it exists). Managers interested in venturing forward must prepare carefully, because people who haven't wet their feet will closely watch what happens to more adventurous colleagues. There are also the inevitable "Yeah, but" types and "door closers," as well as the usual tribe of pooh-poohers who feel uncomfortable around new ideas. These groups default to the downside, revealing themselves with comments such as "Senior management won't buy that," or "Company X tried and failed," or "We don't have the resources," or "I must solve the problem this week, not next week," and even "It just won't work."

"Yeah, buts" crop up most frequently in unhealthy organizational climates, those that penalize risk taking. Keep in mind that "Yeah, but" types aren't fools, which is why they succeed in discouraging others. They point out possible obstacles that merit consideration but can convince innovative thinkers that these *potential* obstacles are unavoidable and insurmountable. Here lies the greatest danger of "Yeah, but" thinking: It oozes into the minds of people who would otherwise innovate but lack the courage of their own convictions. It therefore stifles innovation. William McComb, president of McNeil Consumer Healthcare, deals with "Yeah, buts" by accepting them—and then challenging the naysayers to resolve the issues raised. In this way, "Yeah, but" thinkers gradually develop a constructive "But we could" attitude *without* depriving their company of their critical-thinking skills.

Ask Generic Questions

In any research effort, marketers can stimulate their own creativity by formulating the generic question behind that effort. The *generic question* is the fundamental human or social process that the research seeks to examine. For example, generic questions about brand loyalty would ask, "How do norms of reciprocity (beliefs that if I give you something, then you give me something in return) contribute to enduring social commitments by establishing patterns of exchange and mutual dependence?" or "How do beliefs and expectations shape consumers' perception of their own experiences?"

How can managers craft generic questions? Start by posing a query like, "Why would someone in a different discipline—say, religious studies—want to read research results from a project on air fresheners or the meaning of clean taste?" Asking this kind of question has two benefits. First, it helps managers identify other domains of study that may relate to marketing, like the generic issues surrounding the creation, maintenance, and loss of community that can affect the use of computer-mediated communication as a marketing tool. Therefore, literature on community development and volunteerism could help companies design more effective communication technologies.

Second, posing generic questions helps managers identify new ways to apply seemingly unrelated disciplines to marketing challenges. For example, General Mills has used insights from its generic questions to design several breakfast-product lines that resonate with mothers' feelings about their children's life-stage transitions. When a company attends to generic issues for one brand, it may identify important applications of those insights for several other brands as well.

As another way of asking generic questions, companies can invite people from diverse disciplines to bring their various perspectives to bear on a problem. Box 11-3 shows how rental car company Avis, working with Lou Carbone and Experience Engineering, Inc., did just that.

Avoid Premature Dismissal

The tendency to dismiss ideas without asking what the consequences would be if they were true also causes narrow thinking. Managers can avoid this pitfall by asking, "Would there be significant consequences for my work if this idea or theory had substantial support?" If the answer is yes, then it pays to assess the idea's validity and potential value. For example, when reading about new research in neuroscience, marketers can ask themselves, "If these findings are correct, then what do they imply for my company's efforts to surface consumers' mental models or design more effective advertising?" By exploring the pragmatic validity of a new idea, managers guard against premature dismissal.

A major international bank looked at research concerning placebo effects in medicine. Although the company initially dismissed the research as irrelevant and unfounded, a division vice president used it as an intellectual exercise for some managers in a knowledge-management program: Let's act as if these ideas about placebos have valid application for the banking industry, he proposed.

To the managers' surprise, the research could indeed have enormous value if the basic findings had scientific merit and the group could generalize the findings to banking services. The vice president then assembled a small task force to investigate the issue further. Within

Box 11-3

Customer-Experience Management at Avis

Business Issue

Avis Rent A Car competes with Hertz and National with more than 2,700 locations worldwide. In the early 1990s, Avis brand loyalty ranked third among the three car rental companies, and the company experienced declining customer-satisfaction scores. In 1995, Avis applied experience-management principles and techniques to its office in Newark International Airport in New Jersey—one of the company's largest operations and a major business hub.

Implementation

A fundamental principle of experience management is for companies to connect emotionally with their customers. This connecting starts when a company determines customers' most prominent emotional needs through a wide range of observation and interview techniques. For Avis, the process yielded surprising insights that ultimately influenced the company's marketing strategy and, most important, strengthened customer loyalty.

Working with Experience Engineering, Avis began by studying its customers' current rental experience, examining all aspects through videos from stationary cameras and pinhole cameras embedded in customers' wristwatches and clothing as they rented the cars. The research team, comprised of a futurist, psychologist, and cultural anthropologist, wanted to see and feel exactly what the customer did at every stage of the rental experience; and they studied customers' body language, voice inflection, and word choice at all critical *emotional* junctures. The team also conducted in-depth interviews with both customers and employees to define customers' emotional associations along the way.

To Avis's surprise, customers' most prominent emotional need was to reduce the stress and anxiety associated with traveling. They cared much less about speed of service, cleanliness of cars, or even convenience. This insight became the unifying element for new clues that Avis subsequently developed to restyle the rental experience.

For example, locating one's departure gate and flight status was a major source of stress. So, in the entrances of its rental car return facilities, Avis installed video monitors of flight departure times and gate numbers. Other clues included special doors to accommodate oversized luggage and a business center that customers could use to make calls, send faxes, and plug in their laptops. Avis embedded several hundred new clues into the rental experience, all of which helped to relieve customers' stress and anxiety in some way.

The redesigned rental experience also included new human clues. For example, Avis changed the roles of staff members who worked in the company's frequent-renter express program. Over time, the growth of this program had shifted the bulk of the company's personal contact with top customers from counter personnel to the security guards and roving agents who checked in cars as customers returned them. Avis changed several aspects of the program to relieve customers' anxiety. For example, it renamed the security guards "customer courtesy representatives" and coached these personnel to behave and talk with customers in ways that reduced their stress and anxiety. These courtesy reps were told, for instance, that providing directions to a customer was just as important, if not more important, than checking a driver's license and verifying an assigned rental vehicle. Even these staff members' uniforms and workstations were reconfigured to reinforce their ability to meet that emotional need.

Results

After implementing these changes, Avis's Newark Airport office moved from last place (in a survey of more than sixty airports) to first place in customer satisfaction and experienced a 9 percent increase in overall employee retention.

(continued)

Management rolled out the prototype experience to other key locations that constituted more than 65 percent of Avis's business. By 1998, Avis ranked first in the industry in customer satisfaction and loyalty. Additionally, in an independent study of 147 top worldwide brands in twenty-six categories, Avis ranked first two years in a row for its ability to consistently meet customer expectations.

Ron Masini, a senior vice president who championed the experience project, states: "The insights we gained were significant. Areas where we had beat ourselves up for years to improve turned out not to make any difference. A whole new set of items, many of which we'd never have unearthed, have become key drivers in our ability to generate preference."

Source: Used with the permission of Experience Engineering, Inc., and Avis Rent A Car.

three months, the bank had implemented several of the task force's ideas, like the brochure that detailed why a particular service was superior to that of the bank's competitors. This strategy was based on placebo research indicating that knowledge about how a medication works increases its efficacy. The bank saw results almost immediately. Clients who'd received this new material reported significantly greater satisfaction with the service than clients using the same service who lacked the more detailed information.

Similarly, managers at the Coca-Cola Company's Germany office found that new research on memory contradicted many of their prevailing assumptions about how memory works and how to design the most effective advertising campaigns. They determined whether these findings were grounded in solid research and whether the contradictions had significant implications for their business. By applying several key findings about memory well-grounded in scientific research, the managers launched a successful marketing program in that country. Specifically, the company created more meaning and effective advertising by understanding the reconstructive nature of memory and the various factors affecting the encoding and retrieval of memory.

Integrating Creative-Thinking Principles

The preceding ten creative-thinking principles share certain underlying themes that can help managers tailor the principles to their own habits of mind. For example, several principles imply a sense of *restlessness,* especially those suggesting that marketers should make their own work out of date and view conclusions as new beginnings rather than endings. To apply these principles to your own thinking, ask yourself, "What makes me restless?" Whatever your answer is, make sure you've got plenty of it in your work life.

The principle about the cow's crumpled horn evokes *an appreciation of the irregular* and *an eye for the odd.* To leverage this theme, welcome the unexpected. Ask, "How can I better detect anomalies?" or "How do I *create* anomalies?" The principles of cool passion, of being more committed to the process of generating quality ideas than to the ideas themselves, of seeking knowledge from other domains, and of maintaining the courage of your convictions all share the notion of *reasoned but visceral stubbornness.* When you believe you are right, be stubborn and strong enough to tolerate those who disagree. It's much easier to be stubborn when you possess deep knowledge of other disciplines seemingly unrelated to marketing. To cultivate this quality, ask, "What 'foreign' fields are most interesting, enjoyable, and important to visit?" Whatever these are, visit them often—and stay awhile.

The principles of asking generic questions and avoiding premature dismissal share the theme of helping you achieve *wide cognitive peripheral vision* in your research. Widening your research lens sometimes means you must crumple a horn or two. To apply these principles, ask yourself, "What makes me curious and nosy to the point of being mischievous?" or "What tempts me to break things that appear to be working just fine?"

Taken together, the above crowbars evoke the theme of *thought contagion.* These principles don't exist in isolation. Rather, managers apply them in social settings that can either help or hinder their practice. As you saw in some of the company examples, some firms even *require* their managers to put these principles into action. The principles can infect employees only if the environment truly values fresh thinking and encourages error (rather than merely tolerating it), and recognizes that knowledge flows from ignorance.

For example, a senior vice president at Unilever allows his staff to make decisions that are probably mistakes. When a decision does prove to be a mistake (that is, it doesn't produce positive results), the manager who made it visits the VP's office and expresses remorse. But the VP discourages that posture and asks the manager to develop one or more lessons learned from the experience to share with others. He views the cost of the error as tuition—and a great bargain in terms of the knowledge gained. Vincent P. Barabba at General Motors has created an inquiry center that systematizes learning from such errors. Barabba asserts that a failure to learn from mistakes is like paying expensive tuition but never showing up for school.

High-quality thinking depends on an intellectual agility that remains latent among most managers today. This latency stems in part from restrictive work environments, an inability to engage in out-of-the-box thinking, and lack of wisdom about where to look for alternative boxes and what to do with their contents once they are found.

Our habits of mind—whether they generate creative or stale thinking—have a neurological underpinning, just as our physical movements and systems do. Thus they usually lie beyond our awareness and may resist testing and change. Though our normal habits of mind help us, they also inhibit our ability to think in new ways. An example is premature dismissal, discussed earlier, which tends to occur when we ask whether an idea is true before asking whether it is potentially important. This predisposes us to dismiss too quickly potentially relevant and valid ideas.

Journeys into unfamiliar areas of knowledge demand time—perhaps the scarcest of all valued resources for many managers. That's because new ideas don't come prepackaged and assembled. Marketers must figure out just where to start their journey—for example, in anthropology? psychology? neuroscience? They also must master the unfamiliar terminology that will help them understand and communicate about the new ideas they encounter during their venturing. In addition, they need time to play with the possible applications of an intriguing insight. Finally, they need patience to tolerate jargon and presentation styles that clearly were not created with their needs in mind. Time is necessary to view research questions and findings through the lens of multiple disciplines. Problems and ideas don't belong to disciplines; they don't have a community membership.

To make the most out of diverse bodies of thought, managers must define the generic question they themselves are seeking to address. Specifically, they must ask, "What version of my research question would catch the attention of thinkers in the humanities, natural sciences, and arts?" By answering that question, managers can then seek out research in those disciplines that may shed important light on their question.

For example, the quest to understand needs that consumers have difficulty expressing evokes the generic question: "How does the mind represent its content?" This question in turn may encourage a manager to examine principles of art history and criticism, which could lead to investigations into art therapy, which could in turn inspire research on visual systems, the mind, and ultimately neuroscience. Existing knowledge in these disciplines may reveal new ways that companies can help consumers express hard-to-articulate needs. By understanding those needs, firms can more effectively design valuable products and services to meet them.

The managers featured in this chapter explore other disciplines in part because they find them inherently interesting, even if those disciplines have no immediate connection to their daily responsibilities. They let their minds randomly connect disparate fields of study; they enjoy wondering about and exploring unfamiliar ideas—and then they transform the seemingly idle curiosity into hard-core business results. Meandering onto the playgrounds of other disciplines and playing with their "toys" satisfies the curious mind.

In all cases, a firm's top leaders must model commitment to these creative-thinking principles if they hope to inspire similar commitment among managers. This modeling requires a high degree of self-confidence, the willingness to reveal one's own lack of answers, the courage to reveal errors in one's thinking, and an intense, underlying curiosity. This final dimension—curiosity—prevents confidence from morphing into arrogance.

Answer:

Chapter Twelve

Quality Questions Beget Quality Answers

If it weren't for questions, where would answers be?

THE ABOVE EPIGRAPH, attributed to Gertrude Stein, reflects the essential role of questions in developing marketing knowledge. Questions beget answers. They help us interpret information that we encounter serendipitously, and they drive our search for deeper meaning. Equally important, the *sequence* of the questions asked determines the information acquired and the knowledge gained or missed. In this way, a marketing manager's questioning strategy shapes his ultimate learning about consumers. Different strategies beget different insights.

However, most managers focus more on answers and conclusions than on questions and beginnings. To reengineer the mind of the market, managers must attend equally to both processes. They must also appreciate the interdependency of questions and their answers. Our very framing of a question foreshadows the answer.

Which Question, Which Method?

Formulating the right research questions is both art and science—a combination of tacit sensing and thoughtful, explicit reasoning. As managers craft questions, they risk posing the wrong question, leading to what is called *post-survey regret:* After collecting all the data, regardless of the data collection method used, we often discover that we should have pursued a different basic question or asked important, more focused questions.

Even small nuances in the framing of a question can produce different insights—some unexpected or undesired. Consider the question, "Of all the products and services that you've used in the past month, which one disappointed you the most?" This query will yield considerable insight about specific events that disappointed respondents. However, it won't help marketers draw accurate, useful conclusions about disappointing consumer experiences overall. To do that, the researcher must ask something like, "How do you feel when a product or service fails to meet your expectations?" Of course, this new question wouldn't generate as many specific details as the earlier query. Research questions, like the methods used to answer them, involve trade-offs.

Because different methods involve different question styles, the chosen research method will influence the answers. For example, researchers often use surveys when they want to track changes over time, such as trends in consumer disappointment with well-established products like computers. For an established product category, most respondents will have had numerous satisfactory and unsatisfactory experiences and considerable exposure to product information. Thus they'll have plenty of background information on which to draw in answering the survey questions.

However, if the researchers want to understand consumers' satisfactory and unsatisfactory experiences in a relatively new product category, like Internet-ready cell phones, personal interviews may yield more than surveys.

Although open-ended survey questions may accomplish some of the same goals as interviews, marketers can't ask people to respond to more than a few such questions. Also, researchers can't ask follow-up questions to clarify particular comments. Indeed, surveys involving open-ended questions are costly to code and time-consuming for respondents, increasing the chance that they'll not complete the questionnaire.

Survey research can illuminate consumers' basic thinking about goods and services and reveal the magnitude of a change in an existing attitude.[1] Nevertheless, it won't generate information about previously missed or new attitudes—both of which may interest marketers. Surveys can provide precision, but one-on-one, in-depth personal discussions (such as metaphor-elicitation interviews) produce more surprises and nuanced responses.

Regardless of the method of questioning, the point of view used in wording the study's questions can greatly affect the results. For example, asking consumers about a particular brand (a commonly used question) will often produce markedly different information than asking about what the *brand* thinks of *them* (a more counterintuitive approach). Yet consumers have much to say in both cases; and their thoughts and feelings about what a brand (or company) thinks of them strongly influence how they evaluate a firm's offerings.

For example, when asked what they thought of the brand Mercedes, consumers in one study responded mostly with positive answers, such as "good styling," "comfort," and "good maintenance records," along with few negative answers. However, when the same consumers were asked what they thought the Mercedes brand thinks of them, many negative answers surfaced. Respondents made comments such as, "They don't [think of us]," "We are sheep," "[They think] I have money to burn," and "[They think] I'm a child that doesn't know better." Consumers' decisions about whether to buy a Mercedes vehicle emerge from the blend of both sets of judgments. If the researchers in charge of this study had explored only the first question, they would have missed the more negative—and equally important— thoughts that the second question unearthed. That second question not only added valuable information, it also suggested that the generally positive evaluation consumers provided while answering the first question was actually fragile. Thus you should ask whether the consumer's other points of view are relevant. For example, when loyal consumers of a men's shaving gel were asked why they might stop using the brand, entirely new insights were obtained that had been missed when consumers were asked only why they continued to use the brand.

Framing Effective Research Questions

The following guidelines can help you frame the basic question to explore:

1. Determine the generic question you want to explore.
2. Determine whether the basic question should be specific to brand, category, or problem.
3. Pose more general and more specific versions of the first question that occurs to you.
4. Determine whether you need to know direction, velocity, or both.
5. Allow for surprises.
6. Convert assumptions into questions.
7. Employ a clairvoyant.
8. Employ a wizard.

We examine these guidelines more closely in the following sections.

Determine the Generic Question You Want to Explore

When one firm set out to research the potential market for a new system for cleaning cars, it chose to examine consumers' generic experiences with cleaning as well as their more specific, car-related experiences. To explore generic experiences, the company asked broad-brush questions, such as, "What is the meaning of 'washing'?" and "What is the meaning of 'clean'?" By exploring consumers' generic attitudes about "washing" and "clean," this company could identify fundamental thoughts or emotions relevant to many contexts, including one's home and clothing as well as one's car. Attitudes and perceptions that crop up in diverse contexts are likely to be highly relevant to consumers and deeply embedded in their thinking. Therefore, these same thoughts will play an especially important role in any specific context, such as car washing. Though the company could have explored generic attitudes in a survey designed specifically to ask about car washing, the results would not have revealed the basic underlying beliefs that make having a clean car relevant in the first place.

In a similar vein, a major provider of bottled water addressed several generic questions when planning the introduction of its brand. These questions included discovering consumers' perceptions of the concepts "clean," "pure," and "water." Such concepts have deep and complex significance for consumers that spills into their purchase decisions and their responses to marketing communications. Exploring consumers' thoughts and feelings about each concept helped the company to place bottled water within the complex system of ideas consumers have about (for example) purity, and to create a compelling message about the pure, clean taste of their brand of bottled water.

Firms can also gain important insights about generic concerns inexpensively, by examining published resources or consulting experts from various disciplines. For instance, a company can learn much about the generic concept "clean taste" by reviewing research on eating disorders, the human sense of smell (closely related to taste), cultural history (how the meanings of "clean" and "pure" have changed over time in different societies), religious practices (in which water and purity play a prominent role), and anthropology. In fact, the firm that introduced its brand of bottled water convened a group of experts from these same fields to formulate questions to explore with consumers in subsequent research.

Likewise, when Hallmark was developing a new division to focus exclusively on products relating to the role of memories in consumers' lives, it commissioned an expert forum program.[2] The forum included memory researchers from several disciplines who explained the way memory actually works and helped the firm identify misperceptions among consumers as well as themselves. The forum also helped the company identify additional generic questions to explore in subsequent market research.

As a final example, when managers at a European-based manufacturer were evaluating a radical new kitchen-appliance concept, they asked themselves an intriguing generic question: How might the basic idea of the hero's journey (see chapter 9) play a role in the appliance-buying experience? Initial research revealed that certain journey-like elements influenced consumers' experiences with a particular problem the new product was aiming to address. By exploring the essence of the classic hero's journey and seeing how it played out in consumers' experiences, managers were able to hone the new concept so that it promised to satisfy more consumer needs.

Determine Whether the Key Question Should Be Specific to Brand, Category, or Problem

It is also important to decide whether you should be asking about the brand, the product category, or about the basic problem making the brand and category relevant in the first place. For example, should you be asking consumers about your brand of tooth whitener, about tooth whiteners in general, or about how consumers experience the problem that tooth whiteners address. All three questions may be relevant to a specific brand, but each provides different kinds of insights. Knowing more about the basic problem consumers experience may be helpful in creating a new story about the brand. Knowing more about your specific brand may be helpful in understanding how consumers perceive the brand story now and whether it should be changed. Knowing more about the category may help in understanding brand positioning issues.

When a question is category specific rather than brand specific, researchers should phrase the question to focus on the underlying consumer need that the category seeks to satisfy. For example, if a company wants to introduce a new system for washing cars, it might first learn how people who wash their car at least once a month feel when their car is dirty and what "problem" having a dirty car poses. If the company has already developed the new system, exploring consumers' general feelings about cleanliness is more useful than knowing what they think of existing car-washing solutions.

Sometimes consumers' thoughts and feelings about a brand *and* its category may be similar. For instance, consumers' perceptions of Nestlé Crunch Bars at one time strongly resembled their perceptions of candy bars in general. If such similarities exist, companies had better be aware of them. The more consumers' thoughts about a specific brand and category are aligned, the more vulnerable the brand is to competition, because the brand has few unique qualities. On the other hand, if no other brand has these same qualities, then the brand that does embody them will have a major strategic advantage.

If resources are limited, researchers must make a trade-off in deciding whether to explore consumers' perceptions of the brand in question or of the larger category or even the general need or problem. Generally, the more crowded a category is with alternative brands, the more useful for companies to understand consumers' experiences at the category level or even the more basic problem level rather than brand level. This may identify important but unleveraged thoughts and feelings.

Pose More General and More Specific Versions of the First Question That Occurs to You

When a manager begins thinking about a particular market research project, often a particular question will pop into his or her mind immediately. Rather than proceeding with that question, the manager should instead explore more general and specific versions of it. For example, before proceeding to ask consumers, "What are your thoughts and feelings about keeping a clean car?" the manager should rephrase the question in more general language, such as, "What are your thoughts and feelings about keeping the things you own clean?" He or she should also rephrase it in more specific language, such as, "What do you enjoy most and least about keeping your car clean?" Each version produces somewhat different—and equally valuable—insights. Researchers must therefore decide which version will yield the most important information. They should view the first question that comes to mind through the lens of alternatives framed at *other* levels. Although this screen may seem obvious, researchers rarely use it; they usually debate alternative framings of a question at the *same* level.

In designing a new microwave oven, Samsung Electronics followed this guideline. The company had initially considered asking consumers, "What is your experience when using a microwave oven?" It then devised the more general question, "When you think about cooking in your kitchen, what thoughts and feelings come to mind?" It also created the more specific question, "Tell us about how you use your microwave oven when preparing meals." After debating the merits of all three questions, the company decided to use the more general question because it allowed for surprising results. Had it stuck with its initial question, it would have missed valuable insights. Also, when consumers have prepared for a one-on-one interview, the interviewer can more easily move from the general to the specific than vice versa. For example, before interviews, Nokia has found it better to ask people to think about electronic communication in general rather than cell phones in particular, even when the latter is of greatest interest. Their researchers then gradually move the discussion toward the more specific topic of cell phone use.

Similarly, the Walt Disney Company frames questions at various levels of specificity. Initially, managers had planned to ask metaphor-elicitation interview participants, "What does Mickey Mouse mean to your children?" But by bracketing this question with more general and more specific variations, they created a wide menu of inquiries, each promising a different bundle of insights. The very process of designing the different versions of the question helped the managers to clarify the exact nature of the information they desired. In the end, they decided to ask participants the more general question, "When you think or hear about Mickey Mouse, what thoughts and feelings come to mind?" The participants' responses yielded some surprising insights that prompted the managers to consider new strategic directions in selling Mickey Mouse properties. It is unlikely that the initial question would have yielded these insights.

Determine Whether You Need to Know Direction, Velocity, or Both

When you're sailing into new territory, sometimes you need to know only the direction of the wind; other times, you must figure out the wind's velocity. Sometimes you must know both. Exploring a new concept or product through market research is akin to navigating uncharted waters. You must decide what's most important to learn: the attractiveness or appeal of a concept or product (the wind's direction) or its likely unit initial sales (the wind's velocity). The former is essential for development and launch decisions; the latter, for production decisions. Or, if you are certain about the important features that need to be incorporated (the wind's direction) but need to make improvements in the product with limited resources, it then becomes necessary to pursue questions that address the relative importance (wind velocity) of these features.

Distinguishing between direction versus velocity is crucial, because each suggests different methodologies. In one proprietary study, a Midwestern U.S. bank used a survey to estimate the number of their existing customers who would likely enroll in the new plan. The survey presented the concept and asked respondents to evaluate it and indicate whether they were likely to enroll immediately. The responses were very positive and indicated a high likelihood of enrollment among the client segment of greatest interest. Therefore, the bank introduced the plan—only to withdraw it eight months later after few customers enrolled. It turned out that the precise measures of whether people liked the plan completely missed another critical dimension of consumers' needs for savings plans. In effect, this other dimension represented the critical *direction* in which consumers' attention was focused but which the bank had not identified. The bank made the common mistake of trying to gather too precise data too soon. By using *velocity* measures to assess *direction,* it gathered misleading data, and the new product failed.

The reverse can also occur. Firms have unwisely used focus groups to estimate likely sales (velocity) when they should have been measuring general attitudes (direction). Often companies need answers to directional questions first and velocity issues later. Yet many managers feel tempted to address both at once with the same investigation. Although this approach sometimes works, it often doesn't, and the quality of both kinds of information is compromised.

By approaching these questions in the proper sequence, companies can generate the most valuable data. For example, the bank that introduced the new savings plan subsequently conducted a "directional" study to correct its earlier error. Using the new data, it then implemented a "velocity" survey involving a conjoint analysis. The insights from that study, which was designed with a deeper understanding of consumers, produced a newly configured savings plan that became a huge success.

Allow for Surprises

As noted earlier, most market research is confirmatory; that is, managers conduct it to prove a point rather than explore an idea, thereby forfeiting the chance to surface confirming as well as disconfirming evidence. It also forces consumers *to tell you that they think about whatever you suppose they're thinking about.* Consumers probably won't express relevant thoughts and feelings that the manager hasn't anticipated. So how do you stay open to surprises? Ask interviewees whether they would like to share any other information—something important that the survey or interview didn't address, or that *they* would ask in conducting the research. For example, at the end of formal interviews about the use of advertising research, a Shell Oil team found that participants often gave "parting gifts" in the form of "You know, something we didn't discuss was. . . ." The team pursued these surprises in subsequent interviews— and generated some of the study's most significant insights.

In conducting surveys, managers can capture the value of surprising findings by first simulating possible results. They can then select those scenarios with the most serious consequences for them and ask, "What else must I know to interpret and act on these results? Have I allowed for discovery?" Simulating final results, even if generated randomly, almost always results in timely changes to the survey. The use of more sophisticated statistical tools, together with an attitude of serious play, can yield important surprises. For instance, by experimenting with a new model for segmenting consumers using an existing database, one of the leading telephone service providers in the United States discovered that it had missed an entire market segment.

In one-on-one interviews, managers can generate vital, surprising information by enabling consumers to use their imaginations. For example, an interviewer could ask, "What if, by magic, you never had to wash your car? How would you feel?" In a metaphor-elicitation project on the "soul of Mickey Mouse," interviewers asked participants, "Suppose you were Mickey Mouse and could create just one memory for a child. What would it be?" Questions of this nature uncover thoughts and feelings by assisting the consumer's inward look.

Convert Assumptions into Questions

You know the old saying: "It isn't what we don't know that gets us into trouble; it's what we know that isn't so." Managers face just such a predicament in letting their prior knowledge and assumptions inform their market research. All research inevitably rests on assumptions that inform core questions, the method selected, and the implementation. But sometimes these assumptions are incorrect. For this reason, researchers must identify their underlying assumptions *early* in the study design and test their accuracy.

One food manufacturer's experience illustrates the importance of testing assumptions. This company's market researchers always recruited consumer participants based on the managers' usage criteria. Their definitions of heavy and light product usage guided their research for several years. However, a new VP from another firm challenged the criteria and asked consumers to describe *themselves* in terms of usage. It turned out that allowing consumers to select their own usage criteria provided more meaningful insights than when managers applied theirs. Enough discrepancies existed between the managers' and consumers' definitions that the composition of the self-selected consumer groups differed markedly from those formed through the managers' criteria. In fact, allowing consumers to define themselves as light or heavy users of frozen foods produced more significant insights than did research using managers' criteria. Subsequent research led to significant extensions of its current product line as well as a new communications strategy.

Employ a Clairvoyant

In designing effective survey or interview questions, managers can also engage in an imaginative thought exercise: Suppose you had access to a clairvoyant—someone who can see into the future and who will answer just one question for you. This clairvoyant won't take simple questions, such as, "Will this product succeed?" or "How many units will it sell?" Rather, he or she answers only deeper questions, such as, "What do consumers fear most when they use this product?" or "What key emotions 'converse' with one another when consumers think about my brand?"

A leading alcohol manufacturer used this exercise to define the core question that it wanted to explore through market research. The company's overall goal was to reposition one of its brands. The obvious, simple question—which the clairvoyant would *not* address—was "What is the best positioning for this brand?" Instead of posing this query, the company brainstormed several more complex questions, such as: "What do consumers consider to be an exciting taste experience?" "How does the social setting of beverage consumption affect the definition of an appropriate beverage choice?" "What is the role of alcohol in the overall daily diet?" Finally, the firm decided to focus its research project on the question, "What is the anatomy of social well-being?" By selecting this question, the company was able to concentrate on the factors affecting consumers' thinking and behavior, such as sharing secrets, as opposed to gathering mere descriptions of those thoughts and behaviors in the form of "spending time with friends." Armed with that information, it proceeded to develop one of the most effective advertising campaigns in the brand's history.

Employ a Wizard

A wizard is someone who can fix things that are broken. Of course, waiting for something to be broken before consulting a wizard is a costly strategy. A better strategy is to imagine that a particular decision has proven ineffective and that a wizard needs to be called in. "What one thing would a wizard most likely fix to correct this problem?" By asking themselves this question in advance, managers can identify potential, important knowledge deficiencies before implementing a decision. Once these are identified, managers can assess whether they have sufficient information to either (1) know that it won't occur or (2) know how to respond to it if it does occur. If sufficient information is lacking for these purposes, then the critical information can be gathered in advance, lessening the likelihood that a wizard will be needed later.

What Do Data "Tell" Managers?

Before discussing whether data by themselves actually say anything, a few words about the nature of data and answers will be helpful.

What Are Data?

When asked what data are, most people respond with numeric examples, such as age, price, frequency, correlation coefficient, and so on. When pressed a bit further, they may make distinctions between "hard" data and "soft" data, such as attitudes measured in a three-hundred-person survey versus the same attitudes expressed in focus groups.

But examples are not definitions. Despite the frequency with which the word *data* crops up in marketing discussions, many people have difficulty pinning down what a unit of data actually *is*. One way to clear this up is to figure out what the various pieces of information that we gather through statistics, personal observations, and other data sources have in common. As it turns out, these pieces of information—these data—are all stimuli that influence our thoughts, feelings, and behaviors. By viewing data in this way, most managers suddenly see the value of collecting multiple kinds of data.

What Are Answers?

As stimuli, data provide the raw material for answers to market research questions. The topic of answers is complex, and only a brief comment is possible here. For our purposes, we can think of an answer as a packet of learning that fills the empty "container" of a question. The better designed the container, the more robust the answers it can hold. A small (that is, narrow) question can never hold a large answer. Likewise, a small answer will rattle around hollowly inside a large (that is, broad) question. Thus the "size" of a question and its answer must correspond.

Data Say Very Little without Managers

Many managers wonder whether market research data will clearly tell them what to do next. According to Vincent P. Barabba of General Motors and author of *Meeting of Minds*, "Data don't say anything; only people do." That is, data have meaning only to the extent that managers or researchers bring meaning to them. Barabba has another, related observation: "Never say 'the model says.'" Models only capture and express the information defined by the model maker's assumptions. Rather than saying "The model says . . ." or "The data say . . ." managers might better say, "According to the assumptions built into this model . . ." or "given my prior experience with . . . this is what these data mean to me." As noted neuroscientist Antonio Damasio puts it: "Whether one likes it or not, *all* the contents in our minds are subjective, and the power of science comes from its ability to verify objectively the consistency of many individual subjectivities."[3] That's why we must bring multiple perspectives to bear on the same data. When people with different viewpoints perceive the same or similar meanings or when they can challenge one another with regard to their differences, we can be more confident in any given interpretation.

Contrary to popular wisdom, then, data don't speak for themselves. Managers' *interpretation* of data is the meaning they extract from the data. For example, consider the seemingly straightforward question, "Do significantly more women than men purchase computer hardware on the Internet?" A company could answer this question fairly readily by simply surveying the customers who buy hardware through the Internet. The resulting numbers might be important if the firm is trying to decide whether to advertise a new online source for computer purchases in women's or men's magazines. However, the definition of "significantly more" is still largely a matter of judgment. In this case, the "data" alone can provide answers only at the unlikely extremes; for example, women account for 90 percent or 2 percent of all online computer purchases. Rarely does a number by itself have meaning. It is a manager's prior experience or the consensus among a group of managers that makes a number meaningful.

Thus the meaning of certain language in a research question is also a matter of judgment. In fact, such judgments will strongly shape the way managers interpret the data resulting from the question. The more important they judge a question, the more closely they will examine the data—and the more effort they'll expend to make sense of it. Disagreements among managers about what data mean often cover up more fundamental disagreements about the importance of the research question.

Even when managers agree on a question's importance and the meaning of the language used in it, they still face a daunting task in determining the resulting data's message and conclusiveness. For example, the outcome of a conjoint analysis might reveal that consumers prefer a rectangular, hard-plastic product package with a viewing strip through which to see its contents more than a square, soft-plastic package with no viewing strip. However, these data will be meaningful only if managers have identified the most appropriate packaging dimensions or attributes to measure, the correct options for each dimension, the right study participants, eliminated biases in the framing of the survey questions, and so on. The only meaning these data are capable of communicating is that these particular study participants seem to prefer one set of ideas over another—both of which were provided by the market researchers. It's very possible that the participants would have selected an entirely different package design if the researchers had presented them with one.

To illustrate further, an increase in store traffic during a special sale or the average income of people applying for a mortgage at a branch bank both seem to represent straightforward, easy-to-interpret data. Yet by themselves, these data don't "tell" a manager whether to hold a sale, when, and for how long, or whether to encourage or discourage more risk taking (and just how much) in mortgage-lending practices at a particular branch. Managers can find these "answers" only by merging the data with the tacit knowledge they have already acquired through hardearned experience.

How Objective Are Numbers?

As you may have gathered from the above discussion, *there is nothing more subjective than a number*. The only *objective* aspect of a number is its derivation (as through particular calculations). Before ever "crunching numbers," managers make crucial judgments about which target markets to sample, how to sample them, when to do so, what topics or questions to explore, and which analyses to perform on the data. All of these human judgments affect the actual results obtained.

To interpret data as objectively as possible, many managers emphasize the need to determine statistical significance. Attending to statistical significance is beneficial. For example, managers ascertain whether a given finding could have cropped up randomly. After assessing statistical significance, managers and researchers might wrongly conclude that the data have a 95 percent likelihood of being "true" and therefore "objective." Yet this reasoning poses a problem: Even if the results of all 100 replications of a study are identical, each iteration still repeats the bias or error in the original study design. How can 95 (or even 100) consistent conclusions be valid if they all contain the same design flaw? In fact, in one famous study involving laboratory experiments where researchers could control bias and other kinds of error, psychologists Robert Rosenthal and Ralph Rosnow concluded that *the probability of a researcher's expectations having no effect on the people being studied was less than 0.0000001.*[4] What a researcher *thinks* he might find (that is, his prior interpretation of the data) can subtly or flagrantly influence his findings.

Once researchers collect and process data, their assumptions and expectations continue to shape their interpretation of findings. For example, when asked what verbal description would most express a purchase intent of 90 percent, two-thirds of all managers (and consumers) use terms ranging from "somewhat likely" to "definitely." But "somewhat likely" differs significantly from "definitely."

For instance, when a comparable group of people are asked to assign a probability to "somewhat likely to buy," most responses fall fairly evenly between 30 percent and 90 percent. For "definitely will buy," most responses fall between 50 percent and 100 percent. These are huge ranges. When 55 percent of a study's participants indicate they will "definitely buy" a new product, the probability that managers unconsciously assign to this observation (50 percent, 70 percent, etc.) has immense significance for decisions about production levels, pricing, sales quotas, promotion budgets, and so on.

Shaping the Meaning of a Number: Frames of Reference

The following slightly disguised example illustrates this phenomenon. Researchers asked three groups of newspaper readers who differed only in their geographical location to state how many hours they had spent reading newspapers in the past seven days. Readers in region I reported an average of 5 hours, those in region II reported about 4.3 hours, and readers in region III reported about 3.2 hours. The researchers then gave a group of professional news personnel all three numbers and asked them to describe the readers using consistently defined terms provided by the researchers. Each professional described each group differently and in a way that was largely consistent with his or her colleagues' descriptions. For example, the news personnel described the readers in the three regions as follows:

Region I: "heavy readers, dedicated, highly involved"
Region II: "moderate readers, active readers, somewhat engaged"
Region III: "disengaged, passive, somewhat involved"

Now let's see what happened when the researchers changed one aspect of the study. In the second part of the experiment, the researchers asked three other groups of news professionals, all comparable to the first groups, to respond to the data but gave each group the reading-hour number from just one of the regions. Then they asked the news professionals to describe the readers in that region. Here's a representative list of their responses:

Region I: "active readers, interested, moderate readers, serious"
Region II: "heavy readers, highly engaged, dedicated, quite
    involved"
Region III: "light readers, heavy readers, serious, dedicated"

In the absence of contrasting information from the other two regions—that is, a *frame of reference*—the news professionals tended to describe their particular reader group in similar, generally favorable ways. Their responses contrast with the far sharper distinctions the first group of news professionals made when they saw all three sets of results at once.

The first group of news people had a frame of reference that contained contrasts. The data they saw for one region shaped their thinking about the other regions, and different descriptors of readers in the three regions emerged. The second group had no explicit frame of reference. Thus they used only their prior and somewhat different expectations to form conclusions about their reader group.

Now let's consider another widely reported example of the framing effect. Imagine that a rare disease has broken out in your community and is expected to kill six hundred people. Members of the community can select one of two programs available to deal with the threat. The programs are described in two different ways, as shown below:

DESCRIPTION 1

- Program A would save 200 people.
- Program B would give a 33 percent probability that everyone in the community will be saved and a 67 percent probability that no one will be saved.

DESCRIPTION 2

- With program A, 400 of the 600 people would die.
- With program B, there would be a 33 percent probability that no one would die and a 67 percent probability that 600 would die.

Based on these two descriptions of the programs, which plan would you choose—A or B? Among people who see only the first description of the two programs, the great majority choose program A. Among those who see only the second description, the great majority choose program B.

However, the two different descriptions in each pair would actually yield identical outcomes for each program. For example, in the descriptions of program A, "saving 200 people" and "400 of the 600 people would die" are two different ways of saying the same thing. Yet "saving 200 people" sounds more positive than "400 of the 600 people would die." Thus the way the programs are described provides a frame of reference that strongly influences people's perceptions and choices.

Using Data as Advisors

Although data can't "tell" a manager what to do, they can at least offer wise "advice" for judging research findings. This advisory role raises some valuable points about the discovery process.

The general process of discovery can take numerous forms. For example, picture a painting of a bowl of fruit by an artist from the school of realism. The meaning in the image would be relatively straightforward: You'd gaze at the painting in a rather passive way and conclude, "a bowl of fruit." Now picture an abstract painting consisting of shapes, colors, and textures that relate to nothing that you've seen before. In this case, you'd work at the meaning of image. You might even *create* your own meaning: "It makes a statement about human despair."

Much market research is of the passive, "realistic school" sort. For instance, marketers tend to ask consumers straightforward questions— such as "How likely are you to buy this product?"—and then draw straightforward meaning from the answers. For simplicity's sake, assume that we posed the above question to a large number of people from the right target market and that most respondents indicated a purchase probability of 0.4. We have "discovered" an answer. We might conclude that 40 percent of the larger population would be inclined to buy the product. Though we may not expect an exact 40 percent purchase rate, we may have other data that also signal a positive reaction to the new product; thus we proceed to introduce it. Later, we find that only a disappointing 8 percent of the target market purchased the product.

Was the 40 percent wrong? To find out, we investigate possible explanations for the disappointing sales. We learn a number of surprising things. For example, consumers were insufficiently informed about the product, word-of-mouth communication did not operate as we expected, consumers found the product's price too high, a competitor timed a special promotion to coincide with our product's introduction, shoppers couldn't find the product easily in stores, our advertising campaigns didn't engage people, and so on.

Thus the actual 8 percent sales figure doesn't necessarily mean that the predicated 40 percent figure was either right or wrong. Rather, it reflects our failure to play the kind of active role that understanding "abstract art" demands. The managers in this example never consulted a wizard; they never asked what could cause the 40 percent projection to go wrong or what special action was needed to make it right. In short, they failed to use their imagination.

Actions based on research results or other forms of data, at least concerning more complex and uncertain situations, require an inventive form of discovery. There is no 40 percent out there, orbiting like an undiscovered planet. The 8 percent reflected the way the firm intervened in the marketplace. The estimate of 40 percent simply suggests that creative decisions involving pricing, distribution, and communication strategy, for example, and equally creative implementation are both worthwhile.

Creativity plays a central role in designing effective market research questions and interpreting their answers in ways that lead to successful marketing. The process requires a markedly different attitude and thinking style than the more common, passive approach to data that currently characterizes much research. Creative thinking also suggests that managers don't unearth meaningful answers in the marketplace simply by looking hard for them. Rather, they generate valuable answers by asking new kinds of questions. The manager who concedes, "Okay, we can expect 40 percent trial purchase" is thinking very differently (and far more passively) than the one who asks, "How can we make sure we achieve 40 percent potential or more?" This point may seem obvious. Yet in the face of a marketing failure, too many managers blame the data rather than the way they interpreted them and the actions based on those interpretations.

Market-research questions foreshadow the outlines of their own answers. That's because no matter how broad a question is, it inevitably restricts both managers' and consumers' attention. No matter how narrowly focused a question is, it will always simultaneously exclude certain kinds of answers and overemphasize other kinds. In addition, the framing of a question foreshadows the choice of research method; hence framing favors certain types of answers and discourages others. Like the research methods used to answer them, questions require trade-offs. Managers have only so much time, money, and energy, as well as limits on their imagination and knowledge. Not surprisingly, many managers avoid designing creative research questions and interpreting the answers in more thoughtful ways.

A well-designed research question can be a thing of beauty and can open new doors onto consumers' thinking. But equally important, the very process of developing a good question can be highly instructive and engaging. To frame a research question effectively, managers must carefully assess what they know and don't know, as well as what's most important to them and what isn't. Sometimes creating the right research question can yield so much insight about a problem that a manager doesn't even need to collect further data. The act of thoughtfully framing a question can expose a hidden wellspring of assumptions, knowledge, and experience that managers never realized they had. Question your questions, and your answers will flow with abundance.

Chapter Thirteen

Launching a New Mind-Set

Few occasions intimidate and excite us as much as beginnings.

W E HAVE NOW completed our fantastic voyage. Along the way, we've sampled knowledge from several disciplines and met managers from around the globe who've applied crowbars to their own thinking. Managers who ignore available knowledge or fail to experiment imaginatively with interdisciplinary applications to their marketing decisions risk their livelihoods, just as Captain Edward John Smith of the *Titanic* did.

A New Product Launch and the Failure of a Paradigm

At noon on April 10, 1912, the new Royal Mail Steamer *Titanic,* flagship of the White Star Line, launched from Southampton, England, with great fanfare on her maiden voyage to New York. At 11:40 P.M. on Sunday, April 14, 1912, the *Titanic* hit an underwater iceberg spur, causing, as later photographic explorations would show, poorly installed rivets to pop open. Two hours and forty minutes later, the *Titanic* broke in two and sank, taking with her 1,500 lives, more than two-thirds of those on board.

The ship was doomed in the first ten minutes following the collision.[1] Neither the *Titanic's* pumps nor its structural design could cope with the volume and location of water taken on in those few minutes. Many passengers had no chance to survive, since there were lifeboats for only half of them.

The official inquiries established the following points:

- The *Titanic*'s officers knew about the presence of icebergs in their vicinity that Sunday evening. One of the warnings placed icebergs within five miles of the *Titanic*'s path. Another referred to "growlers," icebergs with deceptively small surfaces and massive underbellies. The ship received the last known warning an hour before the accident. Despite the detail and frequency of the warnings, the crew treated them routinely.
- The ship's officers knew that they'd encounter ice that evening, yet no one arranged a meeting to discuss the warnings. The officer of the watch issued instructions to the crew to keep "a sharp lookout for ice." But visible icebergs weren't the issue; hidden underwater spurs were.
- The ship's officers believed that the evening weather conditions allowed them to spot potential trouble with enough notice to adjust course or speed in a timely way—traditional practice for night travel in these waters. Consequently, they didn't increase the lookout.
- Two clear precautionary actions were available; alter course or reduce speed as night approached. Neither was chosen. The officers assumed that the ship's integrity could handle the modest consequences of a tardy response to an unexpected collision.

In short, it was business as usual on board. The captain, officers, and crew worked according to the existing paradigm on this maiden voyage. The officers didn't doubt that their actions constituted sound procedure for passenger vessels in the waters in question, during the time in question. Obviously, they were wrong.

The British Wreck Commissioner's Inquiry final judgment about the catastrophe could describe any new product launch these days:

With the knowledge of the proximity of ice which the Master had, two courses were open to him: The one was to stand well to the southward instead of turning up to a westerly course; the other was to reduce speed materially as night approached. He did neither. . . . Why, then, did the Master persevere in his course and maintain his speed?

For a quarter of a century or more, the practice of liners using this track when in the vicinity of ice at night in clear weather had been to keep the course, to maintain the speed and to trust to a sharp lookout to enable them to avoid the danger. This practice, it was said, had been justified by experience, no casualties having resulted from it. . . . But the event has proved the practice to be bad.

It is, however, to be hoped that the last has been heard of the practice and that for the future it will be abandoned for what we now know to be more prudent and wiser measures. What was a mistake in the case of the "Titanic" would without doubt be negligence in any similar case in the future.[2]

A Lesson in Hubris

The *Titanic's* story, like so many of the sea, is one of courage and cowardice, determination and hesitation, good luck for some and ill fortune for many others. It is also a story about the inadequacies of conventional wisdom, the limitations of business as usual, and management's Achilles' heel—a reluctance to rethink basic assumptions because of excessive confidence in their soundness. These are the parts of the story of interest here. The decisions made by the ship's officers were the tragic causal forces whose cumulative effect was the sinking of the *Titanic,* sacrificing many lives in the process. The iceberg, the limitations of the pumps, poorly welded rivets, the designs that distributed incoming water in unanticipated ways, and the pitiful supply of life boats were merely the agents through which flawed conventional thinking wreaked its havoc.

Captain Smith of the *Titanic* and his fellow officers, like so many managers in large and small companies around the globe today, were following standard operating procedure: procedures whose terrible flaws were waiting for an opportunity to assert themselves. No system was in place that allowed for questioning the wisdom of simply doing what other vessels did in these circumstances. The officers did what they had done themselves in the past: maintained course and standard speed and kept a "sharp lookout" in the dark of night for cues on the water's surface that might suggest hidden threats below.

This procedure assumed several things: what appeared at the surface adequately represented what lay beneath; the lookout's abilities were reliable; and the crew could alter the ship's direction and speed fast enough after receiving a warning. Most troubling, they believed that their existing practices were so sound and universal—despite the uniqueness and the newness of the vessel—that they didn't merit reexamination.

The Titanic *Effect, then, is the sinking of a company or brand due to managers' unquestioned confidence in customary, surface-oriented thinking about consumers—as if the old paradigm sufficed for both understanding the market and adjusting quickly to market conditions.* This failure to think differently—particularly to think deeply about business consumers and ultimate consumers—is a failure to question the so-called conventional wisdom. Please use this book as a guide for avoiding the *Titanic* Effect. Look at the *Titanic*'s journey as a reflection of the mind of the market, the interactions of two sets of forces: the natural force above and beneath the water's surface, and the human force consciously and unconsciously guiding the decisions of the ship's officers.

Managers must find ways to dive deeper and explore those submerged thoughts and feelings. Today the *Titanic* is a metaphor of callous thinking and blind belief. New-product failure rates expose the *Titanic* Effect at work in marketing, as do the failed brands that lost their leadership positions, and the celebrated firms that have undergone bankruptcy. The resulting losses in consumer satisfaction and trust, shareholder value, and jobs are among the prices paid for failing to think differently about consumers and for failing to take the time needed to gain a deep understanding of them.

We live in exciting times where the half-life of knowledge in the social and biological sciences and humanities is getting shorter and shorter. Not every field can claim, as Antonio Damasio does for neuroscience and psychology, that it has learned more in the 1990s than in the previous history of those fields. But every field of inquiry ranging from literary studies to evolutionary biology has developed insights in recent years that have substantially changed their respective landscapes. And, as I have argued, many of these changes have enormous implications for how we think about the mind of the market—the interaction of the conscious and unconscious mind of the consumer with that of the manager. These changes suggest new beginnings in our efforts to become customer-centric. Yet most knowledge in use in marketing today is at best half right. Let us hope that new product and service failure rates currently at 80 percent or more will become a thing of the past as smarter courses of action are plotted using new insights, an openness of mind, and a willingness to continually challenge what is "known."

Notes

Preface

1. Peter Drucker, "The Next Society," *The Economist,* 3 November 2001, 3.

2. Quoted in F. T. McCarthy, "Who's Wearing the Trousers?" *The Economist,* 8 September 2001, 28.

3. Ibid.

4. See Jerome Kagan, *Surprise, Uncertainty and Knowledge Structures* (Cambridge, MA: Harvard University Press, 2002); Rohit Deshpandé, ed., *Using Market Knowledge* (Thousand Oaks, CA: Sage Publications, 2001).

5. For more insight on this see Jeffrey Pfeffer and Robert Sutton, *The Knowing-Doing Gap: How Smart Companies Turn Knowledge into Action* (Boston, MA: Harvard Business School Press, 2000).

6. Andy Clark, *Being There: Putting Brain, Body, and World Together Again* (Cambridge, MA: MIT Press, 1997).

7. The terms used here are consistent with the two standard texts in psychology and neuroscience: Stephen M. Kosslyn and Robin S. Rosenberg, *Psychology: The Brain, the Person, the World* (Needham Heights, MA: Allyn and Bacon, 2001); and Mark F. Bear, Barry W. Connors, and Michael A. Paradiso, *Neuroscience: Exploring the Brain* (Baltimore: Williams & Wilkins, 1996).

Chapter 1

1. Vicki G. Morwitz, Joel H. Steckel, and Alok Gupta, "When Do Purchase Intentions Predict Sales?" working paper 97–112, Marketing Science Institute, Cambridge, MA, 1997; see also Gerard J. Tellis and Peter N. Golder, *Will and Vision: How Latecomers Grow to Dominate Markets* (New York: McGraw-Hill, 2002).

2. See, for example, Robert F. Hartley, *Marketing Mistakes and Successes,* 8th ed. (New York: John Wiley, 2000); Dorothy Leonard-Barton, *Wellsprings of Knowledge: Building and Sustaining the Sources of Innovation* (Boston, MA: Harvard Business School Press, 1995); Clayton M. Christensen, *The Innovator's Dilemma: When New Technologies Cause Great Firms to Fail* (Boston, MA: Harvard Business School Press, 1997); G. Clotaire Rapaille, *7 Secrets of Marketing in a Multi-Cultural World* (Provo, UT: Executive Excellence Publishing, 2001).

3. For an explanation of this see Donald D. Hoffman, *Visual Intelligence: How We Create What We See* (New York: W. W. Norton, 1998).

4. George S. Day, "Marketing and the CEO's Growth Imperative" (speech delivered to the Marketing Science Institute, Boston, MA, 25 April 2002).

5. Antonio Damasio, "How the Brain Creates the Mind," *Scientific American* 12, no. 1 (2002): 4.

6. Vincent P. Barabba, *Meeting of the Minds: Creating the Market-Based Enterprise* (Boston, MA: Harvard Business School Press, 1995); Stephan Haeckel, *The Adaptive Enterprise* (Boston,

MA: Harvard Business School Press, 2000); and Robert C. Blattberg, Gary Getz, and Jacquelyn S. Thomas, *Customer Equity: Building and Managing Relationships as Valuable Assets* (Boston, MA: Harvard Business School Press, 2001).

7. See, for example, Chris Argyris, *On Organizational Learning* (Cambridge, MA: Blackwell Publishing, 1992); Chris Argyris, *Flawed Advice and the Management Trap* (Oxford, UK: Oxford University Press, 2000); and Chris Argyris, *Knowledge for Action: A Guide to Overcoming Barriers to Organizational Change* (San Francisco: Jossey-Bass, 1993).

8. Rohit Deshpandé, *Using Market Knowledge* (Thousand Oaks, CA: Sage Publications, 2001).

9. Jeffrey Pfeffer and Robert I. Sutton, *The Knowing-Doing Gap: How Smart Companies Turn Knowledge into Action* (Boston, MA: Harvard Business School Press, 2000).

10. David A. Garvin, *Learning in Action: A Guide to Putting the Learning Organization to Work* (Boston, MA: Harvard Business School Press, 2000); Leonard-Barton, *Wellsprings of Knowledge;* and Gerard J. Tellis and Peter N. Golder, *Will and Vision.*

11. For further critique in an advertising context, see William M. Weilbacher, "Point of View: Does Advertising Cause a 'Hierarchy of Effects'?" *Journal of Advertising Research,* November/December 2001, 19–26; see also Jerome Kagan, *Surprise, Uncertainty, and Mental Structures* (Cambridge, MA: Harvard University Press, 2002).

12. George Lowenstein, "The Creative Destruction of Decision Research," *Journal of Consumer Research* 28, no. 3 (December 2001): 499–505. See also Daniel Wegner, *The Illusion of Conscious Will* (Cambridge, MA: Harvard University Press, 2002).

13. Antonio Damasio, *Descartes' Error: Emotion, Reason, and the Human Brain* (New York: G. P. Putnam, 1994), chapter 1; Jon Elster, *Alchemies of the Mind: Rationality and the Emotions* (Cambridge, UK: Cambridge University Press, 1999).

14. A common mistake is to assume that because a decision is not well reasoned or "rational" it must be "irrational" and somehow flawed and wrong. As mentioned in this book's preface, I am a member of Harvard University's Mind/Brain/Behavior Initiative, a group of thirty-five faculty from all areas of the university whose mandate is to explore important issues from a multidisciplinary perspective. Not long ago we devoted an entire year to the study of (ir)rationality. One lesson that emerged is that the observer's way of seeing things—that is, the manager's or researcher's viewpoint—is not a particularly reliable lens for judging the "reasonableness" of another person's thoughts and actions. When managers or researchers claim consumers are irrational, they are saying more about their own system of thought than they are about the consumers'. Indeed, they are admitting that they do not have a deep understanding of consumers. Another lesson was that "rationality" is most usefully judged in terms of whether the consequences of a particular behavior are helpful or harmful. This includes the consequences for the consumer as well as others affected by the consumer's actions. Consumers may make decisions that are harmful to themselves and others, which hardly seems rational or reasonable. But perhaps these harmful consequences are offset by other "benefits" not visible using conventional research methods; to know this requires a deep understanding of consumers. By digging more deeply and understanding the connections among the many things that influence consumers, marketers and policy makers can be more effective in helping consumers make decisions in more constructive ways with more constructive outcomes.

15. For an account of this famous case and the larger point it illustrates, see Damasio, *Descartes' Error,* chapter 1.

16. Ibid. For three additional sources on the role of emotion in active decision making, see Antonio Damasio, *The Feeling of What Happens: Body and Emotion in the Making of Consciousness* (New York: Harcourt Brace, 1999); Joseph P. Forgas, ed., *Feeling and Thinking: The Role of Affect in Social Cognition* (Cambridge, UK: Cambridge University Press, 2001), especially chapter 1; and Mary Frances Luce, James R. Bettman, and John W. Payne, *Emotional Decisions: Tradeoff Difficulty and Coping in Consumer Choice* (Chicago, IL: University of Chicago Press, 2001).

17. Scott Robinettte and Claire Brand, *Emotion Marketing: The Hallmark Way of Winning Customers for Life* (New York: McGraw Hill, 2001); and Bernd Schmitt and Alex Simonson, *Marketing Aesthetics: The Strategic Management of Brands, Identity, and Image* (New York: Free Press, 1997). Both books argue the need to start thinking more deeply and carefully about emotions.

18. William Ian Miller, *The Anatomy of Disgust* (Boston, MA: Harvard University Press, 1997).

19. Jerome Kagan, *Surprise, Uncertainty, and Mental Structures.*

20. Lowenstein, "The Creative Destruction of Decision Research," 503.

21. Joseph LeDoux, *The Emotional Brain: The Mysterious Underpinnings of Emotional Life* (New York: Simon and Schuster, 1996).

22. See Damasio, *The Feeling of What Happens,* for a discussion of the unconscious nature of emotions and the distinction between emotions and feelings.

23. Andy Clark, *Being There: Putting Brain, Body, and World Together Again* (Cambridge, MA: MIT Press, 1997); Joseph LeDoux, *Synaptic Self: How Our Brain Becomes Who We Are* (New York: Viking Press, 2002), 13–32.

24. See the special issue of the *American Journal of Public Health* 87, no. 9 (September 1997); see also various volumes of *Body and Society* published by Sage Publications, Thousand Oaks, CA.

25. See, for example, Philip Lieberman, *Human Language and Our Reptilian Brain* (Cambridge, MA: Harvard University Press, 2002); William C. Stokoe, *Language in Hand: Why Sign Came Before Speech* (Washington, DC: Gallaudet University Press, 2001); and Jim Hopkins, "Evolution, Consciousness and the Internality of the Mind," in *Evolution and the Human Mind: Modularity, Language and Meta-Cognition,* eds. Peter Carruthers and Andrew Chamberlain, (Cambridge, UK: Cambridge University Press, 2000), 276–298.

26. Leonard L. Berry, Lewis P. Carbone, and Stephan H. Haeckel, "Managing the Total Customer Experience," *Sloan Management Review* 43, no. 3 (Spring 2002): 85–89.

27. Jerome L. Singer, "Imagination," in *Encyclopedia of Creativity,* vol. 2 (New York: Academic Press, 1999), 13–25.

28. Emily Eakin, "Penetrating the Mind by Metaphor," *New York Times,* 23 February 2002.

Chapter 2

1. For a general introduction, see *The Scientific American Book of the Brain* (New York: Lyons Press, 1999); and Rita Carter, *Mapping the Mind* (Berkeley, CA: University of California Press, 1998).

2. See, for example, Daniel C. Dennett, "Making Tools for Thinking," 17–30, Robert A. Wilson, "The Mind Beyond Itself," 31–52, and Led Cosmides and John Tooby, "Consider the Source: The Evolution of Adaptations for Decoupling and Metarepresentation," 53–116, in *Metarepresentations: A Multidisciplinary Perspective,* ed. Dan Sperber (New York: Oxford University Press, 2002); Evitar Zerubavel, *Social Mindscapes: An Invitation to Cognitive Sociology* (Cambridge, MA: Harvard University Press, 1997); Kay Kaufman Shelemay and Sarah Coakley, eds., *Pain and Its Transformations: The Interface of Biology and Culture* (Cambridge, MA: Harvard University Press, in press).

3. Peter R. Huttenlocher, *Neural Plasticity: The Effects of Environment on the Development of the Cerebral Cortex* (Cambridge, MA: Harvard University Press, 2002).

4. Michael Tomasello, *The Cultural Origins of Human Cognition* (Cambridge, MA: Harvard University Press, 1999), 3–4. See also Richard Lewontin, *Human Diversity* (New York: American Scientific Library, 1995). Readers have varying beliefs about human evolution. There are many variations of evolutionary and creationist positions and each has difficulty answering certain questions. While this book favors various explanations, the basic ideas are valid even if one prefers a creationist view to account for them.

5. Shira P. White, *New Ideas About New Ideas* (New York: Perseus Publishing, 2002).

6. For further comment on this see William M. Reddy, *The Navigation of Feeling: A Framework for the History of Emotions* (Cambridge, UK: Cambridge University Press, 2001).

7. Anne Harrington, "Getting Under the Skin," working paper, Harvard University, Cambridge, MA, 2001.

8. See Cosmides and Tooby, "Consider the Source," especially 72; David Papineau, "The Evolution of Knowledge," in Carruthers and Chamberlain, *Evolution and the Human Mind*.

9. See Max Bazerman, *Judgment in Managerial Decision Making*, 4th ed. (New York: John Wiley, 1998); and John C. Mowen, *Judgment Calls: High-Stakes Decisions in a Risky World* (New York: Simon and Schuster, 1993). Several relevant essays can be found in Colin Eden and J.-C. Spender, eds., *Managerial and Organizational Cognition: Theory, Methods and Research* (Thousand Oaks, CA: Sage Publications, 1998).

10. Gerald Edelman and Giulio Tononi, "Reentry and the Dynamic Core: Neural Correlates of Conscious Experience," in *Neural Correlates of Consciousness: Empirical and Conceptual Questions,* ed. Thomas Metzinger (Cambridge, MA: MIT Press, 2000), 121–138; Antonio Damasio, *The Feeling of What Happens: Body and Emotion in the Making of Consciousness* (New York: Harcourt Brace, 2000); Antonio Damasio, *Descartes' Error: Emotion, Reason, and the Human Brain* (New York: G. P. Putnam, 1994).

11. S. M. Kosslyn, M. C. Segar, J. Pani, and L. A. Hillger, "When Is Imagery Used? A Diary Study," *Journal of Mental Imagery* 14 (1990): 131–152.

12. See, for example, William Benzon, *Beethoven's Anvil: Music in Mind and Culture* (New York: Basic Books, 2001), especially chapters 2–4, 23–92.

13. Stephen Pinker, *The Language Instinct* (New York: Harper Collins, 1994); Philip Lieberman, *Human Language and Our Reptilian Brain: The Subcortical Bases of Speech, Syntax, and Thought* (Cambridge, MA: Harvard University Press, 2000).

14. See the essays in Albert Galaburda and Stephen M. Kosslyn, *Languages of the Brain* (Cambridge, MA: Harvard University Press, 2002); Leonard M. Shlain, *Art and Physics: Parallel Visions in Space, Time, and Light* (New York: William Morrow, 1991); Jim Hopkins, "Evolution, Consciousness and the Internality of the Mind," in Carruthers and Chamberlain, *Evolution and the Human Mind,* 276–298; Jerome Kagan, *Surprise, Uncertainty, and Mental Structures* (Cambridge, MA: Harvard University Press, 2002); and Marc D. Hauser, *Wild Minds: What Animals Really Think* (New York: Henry Holt, 2000).

15. Jonathan H. Turner, *On the Origins of Human Emotions: A Sociological Inquiry into the Evolution of Human Affect* (Stanford, CA: Stanford University Press, 2000), 109.

16. Stephen Kosslyn, *Image and Brain: The Resolution of the Imagery Debate* (Cambridge, MA: MIT Press, 1994); Harlan Lane, *When the Mind Hears: A History of the Deaf* (New York: Random House, 1989).

17. Gerald Edelman, *Bright Air, Brilliant Fire: On the Matter of the Mind* (New York: Basic Books, 1992), 108; see also Dan Sperber, "Metarepresentations in an Evolutionary Perspective," in Sperber, *Metarepresentations*, chapter 5, 117–137, esp. 121.

18. Pinker, *Language Instinct,* 56–58.

19. Dan Sperber, *Explaining Culture: A Naturalistic Approach* (Oxford, UK: Blackwell Publishing, 1996).

20. For examples of ZMET collages see Emily Eakin, "Penetrating the Mind by Metaphor," *New York Times,* 23 February 2002; Gardiner Morse, "Hidden Minds: A Conversation with Gerald Zaltman, *Harvard Business Review* (June 2002); Jamie Seaton, "Stateside," *Marketing Business,* June 2002; Sandra Yin, *American Demographics,* November 2001; Daniel Pink, "Metaphor Marketing," *Fast Company,* April–May 1998.

21. See, for example, Jeffrey Pittam, *Voice in Social Interaction: An Interdisciplinary Approach* (Thousand Oaks, CA: Sage Publications, 1994); Lane, *When the Mind Hears;* and James V. Wertsch, *Voices of the Mind: A Sociocultural Approach to Mediated Action* (Cambridge, MA: Harvard University Press, 1991).

22. Edward T. Hall, *The Silent Language* (New York: Fawcett World Library, 1961).

23. Robin Dunbar, *Grooming, Gossip, and the Evolution of Language* (Cambridge, MA: Harvard University Press, 1996); Pinker, *Language Instinct*.

24. George Lakoff and Mark Johnson, *Philosophy in the Flesh: The Embodied Mind and Its Challenge to Western Thought* (New York: Basic Books, 1999).

25. Raymond W. Gibbs, Jr., "Categorization and Metaphor Understanding," *Psychological Review* 99, no. 3 (1992).

26. G. Bottini, R. Corcoran, R. Sterzi, E. Paulesu, P. Schenone, P. Scarpa, R. S. J. Frackowiak, and C. D. Frith, "The Role of the Right Hemisphere in the Interpretation of Figurative Aspects of Language: A Positive Emission Tomography Activation Study," *Brain* 117 (1994): 1241–53, The authors suggest that, using PET scans, cerebral activations during metaphor comprehension activate several areas of the right hemisphere (as well as the left). In the right hemisphere this includes the right middle temporal gyrus. Although not much is known about this area, it appears to be active during complex information processing tasks such as those involved in appreciating metaphor. The precuneous is also activated. No one understands it well, although some evidence suggests that it may affect the functioning of long-term memory, which processes metaphors. There may be a significant basic relationship between metaphor, categorization, and memory processes: Metaphors may reflect conceptualizations of experiences in long-term memory, and knowledge may be structured as metaphorical associations in long-term memory. The frontal lobe, especially right prefrontal cortex, is also activated during metaphor processing (the same area on the left is activated when processing literal language). This suggests that retrieval of information (experiences) from episodic memory may be important: Retrieval from episodic memory helps determine whether the sentence is meaningful even if literally untrue, that is, a denotative violation. Activity in the right frontal lobe area (prefrontal cortex and the frontal eye field) have been associated with mental imagery, which may also be essential for metaphor comprehension.

27. Arthur I. Miller, *Insights of Genius: Imagery and Creativity in Science and Art* (Cambridge, MA: MIT Press, 2000).

28. Alvin I. Goldman, *Epistemology and Cognition* (Cambridge, MA: Harvard University Press, 1986), 247–249.

29. Mark Johnson, *The Body in the Mind: The Bodily Basis of Meaning, Imagination and Reason* (Chicago: University of Chicago Press, 1987), ix.

30. Miller, *Insights of Genius*.

31. An excellent source for researchers is Lynne Cameron and Graham Low, eds., *Researching and Applying Metaphor* (Cambridge, UK: Cambridge University Press, 1999).

32. Joyce L. Ingram, "The Role of Figurative Language in Psychology: A Methodological Examination," *Metaphor and Symbolic Activity* 9, no. 4 (1994): 271–288; Richard R. Kopp, *Metaphor Therapy: Using Client-Generated Metaphors in Psychotherapy* (New York: Brunner/Mazel, 1995); and Judy Weiser, *PhotoTherapy Techniques: Exploring the Secrets of Personal Snapshots and Family Albums* (San Francisco: Jossey-Bass, 1993).

33. Marcel Danesi, "Thinking Is Seeing: Visual Metaphors and the Nature of Abstract Thought," *Semiotica* 80, no. 3–4 (1990): 221–237; Johnson, *The Body in the Mind*; Lawrence E. Marks, "On Perceptual Metaphors," *Metaphor and Symbolic Activity* 11, no. 1 (1996): 39–66.

34. See Pia Lindell, Leif Melin, Henrik J. Gahmberg, Anders Hellqvist, and Anders Melander, "Stability and Change in a Strategist's Thinking," in Eden and Spender, *Managerial and Organizational Cognition*, chapter 5, 77–92; Narakesari Narayandas and Gerald Zaltman, "The Human Element in Marketing Strategy: A Look at the Creative and Subjective Side," note 598-105 (Boston: Harvard Business School, 1999); and John C. Mowen, *Judgment Calls*, especially chapter 9, 211–238.

35. Paul L. Harris, "Understanding Emotion," in *The Handbook of Emotions*, eds. Michael Lewis and Jeannette M. Haviland (New York: Guilford Press, 1993), 237–246; Aaron Ben-Ze'ev,

The Subtlety of Emotions (Cambridge, MA: MIT Press, 2000); Joseph LeDoux, *The Emotional Brain: The Mysterious Underpinnings of Emotional Life* (New York: Simon and Schuster, 1996); and Alice M. Isen, "Positive Affect and Decision Making," in Lewis and Haviland, *Handbook of Emotion* (New York: Guilford Press, 1993).

36. Turner, *On the Origins of Human Emotion,* 59. Italics added.

37. Damasio, *Descartes' Error,* xiii.

38. Ben-Ze'ev, *The Subtlety of Emotions.*

39. Daniel M. Wegner, *The Illusion of Conscious Will* (Cambridge, MA: MIT Press, 2002); Lakoff and Johnson, *Philosophy in the Flesh;* Damasio, *The Feeling of What Happens;* Edelman and Tononi, "Reentry and the Dynamic Core"; Bernard J. Baars, *A Cognitive Theory of Consciousness* (New York: Cambridge University Press, 1988); LeDoux, *The Emotional Brain;* Searle, *The Rediscovery of the Mind;* and Walter J. Freeman, *How Brains Make Up Their Mind* (New York: Columbia University Press, 2000), 13–36.

40. LeDoux, *The Emotional Brain,* 29–39.

41. Ibid., 32.

42. Josef Perner, *Understanding the Representational Mind* (Cambridge, MA: MIT Press, 1991); Elijah Millgram, *Practical Induction* (Cambridge, MA: Harvard University Press, 1997); and the essays in George R. Lockhead and James R. Pomeranz, eds., *The Perception of Structure* (Washington, DC: American Psychological Association, 1991).

43. Kagan, *Surprise, Uncertainty, and Knowledge Structures.*

44. Robert A. Wilson, "The Mind Beyond Itself," in Sperber, *Metarepresentations,* 31–52; Scott Atran, "Folk Biology and the Anthropology of Science: Cognitive Universals and Cultural Particulars," *Behavioral and Brain Sciences* 21 (1998), 547–569; Zerubavel, *Social Mindscapes.*

45. Glenn L. Christensen and Jerry C. Olson, "Mapping Consumers' Mental Models with ZMET," *Psychology & Marketing* 19, no. 6 (June 2002): 477–502; Giep Franzen and Margot Bouwman, *The Mental World of Brands: Mind, Memory and Brand Success* (Oxfordshire, UK: World Advertising Research Center, 2001).

46. See Christensen and Olson, "Mapping Consumers' Mental Models with ZMET."

47. Elizabeth F. Loftus, *Eyewitness Testimony* (Cambridge, MA: Harvard University Press, 1979). For a general introduction, see *The Scientific American Book of the Brain* (New York: Lyons Press, 1999); and Rita Carter, *Mapping the Mind* (Berkeley, CA: University of California Press, 1998).

Chapter 3

1. This important point is made by several treatments of consciousness such as those cited in endnote 3. See also the several essays in Robert F. Bornstein and Than S. Pittman, eds., *Perception without Awareness* (New York: Guilford Press, 1992); Michael Leyton, *Symmetry, Causality, Mind* (Cambridge, MA: MIT Press, 1992); Jerome Kagan, *Surprise, Uncertainty, and Mental Structures* (Cambridge: MA: Harvard University Press, 2002); and Paul R. Lawrence and Nitan Nohria, *Driven: How Human Nature Shapes Our Choices* (Boston, MA: Harvard Business School Press, 2002).

2. Doris-Louise Haineault and Jean-Yves Roy, *Unconscious for Sale: Advertising, Psychoanalysis, and the Public* (Minneapolis: University of Minnesota Press, 1993); Dennis Rook, ed., *Brands, Consumers, Symbols, and Research* (Thousand Oaks, CA: Sage Publications, 1999).

3. See the essays in Tetsuro Matsuzawa, ed., *Primate Origins of Human Cognition and Behavior* (Tokyo: Springer-Verlag, 2001).

4. Edward O. Wilson, *In Search of Nature* (Washington, DC: Island Press, 1996).

5. Henry Plotkin, *Evolution in Mind: An Introduction to Evolutionary Psychology* (Cambridge, MA: Harvard University Press, 1997); Marc D. Hauser, *Wild Minds: What Animals Really Think* (New York: Henry Holt, 2000).

6. Joseph LeDoux, *The Emotional Brain: The Mysterious Underpinnings of Emotional Life* (New York: Simon and Schuster, 1996); Matsuzawa, *Primate Origins of Human Cognition.*

7. Janet Wilde Astington, *The Child's Discovery of the Mind* (Cambridge, MA: Harvard University Press, 1994), 27.

8. Astington, *The Child's Discovery of the Mind,* chapter 4.

9. Robert Nozick, personal communication, April 1998.

10. See, for example, Merlin Donald, *Origins of the Modern Mind: Three Stages in the Evolution of Culture and Cognition* (Cambridge, MA: Harvard University Press, 1991); Robin Dunbar, *Grooming, Gossip, and the Evolution of Language* (Cambridge, MA: Harvard University Press, 1996); and Plotkin, *Evolution in Mind.*

11. See, for example, Robert Kegan, *In Over Our Heads: The Mental Demands of Modern Life* (Cambridge, MA: Harvard University Press, 1994); Jerome H. Barkow, Leda Cosmides, and John Tooby, *The Adapted Mind: Evolutionary Psychology and the Generation of Culture* (New York: Oxford University Press, 1992); Plotkin, *Evolution in Mind;* Adam Kuper, *The Chosen Primate: Human Nature and Cultural Diversity* (Cambridge, MA: Harvard University Press, 1994), especially chapter 4; and S. L. Hurley, *Consciousness in Action* (Cambridge, MA: Harvard University Press, 1998).

12. Patricia Hawkins, personal communication with author, November 2001, based on QUEST research.

13. Gerald Edelman, *Bright Air, Brilliant Fire: On the Matter of the Mind* (New York: Basic Books, 1992); George Lakoff and Mark Johnson, *Philosophy in the Flesh: The Embodied Mind and Its Challenge to Western Thought* (New York: Basic Books, 1999); John Bostock, *The Neural Energy Constant: A Study of the Bases of Consciousness* (London: Allen and Unwin, 1931); Pascal Boyer, *Religion Explained: The Evolutionary Origins of Religious Thought* (New York: Perseus Books, 2001).

14. John R. Searle, *The Construction of Social Reality* (New York: Free Press, 1996); John R. Searle, *The Rediscovery of the Mind* (Cambridge, MA: MIT Press, 1992). An exception to this point is made by Gerald M. Edelman in *The Remembered Present: A Biological Theory of Consciousness* (New York: Basic Books, 1989), 207.

15. Lakoff and Johnson, *Philosophy in the Flesh;* Steven Pinker, *How the Mind Works* (New York: W. W. Norton, 1997); and LeDoux, *The Emotional Brain.*

16. John Haugeland, *Having Thought: Essays in the Metaphysics of Mind* (Cambridge, MA: Harvard University Press, 1998), 159–160.

17. Gerald M. Edelman and Giulio Tononi, *A Universe of Consciousness: How Matter Becomes Imagination* (New York: Basic Books, 2000), 33.

18. J. Allan Hobson, *Consciousness* (New York: Scientific American Library, 1999), 26.

19. Edelman and Tononi, *A Universe of Consciousness,* 176.

20. Hobson, *Consciousness,* 218.

21. Daniel Wegner, *The Illusion of Conscious Will* (Cambridge, MA: MIT Press, 2002), 145.

22. See Bornstein and Pittman, *Perception without Awareness.*

23. For a helpful commentary on managers' reliance on notions of rationality, see Lawrence and Nohria, *Driven.*

24. Antoine Bechara, Hannah Damasio, Daniel Tranel, and Antonio Damasio, "Deciding Advantageously Before Knowing the Advantageous Strategy," *Science* 275 (February 1997), 1293–1295; Antoine Bechara, Daniel Tranel, Hannah Damasio, Ralph Adolphs, C. Rockland, and Antonio Damasio, "Double Dissociation of Conditioning and Declarative Knowledge Relative to the Amygdala and Hippocampus in Humans," *Science* 269 (1995): 1115–1118.

25. An interesting study conducted by Frank Tong and his colleagues provides further evidence. They presented to one eye of their subjects a picture of a house and to the other eye a picture of a face. This produces what is known as binocular rivalry. The subject sees the

face, for example, and after a while he sees the house. This continues back and forth, first one, then the other object. Seldom do people report seeing both with one superimposed on the other. Using functional magnetic imaging techniques (fMRI), the researchers were able to see the brain activations accompanying the two alternative perceptual states. Interestingly, the brain areas representing houses (or faces) were activated *before* the subjects reported the switch from one image to the other. Frank Tong, James T. Vaughan, and Nancy Kanwisher, "Binocular Rivalry and Visual Awareness in Human Extrastriate Cortex," *Neuron* 21 (1998): 753–749.

26. Rita Carter, *Mapping the Mind* (Berkeley, CA: University of California Press, 1998), especially chapter 7; Kagan, *Surprise, Uncertainty, and Mental Structures*.

27. Andy Clark, *Being There* (Cambridge, MA: MIT Press, 1997); Daniel Dennett, *Kinds of Minds* (New York: Basic Books, 1996); Walter Freeman, *How Brains Make Up Their Mind* (London: Weiderfeld and Nicholson, 1999).

28. Robert Nozick, *Invariances: The Structure of the Objective World* (Cambridge, MA: Harvard University Press, 2001), especially chapter 14; Hobson, *Consciousness,* especially chapter 9; Edelman and Tononi, *A Universe of Consciousness;* David J. Chalmers, *The Conscious Mind: In Search of a Fundamental Theory* (Oxford, UK: Oxford University Press, 1996); Wallace Chafe, *Discourse, Consciousness, and Time: The Flow and Displacement of Conscious Experiences in Speaking and Writing* (Chicago, IL: University of Chicago Press, 1994), especially 35–39; Janet Metcalfe and Arthur P. Shimamura, eds., *Metacognition: Knowing about Knowing* (Cambridge, MA: MIT Press, 1995); and Bernard J. Baars, *A Cognitive Theory of Consciousness* (Cambridge, UK: Cambridge University Press, 1988).

29. See various essays in these three sources: Matsuzawa, *Primate Origins of Human Cognition and Behavior;* Peter Carruthers and Andrew Chamberlain, eds., *Evolution and the Human Mind: Modularity, Language, and MetaCognition* (Cambridge, UK: Cambridge University Press, 2000); and Lawrence and Nohria, *Driven.*

30. Physical and social contexts are critical in shaping behavior. See, for example, Jerry Fodor, *The Mind Doesn't Work That Way: The Scope and Limits of Computational Psychology* (Cambridge, MA: MIT Press, 2000); Leslie Brothers, *Friday's Footprint: How Society Shapes the Human Mind* (New York: Oxford University Press, 1997); and Jonathan Turner, *On the Origins of Human Emotions: A Sociological Inquiry into the Evolution of Human Affect* (Stanford, CA: Stanford University Press, 2000).

31. Andrew F. Leuchter, "Changes in Brain Function of Depressed Subjects During Treatment with Placebo," *American Journal of Psychiatry* 159 (2002): 122–129; see also Helen S. Mayberg, Arturo Silva, Seven K. Brannan, Janet L. Tekell, Roderick K. Mahurin, Scott McGinnis, and Paul Jerbek, "The Functional Neuroanatomy of the Placebo Effect," *American Journal of Psychiatry* 159 (2002): 728–737.

32. V. S. Ramachandran and Sandra Blakeslee, *Phantoms in the Brain: Probing the Mysteries of the Human Mind* (New York: Morrow Press, 1998).

33. Ibid., 52–53.

34. Ibid., 53.

35. Ibid., 227–228. For other accounts devoted to the same conclusion, see Ian Stewart and Jack Cohen, *Figments of Reality: The Evolution of the Curious Mind* (Cambridge, UK: Cambridge University Press, 1997); and Donald D. Hoffman, *Visual Intelligence: How We Create What We See* (New York: W. W. Norton, 1998).

36. John Dowling, *Creating Mind: How the Brain Works* (New York: W. W. Norton, 1998), 119–120.

37. Psychologist Hermann von Helmholtz has used the term "unconscious inferences" for explaining this phenomenon.

38. Fodor, *The Mind Doesn't Work That Way.*

39. Daniel Simons and Christopher Chabris, "Gorillas in Our Midst: Sustained Inattentional Blindness for Dynamic Events," *Perception* 28 (1999): 1059–1074.

Chapter 4

1. No method is above criticism. For example, Jerome Kagan, the Daniel and Amy Starch Research Professor of Psychology at Harvard University, is critical of questionnaire data in ways that apply to marketing, including their inability to reveal tacit or unconscious knowledge. (See Jerome Kagan, *Surprise, Uncertainty, and Mental Structures* [Cambridge, MA: Harvard University Press, 2002].) Still, surveys remain an important mainstay of market research, and there is constant investigation on improving the method. For a critique of methods requiring consumer recall, see Dennis Rook, "Projective Methods Reconsidered," working paper, University of Southern California, Los Angeles, 2002.

2. An example involving one of the more commonly used techniques can be found in Paul E. Green and V. Srinivasan, "Conjoint Analysis in Marketing: New Developments with Implications for Research and Practice," *Journal of Marketing* 54 (October 1990): 2–19.

3. Gerald Zaltman, "Rethinking Market Research: Putting People Back In," *Journal of Marketing Research* 34 (November 1997): 424–437.

4. The title for this section is taken from Emily Eakin, "Penetrating the Mind by Metaphor," *New York Times,* 23 February 2002.

5. Gerald M. Edelman and Giulio Tononi, *A Universe of Consciousness: How Matter Becomes Imagination* (New York: Basic Books, 2000), 176.

6. See, for example, Jerome B. Kernan, "More Than a Rat, Less Than God, Staying Alive," and Dennis W. Rook, "Four Questions about Consumer Motivation Research," in *The Why of Consumption: Contemporary Perspectives on Consumer Motives, Goals, and Desires,* eds. S. Ratneshwar, David Glen Mick, and Cynthia Huffman (New York: Routledge, 2000).

7. Excellent sources about using metaphor to surface unconscious thoughts as well as influence conscious thoughts and actual behavior include the following books, several of which are cited throughout this book, listed alphabetically by author: Lynne Cameron and Graham Low, eds., *Researching and Applying Metaphor* (Cambridge, UK: Cambridge University Press, 1999); Gemma Corradi Fiumara, *The Metaphoric Process: Connections between Language and Life* (New York: Routledge, 1995); Raymond W. Gibbs, Jr., *The Poetics of Mind: Figurative Thoughts, Language, and Understanding* (Cambridge, UK: Cambridge University Press, 1994); Richard R. Kopp, *Metaphor Therapy: Using Client-Generated Metaphors in Psychotherapy* (New York: Brunner/Mazel, 1995); George Lakoff and Mark Johnson, *Philosophy in the Flesh: The Embodied Mind and Its Challenge to Western Thought* (New York: Basic Books, 1999); George Lakoff and Mark Johnson, *Metaphors We Live By* (Chicago, IL: University of Chicago Press, 1980); Jeffery Scott Mio and Albert N. Katz, eds., *Metaphor: Implications and Applications* (Mahwah, NJ: Lawrence Erlbaum, 1996); Linda E. Olds, *Metaphors of Interrelatedness: Toward a Systems Theory of Psychology* (Albany, NY: State University of New York Press, 1992); Andrew Ortony, ed., *Metaphor and Thought,* 2d ed. (Cambridge, UK: Cambridge University Press, 1993); Paul C. Rosenblatt, *Metaphors of Family Systems Theory: Toward New Constructions* (New York: Guilford Press, 1994); and Ellen Y. Siegelman, *Metaphor and Meaning in Psychotherapy* (New York: Guilford Press, 1990).

8. See, for example, the special issue of *Metaphor and Symbol: Models of Figurative Language* 16 (2001): 141–333 (Rachel Biora, guest ed.).

9. Lakoff and Johnson, *Philosophy in the Flesh.*

10. See Sam Glucksberg, Deanna Ann Manfredi, and Matthew S. McGlone, "Metaphor Comprehension: How Metaphors Create New Categories," 327–350; and Raymond W. Gibbs, Jr., "How Language Reflects the Embodied Nature of Creative Cognition," in *Creative Thought: An Investigation of Conceptual Structures and Processes,* eds. Thomas B. Ward, Steven M. Smith, and Jyotsna Vaid (Washington, DC: American Psychological Association, 1997), 351–374.

11. This position is quite important and can be found explained in various ways and levels. Recall that we are treating metaphor broadly as a family including similes, analogies, allegories, proverbs, and the like. For a good introduction, see C. Burgess and C. Chiarello,

"Neurocognitive Mechanisms Underlying Metaphor Comprehension and Other Figurative Language," *Metaphor and Symbolic Activity* 11 (1996): 67–84. See also Rachel Giora, Eran Zaidel, Nachum Soroker, Gila Batori, and Asa Kasher, "Differential Effects of Right- and Left-Hemisphere Damage on Understanding Sarcasm and Metaphor," *Metaphor and Symbol* 15 (2000): 63–84; Skye McDonald, "Neuropsychological Studies of Sarcasm," *Metaphor and Symbol* 15 (2000): 85–98; Ellen Winner, H. Brownell, F. Happe, A. Blum, and D. Pincus, "Distinguishing Lies from Jokes: Theory of Mind Deficits and Discourse Interpretation in Right Hemisphere Brain Damaged Patients," *Brain and Language* 36 (1998): 580–591; K. Fedemeier and M. Kutas, "Right Words and Left Words: Electrophysiological Evidence for Hemispheric Differences in Meaning Processing," *Cognitive Brain Research* 8 (1999): 373–392; and M. J. Beeman, E. M. Bowden, and M. A. Gernsbacher, "Right and Left Hemisphere Cooperation for Drawing Predictive and Coherence Inferences During Normal Story Comprehension," *Brain and Language* 71 (2000): 310–336.

12. Kevin Keller, *Strategic Brand Management: Building, Measuring, and Managing Brand Equity* (Upper Saddle River, NJ: Prentice Hall, 1998). Further accounts can be found in Daniel Pink, "Metaphor Marketing," *Fast Company,* April 1998; Sandra Yin, "The Power of Images," *American Demographics,* November 2001, 32–33; Ronald B. Lieber, "Storytelling: A New Way to Get Close to Your Customer," *Fortune,* 3 February 1997, 102–108; Gwendolyn Catchings-Castello, "The ZMET Alternative," *Marketing Research,* Summer 2000, 6–12; Emily Eakin, "Penetrating the Mind by Metaphor"; John Grant, *After Image: Mind-Altering Marketing* (London: Harper Collins, 2002); and Jonathan E. Schoreder, *Visual Consumption* (New York: Routledge, 2002).

13. Richard E. Cytowic, *Synesthesia: A Union of the Senses,* 2d ed. (Cambridge, MA: MIT Press, 2002), 276.

14. Robin Coulter and Gerald Zaltman, "The Power of Metaphor," in *The Why of Consumption: Contemporary Perspectives on Consumer Motives, Goals, and Desires,* eds. S. Ratneshwar, David Glen Mick, and Cynthia Huffman (New York: Routledge, 2001), 259–281.

15. Pink, "Metaphor Marketing," 78.

16. Pink, "Metaphor Marketing."

17. Cytowic, *Synesthesia.*

18. Antonio R. Damasio, *Descartes' Error: Emotion, Reason, and the Human Brain* (New York: G. P. Putnam, 1994), xiii.

19. Lakoff and Johnson, *Philosophy in the Flesh,* 43.

20. Christopher Collins, *The Poetics of the Mind's Eye: Literature and the Psychology of Imagination* (Philadelphia, PA: University of Pennsylvania Press, 1991); Sik Hung Ng and James J. Bradac, *Power in Language: Verbal Communication and Social Influence* (Thousand Oaks, CA: Sage Publications, 1993), 136–141.

21. Andrew Goatly, *The Language of Metaphors* (London: Routledge, 1997).

22. There are several interesting accounts of this reflecting different perspectives. See, for example, Terrence W. Deacon, *The Symbolic Species: The Co-evolution of Language and the Brain* (New York: W. W. Norton, 1997); Leslie Brothers, *Friday's Footprint: How Society Shapes the Human Mind* (Oxford, UK: Oxford University Press, 1997); Adam Kuper, *The Chosen Primate: Human Nature and Cultural Diversity* (Cambridge, MA: Harvard University Press, 1994); Merlin Donald, *Origins of the Modern Mind: Three Stages in the Evolution of Culture and Cognition* (Cambridge, MA: Harvard University Press, 1991); Robert Boyd and Joan B. Silk, *How Humans Evolved,* 2d ed. (New York: W. W. Norton, 2000); and Daniel McNeill, *The Face: A Natural History* (Boston, MA: Little, Brown, 1998).

23. W. J. T. Mitchell, *Picture Theory: Essays on Verbal and Visual Representation* (Chicago, IL: University of Chicago Press, 1994).

24. Coulter and Zaltman, "The Power of Metaphor"; Robin Coulter, Keith Coulter, and Gerald Zaltman, "In Their Own Words: Consumers' Attitudes Toward Advertising," *Journal of Advertising* (December 2001), 1–21.

25. Stephen Cole, personal communication, March 2002.

26. Francisco J. Varela, Evan Thompson, and Elenor Rosch; *The Embodied Mind* (Cambridge, MA: MIT Press 1992); see also references in endnote 7.

27. A. J. Soyland, *Psychology as Metaphor* (Thousand Oaks, CA: Sage Publications, 1994).

Chapter 4 Appendix

1. A very good general source of guidance can be found in Thomas Reynolds and Jerry C. Olson, *Understanding Consumer Decision Making: The Means-End Approach to Marketing and Advertising Strategy* (Mahwah, NJ: Lawrence Erlbaum, 2001). A source that is still more specific to metaphor is "Thirteen Lucky Tips for ZMET Interviewing," occasional paper no. 3, Olson Zaltman Associates, State College, PA, 2002, revised ed. See also Judy Wieser, *Phototherapy Techniques: Exploring the Secrets of Personal Snapshots and Family Albums* (San Francisco: Jossey-Bass, 1993).

2. Altering the frame introduces a "hiccup" that surfaces yet other ideas. The bases for this can be found in Meyer Schapiro, *Theory and Philosophy of Art: Style, Artists, and Society, Selected Papers* (New York: George Braziller, 1994), especially chapter 1, 1–33; W. J. T. Mitchell, *Picture Theory: Essays on Verbal and Visual Representation* (Chicago, IL: University of Chicago Press, 1994); Rudolf Arnheim, *The Power of the Center: A Study of Composition in the Visual Arts* (Berkeley, CA: University of California Press, 1988).

3. For more information on this issue, see Weiser, *Phototherapy Techniques;* John Willats, *Art and Representation: New Principles in the Analysis of Pictures* (Princeton, NJ: Princeton University Press, 1997); and Rudolf Arnheim, *Art and Visual Perception: A Psychology of the Creative Eye* (Berkeley, CA: University of California Press, 1974).

4. For further guidance on this issue see Shay Sayre, *Qualitative Methods for Marketplace Research* (Thousand Oaks, CA: Sage Publications, 2001).

Chapter 5

1. Philip M. Merikle and Meredyth Daneman, "Conscious vs. Unconscious Perception," in *The New Cognitive Neurosciences,* 2d ed., ed. Michael S. Gazzaniga (Cambridge, MA: MIT Press, 2000), 1295–1304.

2. Vicki G. Morwitz, Joel H. Steckel, and Alok Gupta, "When Do Purchase Intentions Predict Sales?" working paper 97–112, Marketing Science Institute, Cambridge, MA, 1997; see especially Jerome Kagan, *Surprise, Uncertainty, and Mental Structures* (Cambridge, MA: Harvard University Press, 2002) 181. Also see Joseph LeDoux, *The Emotional Brain* (New York: Simon and Schuster, 1996), especially chapters 1–3 for a detailed explanation of why verbal self-report measures are often inconsistent with actual behavior and frequently incomplete concerning important drivers of customer behavior.

3. J. A. Bargh, M. Chen, and L. Burrows, "Automaticity of Social Behavior: Direct Effects of Trait Constructs and Stereotype Activation on Action," *Journal of Personality and Social Psychology* 71 (1996): 230–244.

4. C. N. Macrae and L. Johnston, "Help, I Need Somebody: Automatic Action and Inaction," *Social Cognition* 16 (1998): 400–417.

5. A. Dijksterhuis et al., "Seeing One Thing and Doing Another: Contrast Effects in Automatic Behavior," *Journal of Personality & Social Psychology* 75 (1998): 862–871.

6. D. Maison, A. G. Greenwald, and R. Bruin, "The Implicit Association Test as a Measure of Implicit Consumer Attitudes," *Polish Psychological Bulletin* 32, no. 1 (2001).

7. For more information on this study, see Kathryn A. Braun and Gerald Zaltman, "When What Consumers Say Isn't What They Do: The Case of Ethnocentrism" (Austin, TX: Proceedings of the Association for Consumer Research, 2002).

8. Fred Mast and Nancy Puccinelli, "Mood and Implicit Associations with Brands," unpublished data, Mind of the Market Laboratory, Harvard Business School, Boston, MA, 2001.

9. Steven M. Kosslyn and Robin S. Rosenberg, *Psychology: The Brain, the Person, the World* (Boston, MA: Allyn and Bacon, 2001), 686.

10. An excellent resource is Roberto Cabeza and Alan Kingstone, eds., *Handbook of Functional Neuroimaging of Cognition* (Cambridge, MA: MIT Press, 2001); see also Peter R. Huttenlocher, *Neural Plasticity: The Effects of Environment on the Development of the Cerebral Cortex* (Cambridge, MA: Harvard University Press, 2002), 68–87.

11. See "Neuroimaging as a Marketing Tool," U.S. Patent Number 6,099,319, patent for the use of neuroimaging techniques in marketing, held by Stephen M. Kosslyn and Gerald Zaltman; see also "Metaphor Elicitation Technique with Physiological Function Monitoring," U.S. Patent Number 6,315,569 B1, patent for the use of physiological measures in market research, held by Gerald Zaltman.

12. William R. Uttal, *The New Phrenology: The Limits of Localizing Cognitive Processes in the Brain* (Cambridge, MA: MIT Press, 2001).

13. Stephen L. Crites, Jr., and Shelley N. Aikman-Eckenrode, "Making Inferences Concerning Physiological Responses: A Reply to Rossiter, Silbesteing, Harris, and Nield," *Journal of Advertising Research* 41 (March/April 2001): 23–25.

14. See, for example, Robert Morais, "The End of Focus Groups," in *Quirk's Marketing Research Review* (May 2001): 154; and "Advertising" column by Vanessa O'Connell, *Wall Street Journal,* 27 November 2000.

15. Quoted in Kirsten D. Sandberg, "Focus on the Benefits," Harvard Management Communication Letter (April 2002): 4.

16. See Thomas L. Greenbaum, *The Handbook for Focus Group Research,* 2d ed. (Thousand Oaks, CA: Sage Publications, 1998); and Bonnie Goebert with Herman M. Rosenthal, *Beyond Listening: Learning the Secret Language of Focus Groups* (New York: John Wiley, 2002). See also endnote 17.

17. Perhaps the most constructive treatment of focus groups to help researchers and managers that use this method is Edward F. Fern, *Advanced Focus Group Research* (Thousand Oaks, CA: Sage Publications, 2001). Another very helpful source is Hy Mariampolski, *Qualitative Market Research: A Comprehensive Guide* (Thousand Oaks, CA: Sage Publications, 2001).

18. A widely cited reference about focus groups is Edward Fern's classic article, "The Use of Focus Groups for Idea Generation: The Effects of Group Size, Group Type, Acquaintanceship and the Moderator on Response Quantity and Quality," *Journal of Marketing Research* 19 (1982): 1–13. Fern's reservations have the same force and validity today that they did in 1982.

19. Valerie Janesick, "The Dance of Qualitative Research Design," in *Handbook of Qualitative Research,* eds. Norman K. Denzin and Yvonna S. Lincoln (Thousand Oaks, CA: Sage Publications, 1994).

20. Herbert Rubin and Irene Rubin, *Qualitative Interviewing: The Art of Hearing Data* (Thousand Oaks, CA: Sage Publications, 1995).

21. Steven Taylor and Robert Bogdan, *Introduction to Qualitative Research Methods,* 3d ed. (New York: John Wiley, 1998), 115.

22. Robert B. Brandom, *Making It Explicit: Reasoning, Representing, and Discursive Commitment* (Cambridge, MA: Harvard University Press, 1994); and Jordan B. Petersen, *The Architecture of Belief* (London: Routledge, 1999).

23. Robin Dunbar, *Grooming, Gossip, and the Evolution of Language* (Cambridge, MA: Harvard University Press, 1996), 121.

24. Morais, "The End of Focus Groups."

25. Mark L. Knapp, Gerald R. Miller, and Kelly Fudge, eds., *Handbook of Interpersonal Communication,* 2d ed. (Thousand Oaks, CA: Sage Publications, 1994).

26. Timur Kuran, *Private Truths, Public Lies: The Social Consequences of Preference Falsification* (Cambridge, MA: Harvard University Press, 1995).

27. John Hauser and Abbie Griffin, "The Voice of the Customer," working paper 92–106, Marketing Science Institute, Cambridge, MA, 1993.

28. A related nonproprietary study can be found in Peter R. Dickson and Alan G. Sawyer, "The Price Knowledge and Search of Supermarket Shoppers," *Journal of Marketing* 54 (July 1990): 42–53.

29. I am indebted to Vincent P. Barabba for bringing this example to my attention.

30. Robin Coulter, Gerald Zaltman, and Keith Coulter, "Interpreting Consumer Perceptions of Advertising: An Application of the Zaltman Metaphor Elicitation Technique," *Journal of Advertising* 30 (December 2001): 1–21; Gene Weingarten, "Below the Beltway," *Washington Post*, 14 April 2002; Douglas Rushkoff, *Coercion: Why We Listen to What "They" Say* (New York: Riverhead Books, 1999); and Robin Coulter and Gerald Zaltman, "The Meaning of Marketing," working paper, University of Connecticut, Storrs, 1995.

31. The Zaltman Metaphor Elicitation Technique, employed by Olson Zaltman Associates and its licensees, is a patented research method, U.S. Patent Number 5,436,830.

32. Because these stories can be quite upsetting to the participants and on occasion to the interviewer, interviewers are trained in various ways of handling these situations. Most experienced interviewers develop a personal variant of one of these options that works well for them.

33. The usual assurances of anonymity are provided, of course, and when it applies, consumers are advised that other people may observe portions of the interview through a one-way mirror.

34. Raymond A. Bauer, "The Limits of Persuasion," *Harvard Business Review,* September–October 1958, 107.

35. Indeed, even under the extreme conditions used in famous brainwashing examples involving members of particular sects and war prisoners, the effectiveness of these techniques is varied, sometimes succeeding and sometimes not.

Chapter 6

1. See Mary Frances Luce, James R. Bettman, and John W. Payne, *Emotional Decisions: Tradeoff Difficulty and Coping in Consumer Choice* (Chicago, IL: University of Chicago Press, 2001); and S. Ratneshwar, David Glen Mick, and Cynthia Huggman, eds., *The Why of Consumption: Contemporary Perspectives on Consumer Motives, Goals, and Desires* (New York: Routledge, 2001).

2. For more on this see Walter J. Freeman, *How Brains Make Up Their Minds* (New York: Columbia University Press, 2000), especially chapter 2, 13–36.

3. See Daniel C. Dennett, *Kinds of Minds: Toward an Understanding of Consciousness,* (New York: Basic Books, 1996), especially chapter 1, 1–18, and chapter 6, 119–152.

4. Freeman, *How Brains Make Up Their Mind,* chapter 3; Jerome Kagan, *Surprise, Uncertainty, and Mental Structures* (Cambridge, MA: Harvard University Press, 2002).

5. Clayton M. Christensen, *The Innovator's Dilemma: When New Technologies Cause Great Firms to Fail* (Boston, MA: Harvard Business School Press, 1997).

6. Freeman, *How Brains Make Up Their Mind,* 16; excellent accounts of this issue can also be found in James W. Barrow, ed., *Self-Analysis: Critical Inquiries, Personal Vision* (Hinsdale, NJ: Analytic Press, 1993).

7. See, for example, Kevin J. Chancy and Robert S. Shulman, *Marketing Myths That Are Killing Business: The Cure for Death Wish Marketing* (New York: McGraw Hill, 1994); and Vincent P. Barabba, *Meeting of Minds* (Boston, MA: Harvard Business School Press, 1995).

8. Freeman, *How Brains Make Up Their Mind;* Philip Lieverman, *Human Language and Our Reptilian Brain: The Subcortical Bases of Speech, Syntax, and Thought* (Cambridge, MA: Harvard University Press, 2000), 1–18.

9. Jesse J. Prinz, *Furnishing the Mind: Concepts and Their Perceptual Basis* (Cambridge, MA: MIT Press, 2002).

10. Jerome Kagan, *Three Seductive Ideas* (Cambridge, MA: Harvard University Press, 1998).

11. Jerry Fodor, *The Mind Doesn't Work That Way: The Scope and Limits of Computational Psychology* (Cambridge, MA: MIT Press, 2000).

12. Kagan, *Three Seductive Ideas,* 35.

13. Daniel Miller, *A Theory of Shopping* (Ithaca, NY: Cornell University Press, 1998.

14. Peter Huttenlocher, *Neural Plasticity: The Effects of Environment on the Development of the Cerebral Cortex* (Cambridge, MA: Harvard University Press, 2002); Susan Engel, *Context Is Everything: The Nature of Memory* (New York: W. H. Freeman, 1999); Robert A. Wilson, "The Mind Beyond Itself," in *Metarepresentation: A Multidisciplinary Perspective,* ed. Dan Sperber (Oxford, UK: Oxford University Press, 2000), 31–52; Alexandra Maryanski and Jonathan H. Turner, *The Social Cage: Human Nature and the Evolution of Society* (Stanford, CA: Stanford University Press, 1992); Judith Rich Harris, *The Nurture Assumption: Why Children Turn Out the Way They Do* (New York: Free Press, 1998); Leslie Brothers, *Friday's Footprint: How Society Shapes the Human Mind* (Oxford, UK: Oxford University Press, 1997); Richard Lewontin, The *Triple Helix: Gene, Organism, and Environment* (Cambridge, MA: Harvard University Press, 2000); Shelley E. Taylor and Rena L. Repetti, "Health Psychology: What Is an Unhealthy Environment and How Does It Get Under the Skin?" *Annual Review of Psychology* 48 (1997): 411–447; and Andy Clark, *Being There: Putting Brain, Body, and World Together Again* (Cambridge, MA: MIT Press, 1997).

15. Emily Eakin, "Penetrating the Mind by Metaphor," *New York Times,* 23 February 2002.

16. Several diverse accounts can be found in the following: Pascal Boyer, *The Naturalness of Religious Ideas: A Cognitive Theory of Religion* (Berkeley, CA: University of California Press, 1999); Jan Klein and Naoyuki Takahata, *Where Do We Come From?* (New York: Springer-Verlag, 2002), especially chapter 12, 371–379; Dan Sperber, *Explaining Culture: A Naturalistic Approach* (Oxford, UK: Blackwell Publishers, 1996).

17. Adapted from Donald E. Brown, *Human Universals* (New York: McGraw-Hill, 1991), 157–201.

18. See Kagan, *Three Seductive Ideas,* chapter 1.

19. Kay Kaufman Shelemay, *Soundscapes: Exploring Music in a Changing World* (New York: W. W. Norton, 2001).

20. John Hauser and Abbie Griffin, "The Voice of the Customer," working paper 92-106, Marketing Science Institute, Cambridge, MA, 1993.

21. For example, others report that laddering studies, a special way of interviewing, are able to capture—after eighteen to twenty-two one-on-one interviews—all of the ideas that will be provided by a hundred more such interviews. What is noteworthy about the metaphor-elicitation interviews is that between five and eight interviews are required to identify all the relevant ideas that a larger group would reveal. In one validation study, for example, between four and six participants, selected at random from the completed data files, were required to identify all the relevant constructs in a consensus map based on eighty-one interviews. In other validation studies, the number of participants required to identify relevant constructs has varied between three and seven. This does not mean that only this many people should be interviewed. A larger number of people provide more insight into the many nuances and rich language of thought that surround each construct and associations between constructs. However, for a given group, interviewing more than fifteen to twenty consumers, depending on the topic, will not likely produce significant additional insights.

Chapter 7

1. See John Hauser and Abbie Griffin, "The Voice of the Customer," working paper 92-106, Marketing Science Institute, Cambridge, MA, 1993; Thomas Reynolds and Jerry C. Olson, *Understanding Consumer Decision Making: The Means-End Approach to Marketing and*

Advertising Strategy (Mahwah, NJ: Lawrence Erlbaum, 2001); Gerald Zaltman and Robin Coulter, "Seeing the Voice of the Customer: Metaphor-based Advertising Research," *Journal of Advertising Research* 35, no. 4 (July–August 1995): 35–51.

2. This holds across topics that vary in level of abstraction, substantive issues, and cultural boundaries. For example, in validation studies where more than a hundred people were interviewed, on average only about five consumer data files selected at random are required to generate all constructs included in the complete consensus map generated by the larger set of interviewees. To obtain the same relationships among the constructs as shown in the consensus map developed with the large consumer pool, only eight representative consumers are needed. Other sources of validation included in these studies, which ranged across different cooperating firms and different topics, involved large-scale surveys involving thousands of consumers, the results of certain proprietary techniques, and focus group studies on the same topics. Still other evidence is provided by research on the use of experts, which shows that only about three experts who do not know each other are needed to identify the relevant issues in a problem areas. See R. T. Clemen and R. L. Winkler, "Limits for the Precision and Value of Information from Dependent Sources," *Operations Research* 33, no. 4 (1985): 427–442; and Donald G. Morrison and David C. Schmittlein, "How Many Forecasters Do You Really Have? Mahalanobis Provides the Intuition for the Surprising Clemen and Winkler Result," *Operations Research* 39, no. 3 (1991): 519–523. The experience of the National Institutes of Health with their Consensus Development Boards also provides support for the idea that a few people with expertise (and each consumer is the leading expert on his or her own thinking) can identify procedures that are appropriate for a large population of medical practitioners to follow most of the time. The NIH Consensus Development Boards follow an intensive procedure not unlike ones consumers participate in as part of the ZMET interviews.

3. Peter R. Huttonlocher, *Neural Plasticity: The Effects of Environment on the Development of the Cerebral Cortex* (Cambridge, MA: Harvard University Press, 2002); See David Perkins, *Outsmarting IQ: The Emerging Science of Learnable Intelligence* (New York: Free Press, 1995); Gerald Edelman, *Bright Air, Brilliant Fire: On the Matter of the Mind* (New York: Basic Books, 1992); Jerome Kagan, *Three Seductive Ideas* (Cambridge, MA: Harvard University Press, 1998), especially chapter 2, 83–150; and Michael Tomasello, *The Cultural Origins of Human Cognition* (Cambridge, MA: Harvard University Press, 1999).

4. An important reminder: The phrase "mind of the market" does not refer to some actual entity like the Magna Carta. It is instead the emergent product of how consumers and managers interact, like the way a sports fan emerges from the interplay of a team, the fan's own reactions to that team, and what the team does (or fails to do) to cultivate those reactions.

5. Gerald Edelman and Giulio Tononi, *A Universe of Consciousness: How Matter Becomes Imagination* (New York: Basic Books, 2000), especially chapter 10, 113–124; and Edelman, *Bright Air, Brilliant Fire,* especially chapter 9, 81–110.

Chapter 8

1. Elizabeth F. Loftus and Katherine Ketchum, *Myth of Repressed Memory: False Memories and Allegations of Sexual Abuse Witness for the Defense* (New York: St. Martin's Griffin, 1996); and Elizabeth F. Loftus, *Eyewitness Testimony* (Cambridge, MA: Harvard University Press, 1996).

2. Daniel L. Schacter, *Searching for Memory: The Brain, the Mind, and the Past* (New York: Basic Books, 1996), 308.

3. Daniel L. Schacter, ed., *Memory Distortion: How Minds, Brains, and Societies Reconstruct the Past* (Cambridge MA: Harvard University Press, 1995), 22. See also Susan Engel, *Context Is Everything: The Nature of Memory* (New York: W. H. Freeman, 1999).

4. Jeffrey Prager, *Presenting the Past: Psychoanalysis and the Sociology of Misremembering* (Cambridge, MA: Harvard University Press, 1998). This book is highly recommended as an account of the role of memory in merging the self, society, and culture.

5. Ibid., 82.

6. Kathryn A. Braun and Gerald Zaltman, "Backwards Framing: A Theory of Memory's Reconstruction," working paper 98–109, Marketing Science Institute, Cambridge, MA.

7. Interestingly, while addressing the topic of memory reconstruction, two other researchers have found that asking consumers certain hypothetical questions in advance of a purchase decision has an unconscious impact, one that is beyond their awareness, on their choices and that this impact is difficult to counteract. See Gavan J. Fitzsimons and Baba Shiv, "Nonconscious and Contaminative Effects of Hypothetical Questions on Subsequent Decision Making," *Journal of Consumer Research* 28 (September 2001): 224–238.

8. Bob Snyder, *Music and Memory: An Introduction* (Cambridge, MA: MIT Press, 2000), 107.

9. Daniel L. Schacter and Tim Curran, "Memory without Remembering and Remembering without Memory: Implicit and False Memories," in *The New Cognitive Neurosciences,* 2d ed., ed. Michael S. Gazzaniga (Cambridge, MA: MIT Press, 2000), 829–844.

10. See, for instance, the first three "sins" in Daniel L. Schacter, *The Seven Sins of Memory: How the Mind Forgets and Remembers* (Boston, MA: Houghton Mifflin, 2001).

11. Roger C. Schank, *Tell Me a Story: A New Look at Real and Artificial Memory* (New York: Scribners, 1990).

12. Two excellent sources on memory and smell are Frank R. Schols and Robert G. Crowder, eds., *Memory for Odors* (Mahwah, NJ: Lawrence Erlbaum, 1995); and Truygg Engen, *Odor Sensation and Memory* (New York: Praeger, 1999). For a review of neuroimaging studies on olfaction, see Christopher F. Chabris and Jennifer M. Shepard, "The Cognitive Neuroscience of Olfaction: A Selective Review," unpublished paper, Mind of the Market Laboratory, Harvard Business School, July 1999.

13. David B. Pillemer, *Momentous Events, Vivid Memories* (Cambridge, MA: Harvard University Press, 1998), 50.

14. See, for example, Israel Rosenfield, *The Invention of Memory: A New View of the Brain* (New York: Basic Books, 1988); and the same author's book, *The Strange, Familiar, and Forgotten: An Anatomy of Consciousness.*

15. Schacter, *Searching for Memory*, 60.

16. Linda J. Levine et al., "Remembering Past Emotions: The Role of Current Appraisals," *Cognition and Emotion* 14, no. 4 (2001): 393–417 (New York: Knopf, 1992).

17. See Paul John Eakin, *How Our Lives Become Stories: Making Selves* (Ithaca, NY: Cornell University Press, 1999); and Ian Stewart and Jack Cohen, *Figments of Reality: The Evolution of the Curious Mind* (Cambridge, UK: Cambridge University Press, 1997). These two sources offer two different approaches reaching the same conclusion about memory in partnership with imagination. For a philosophical perspective reinforcing the idea of a partnership between memory and imagination, see Alvin I. Goldman, *Epistemology and Cognition* (Cambridge, MA: Harvard University Press, 1986).

18. Loftus and Ketchum, *Myth of Repressed Memory;* and Loftus, *Eyewitness Testimony.*

19. Kathryn A. Braun, "Post-Experience Effects on Consumer Memory," *Journal of Consumer Research* 25 (March 1999): 319–334.

20. Ibid.

21. Kathryn A. Braun, Rhiannon Ellis, and Elizabeth F. Loftus, "Make My Memory: How Advertising Can Change Our Memories of the Past," *Psychology & Marketing* 19 (January 2002): 1–23.

22. Schacter, *The Seven Sins of Memory*, 99.

23. Antonio Damasio, *The Feeling of What Happens: Body and Emotion in the Making of Consciousness* (New York: Harcourt Brace, 2000).

24. Joseph P. Forgas, "Mood and Judgment: The Affect Infusion Model (AIM)," *Psychological Bulletin* 117, no. 1 (1995): 39–66.

25. F. G. Ashby, Alice M. Isen, and A. U. Turken, "A Neuropsychological Theory of Positive Affect and Its Influence on Cognition," *Psychological Review* 106 (1999): 529–550.

26. Angeli Y. Lee and Brian Sternthal, "The Effects of Positive Mood on Memory," *Journal of Consumer Research* 26, no. 2 (September 1999): 115–127.

Chapter 9

1. Bob Snyder, *Music and Memory: An Introduction* (Cambridge, MA: MIT Press, 2000).

2. Roger C. Schank and R. P. Abelson, "Knowledge and Memory: The Real Story," *Advances in Social Cognition* 8 (1995): 33. See also Roger C. Schank, *Tell Me a Story: A New Look at Real and Artificial Memory* (New York: Scribners, 1990).

3. See Paul Connerton, *How Societies Remember* (Cambridge, UK: Cambridge University Press, 1999).

4. Robert A. Wilson, "The Mind Beyond Itself," in *Metarepresentations: A Multidisciplinary Perspective,* ed. Dan Sperber (Oxford, UK: Oxford University Press, 2000): 31–52.

5. Susan Engel, *Context Is Everything: The Nature of Memory* (New York: W. H. Freeman, 1999), 10.

6. Edward O. Wilson, *Consilience: The Unity of Knowledge* (New York: Random House, 1998).

7. Andy Clark, *Being There: Putting Brain, Body, and World Together Again* (Cambridge, MA: MIT Press, 1997).

8. Paul Connerton, *How Societies Remember* (Cambridge, UK: Cambridge University Press, 1999).

9. Paul Stoller, *The Taste of Ethnographic Things: The Senses in Anthropology* (Philadelphia, PA: University of Pennsylvania Press, 1989); see also the several essays in David Howes, ed., *The Varieties of Sensory Experience: A Sourcebook in the Anthropology of the Senses* (Toronto, Canada: University of Toronto Press, 1991).

10. See the various essays on odor and memory in Frank R. Schab and Robert G. Crowder, eds., *Memory for Odors* (Mahwah, NJ: Lawrence Erlbaum, 1995).

11. M. Morrin and S. Ratneshwar, "The Impact of Ambient Scent on Evaluation, Attention, and Memory for Familiar and Unfamiliar Brands," *Journal of Business Research* 49 (August 2000): 157–165.

12. See Constance Classen, *Worlds of Sense: Exploring the Senses in History and Across Cultures* (New York: Routledge, 1993); and Constance Classen, *The Color of Angels: Cosmology, Gender and the Aesthetic Imagination* (New York: Routledge, 1998).

13. Several essays that touch upon this can be found in Stephen McAdams and Emmanuel Bigand, eds., *Thinking in Sound: The Cognitive Psychology of Human Audition* (Oxford, UK: Clarendon Press, 1993), especially the essay by Robert G. Crowder, "Auditory Memory," 113–145; and Bob Snyder, *Music and Memory: An Introduction* (Cambridge, MA: MIT Press, 2000).

14. William Benzon, *Beethoven's Anvil: Music in Mind and Culture* (New York: Basic Books, 2001), especially 23–46; Kay Shelemay, *Let Jasmine Rain Down* (Chicago: University of Chicago Press, 1998); and Kay Shelemay, *Soundscapes: Exploring Music in a Changing World* (New York: W. W. Norton, 2001).

15. Shelemay, *Soundscapes,* 7.

16. Susanne Kuchler and Walter Melion, eds., *Images of Memory: On Remembering and Representation* (Washington, DC: Smithsonian Institution Press, 1991), especially Adrienne L. Kaeppler, "Memory and Knowledge in the Production of Dance," 109–120.

17. Jonathan E. Schroeder, *Visual Consumption* (London: Routledge, 2002); and John Grant, *After Image: Mind-Altering Marketing* (London: Harper Collins, 2002).

18. As discussed in the last chapter, some memories are simply false despite their very real feeling. A well-known example is the "lost in the mall" experiment. People for whom it

was established could never have been lost in a mall as a child had the memory of being lost implanted by researchers. Each time the person was asked to describe the experience of being lost in the mall as a child they added more detail such as a security guard buying them an ice cream. The memory of being lost in the mall had great realism for participants.

19. "Consumer Fraud and Deception Among the Elderly" (report to the U.S. Administration on Aging, University of Pittsburgh Marketing Department, 1979).

20. Schank, *Tell Me a Story;* Robert Coles, *The Call of Stories: Teaching and the Moral Imagination* (Boston, MA: Houghton Mifflin, 1989); Elaine Scarry, *Dreaming by the Book* (New York: Farrar, Straus, Giroux, 1999).

21. See especially Daniel L. Schacter and Elaine Scarry, eds., *Memory, Brain, and Belief* (Cambridge, MA: Harvard University Press, 2000); and Paul John Eakin, *How Our Lives Become Stories: Making Selves* (Ithaca, NY: Cornell University Press, 1999).

22. Paul John Eakin, "Autobiography, Identity, and the Fictions of Memory," in Schacter and Scarry, *Memory, Brain and Belief,* 290.

23. Donnel B. Stern, *Unformulated Experience* (Hillsdale, NJ: Analytic Press, 1997).

24. Ibid., 65.

25. Jerome Kagan, *Surprise, Uncertainty, and Mental Structures* (Cambridge, MA: Harvard University Press, 2002).

26. See Antonio R. Damasio, "Thinking about Belief," in Schacter and Scarry, *Memory, Brain and Belief,* 325–333.

27. C. Moorman, Gerald Zaltman, and Rohit Deshpandé, "Relationships between Providers and Users of Market Research: The Dynamics of Trust within and between Organizations," *Journal of Marketing Research* 29 (August 1992): 314–328; and Vincent P. Barabba and Gerald Zaltman, *Hearing the Voice of the Market* (Boston: Harvard Business School Press, 1991).

28. Robert McKee, *Story: Substance, Structure, Style, and the Principles of Screenwriting* (New York: Harper Collins, 1997), 25.

29. Howard Eichenbaum and J. Alexander Bodkin, "Belief and Knowledge as Forms of Memory," in Schacter and Scarry, *Memory, Brain and Belief,* 176–207, especially 204 for quote.

30. Jonathan H. Turner, *On the Origins of Human Emotions: A Sociological Inquiry into the Evolution of Human Effect* (Stanford, CA: Stanford University Press, 2000); and Engel, *Context Is Everything.*

31. Even jazz improvisation, the commonly given example of the totally novel, is the product of a lifetime of preparation and multiple kinds of knowledge involving rigorous musical thinking and constancy of personal style. See, for example, Paul F. Berliner, *Thinking in Jazz: The Infinite Art of Improvisation* (Chicago, IL: University of Chicago Press, 1994).

32. Gerald Zaltman, Karen LeMasters, and Michael Heffring, *Theory Construction in Marketing: Some Thoughts on Thinking* (New York: John Wiley, 1982); and Murray Davis, "That's Interesting! Towards a Phenomenology of Sociology and a Sociology of Phenomenology," *Philosophy of the Social Sciences* 4, no. 3 (1977): 103–117.

Chapter 10

1. See, for example, Margaret Mark and Carol S. Pearson, *The Hero and the Outlaw: Building Extraordinary Brands Through the Power of Archetype* (New York: McGraw-Hill, 2001); John Grant, *After Image: Mind-Altering Marketing* (London: Harper Collins, 2002).

2. Sidney J. Levy, "The Consumption of Stories," unpublished paper, University of Arizona, Tuscon, October 2001.

3. See, for example, Susan Fournier, "Consumers and Their Brands: Developing Relationship Theory in Consumer Research," *Journal of Consumer Research* 24 (March 1998): 343–373; and Susan Fournier and Seth M. Schulman, "Relating to Peapod," Case N9-502-050 (Boston, MA: Harvard Business School, 2002).

4. Wendy Gordon, Foreword in Giep Franzen and Margot Bouwman, *The Mental World of Brands: Mind, Memory and Brand Success* (Oxfordshire, UK: World Advertising Research Center, 2001), xiii.

5. Quote provided by Larry Huston, vice president, Procter & Gamble, January 2002.

6. Robert W. Brockway, *Myth: From the Ice Age to Mickey Mouse* (Albany, NY: State University Press, 1994); and J. F. Bierlein, *Parallel Myths* (New York: Ballantine Publishing Group, 1994). See also the classic work by Joseph Campbell with Bill Moyers, *The Power of Myth* (New York: Doubleday, 1988).

7. Doris-Louise Haineault and Jean-Yves Roy, *Unconscious for Sale: Advertising, Psychoanalysis, and the Public* (Minneapolis/London: University of Minnesota Press, 1993).

8. Elizabeth Hirschman, *Heroes, Monsters, and Messiahs* (Kansas City, MO: Andrews McKeel Publishing, 2000).

9. For example, see Martin J. Gannon, *Understanding Global Cultures: Metaphorical Journeys Through 23 Nations,* 2d ed. (Thousand Oaks, CA: Sage Publications, 2001) for a discussion of twenty-three unique deep metaphors or archetypes capturing the common essence of each of twenty-three countries.

10. Ibid. See also Terrence W. Deacon, *The Symbolic Species: The Co-evolution of Language and the Brain* (New York: W. W. Nortons, 1997), especially chapter 10, 279–320.

11. Jack Zipes, ed., *The Trials and Tribulations of Little Red Riding Hood,* 2nd ed. (New York: Routledge, 1993).

12. An excellent book on this topic is Franzen and Margot, *The Mental World of Brands.*

13. Ulric Neisser, "Five Kinds of Self-knowledge," *Philosophical Psychology* 1 (1988): 35–59.

14. Deacon, *The Symbolic Species.*

Chapter 11

1. See, for example, the essays in Steven M. Smith, Thomas B. Ward, and Ronald A. Finke, *The Creative Cognition Approach* (Cambridge, MA: MIT Press, 1997).

2. See also Arthur I. Miller, *Insights of Genius: Imagery and Creativity in Science and Art* (Cambridge, MA: MIT Press, 2000) for a discussion of the role that visual imagery and metaphor, processes inherent in everyone's everyday thinking, play in scientific breakthroughs.

3. Edward O. Wilson, *Consilience: The Unity of Knowledge* (New York: Random House, 1999).

4. Max Bazerman, *Judgment in Managerial Decision Making,* 4th ed. (New York: John Wiley, 1998).

5. Frank Close, *Lucifer's Legacy: The Meaning of Asymmetry* (Oxford, UK: Oxford University Press, 2000); Michael Leyton, *Symmetry, Causality, Mind* (Cambridge, MA: MIT Press, 1992).

6. David A. Garvin, *Learning in Action: A Guide to Putting the Learning Organization to Work* (Boston, MA: Harvard Business School Press, 2000), chapter 6, especially 211.

7. Ellen Dissanayke, *Homo Aestheticus: Where Art Comes from and Why* (Seattle, WA: University of Washington Press, 1995); and Semir Zeki, *Inner Vision: An Exploration of Art and the Brain* (Oxford, UK: Oxford University Press, 1999).

8. Edward McQuarrie, *Customer Visits: Building a Better Market Focus,* 2d ed. (Thousand Oaks, CA: Sage Publications, 1998). See, for example, the essays in Steven M. Smith, Thomas B. Ward, and Ronald A. Finke, eds., *The Creative Cognition Approach* (Cambridge, MA: MIT Press, 1997).

Chapter 12

1. For a discussion of the limitations of questionnaires in understanding what people think, see Jerome Kagan, *Surprise, Uncertainty, and Mental Structures* (Cambridge, MA: Harvard University Press, 2002), 181–188.

2. Expert Forums are conducted by Olson Zaltman Associates. They involve bringing together experts on a topic who are from different disciplines and a group of managers to review the latest insights outside marketing that are relevant to a specific brand or product issue faced by a company.

3. Antonio Damasio, *The Feeling of What Happens: Body and Emotion in the Making of Consciousness* (New York: Harcourt, Brace, 1999) 83. Italics in original.

4. Robert Rosenthal, *Experimenter Effects in Behavioral Research* (New York: Irvington Press, 1976); also Robert Rosenthal and Robert Rosnow, *Essentials of Behavioral Research: Methods and Data Analysis* (New York: McGraw-Hill, 1991).

Chapter 13

1. All information about the *Titanic* is taken from the proceedings of the U.S. Senate Inquiry and the British Wreck Commissioner's Inquiry. These are the most thorough and accurate records of what transpired. They are available at http://www.titanicinquiry.org.

2. Ibid.

Index

Acknowledgments

I have always had the good fortune of working with thought leaders in academia and in the world of practice. The writing of this book has profited tremendously from this experience.

This book has benefited from critical reviews by numerous people, many of whom were subjected to multiple manuscript drafts. In alphabetical order, they include: Chris Argyris (Harvard Business School and Monitor Company); Vincent P. Barabba (General Motors); Marco Bertini (Harvard University); Maya Bourdeau (Olson Zaltman Associates); Thomas Brailsford (Hallmark); Mary Caravella (Harvard University); Lewis Carbone (Experience Engineering); John Carew (Carew Consulting, Inc.); Eugene Caruso (Harvard University); Clayton Christensen (Harvard University); Stephen Cole (Deployed Solutions, Inc.); Nancy Cox (Hallmark); Suzy Goan (Experience Engineering); Stephan Haeckel (IBM); Nicholas Hahn (Capital Markets Company); Jeffrey Hartley (General Motors); Larry A. Huston (P&G); Joseph Lassiter (Harvard University); Fred Mast (Harvard University); Nancy Puccinelli (Emerson College); Kash Rangan (Harvard University); Malcolm Salter (Harvard University); Robert Scalea (J. Walter Thompson); Elena Siyanko (Capital Markets Company); Robert Summers (Summers Communications); Anne Thistleton (Thistleton Consulting); Tuba Ustuner (Harvard University); Luc Wathieu (Harvard University); Andrea Wojnicki (Harvard University); Steven Wright (Wright Solutions); Lindsay Zaltman (Olson Zaltman Associates); and Jeffrey Zaltman (Ford Motor Company). Three anonymous reviewers also helped shape the content of this book.

Many ideas in this book have benefited from extensive discussions with other thoughtful, sharp-minded people, including (in alphabetical order) Margarita Bahri-Keeton (P&G); Carliss Baldwin (Harvard University); Rita Bartczak (Thomson Marketing Resources); Alex Biel (Biel

Consulting); Kathryn Braun-LaTour (Marketing Memories); Robin Coulter (University of Connecticut); John Deighton (Harvard University); Rohit Deshpandé (Harvard University); Iain Douglas (Gallo Wines); Susan Fournier (Harvard University); Steve Greenspan (Active Communication Technology); Diane Harper (General Mills); Anne Harrington (Harvard University); David Garvin (Harvard University); David Hurvitz (Olson Zaltman Associates); Stephen M. Kosslyn (Harvard University); Roland Kulen (Story Development Studio); Dorothy Leonard (Harvard University); Tom Long (Coca-Cola Company); William McComb (McNeil Consumer Healthcare); Silke Muenster (Coca-Cola Company); Jerry Olson (Olson Zaltman Associates); Djordjija Petkoski (the World Bank); Bianca Philippe (Story Development Studio); Leonora Polansky (P&G); Kay Kaufman Shelemay (Harvard University); Howard Stevenson (Harvard University); Drake Stimson (P&G); John Sviokla (Diamond Cluster); and Robert Worden (Eastman Kodak). Many other executives from Alta Vista, American Century, the Coca-Cola Company, Eastman Kodak, General Mills, General Motors, Hallmark, and Johnson & Johnson influenced my thinking during Mind of the Market Laboratory Advisory Council programs, where many of the book's ideas were explored. The folks mentioned above from Harvard University span a diverse set of disciplines and departments within the university.

The task of helping me make complex and unfamiliar ideas more readable without compromising accuracy fell to Corey Hajim and Lynn Maloney, both former students in my Customer Behavior Laboratory, and especially Laurie Armstrong Johnson. Corey had a major impact on the first draft of this book, while Laurie had an especially significant impact on the last draft. Lynn contributed in a number of ways in between. Others have played an important role in shepherding the manuscript during the writing process. I want to thank Bonnie Murray, Margo McCool, and Al Lemieux, whose talents and patience seem inexhaustible.

Beyond her invaluable contributions as an insightful, clear-eyed, constructive reader, Kirsten Sandberg of the Harvard Business School Press was instrumental in my finally starting the book and in bringing it to conclusion. She has been a delight to work with, and a very special set of thanks goes out to her.

At an institutional level, my experience at the Harvard Business School has been particularly stimulating under the leadership of two deans, John McArthur and Kim Clark, and the school's research directors, F. Warren McFarlan, Dwight Crane, Teresa Amabile, and Krishna Palepu. All have helped make the Harvard Business School unique in encouraging faculty to develop the broad cognitive peripheral vision necessary for discovery.

My colleagues in the Marketing Unit have influenced many ideas in this book. Their occasional puzzled looks, questions, frank criticisms, and encouragement kept me busy refining and clarifying my ideas. The environment in the Marketing Unit, particularly under the leadership of its recent chair, Professor Kash Rangan, is a special and fun place to work. Professor Rangan believes work should be enjoyable, clearly evidenced in his research and teaching, and he goes out of his way to make it so for colleagues. I have been one of those fortunate colleagues.

About the Author

Gerald Zaltman is the Joseph C. Wilson Professor of Business Administration at the Harvard Business School and a member of Harvard University's Mind, Brain, and Behavior Interfaculty Initiative. Prior to joining the Harvard faculty, he held professorships at Northwestern University and the University of Pittsburgh. He is also a partner in the research and consulting firm Olson Zaltman Associates.

Zaltman is the author or coauthor of fourteen books and the editor or coeditor of twelve books. He has published widely in major professional journals, contributed chapters to numerous books, and is a frequent presenter at national conferences. He is a current or past member of the editorial boards of numerous journals in marketing and the social sciences and is a past president of the Association for Consumer Research.

Zaltman has been cited in various surveys of the American Marketing Association as one of the top five scholars in marketing and one whose work is among the most frequently cited in the marketing literature. He is the recipient of several major awards and honors conferred by various professional associations.

Zaltman holds an A.B. from Bates College, an M.B.A. from the University of Chicago, and a Ph.D. in sociology from the Johns Hopkins University.